the
DEVELOPMENT
of the
MODERN FLUTE

the DEVELOPMENT of the MODERN FLUTE

NANCY TOFF

A CRESCENDO BOOK

Taplinger Publishing Company · New York

First Edition

Published in the United States in 1979 by
TAPLINGER PUBLISHING CO., INC.
New York, New York

Copyright © 1979 by Nancy Toff
Printed in the U.S.A. by Vail-Ballou Press, Inc.

Library of Congress Cataloging in Publication Data

Toff, Nancy.
The development of the modern flute.

"A Crescendo book."
Bibliography: p.
Includes index.
1. Flute—History. I. Title.
ML935.T63   788′.51′209   78-57562

ISBN 0-8008-2185-8 (Cloth)   ISBN 0-8008-2186-6 (Paper)

Book design: Mollie M. Torras

954560

To the memory of
PETER HENLE

Acknowledgments

This book would not be complete without grateful acknowledgment of its patron saint, Dr. Dayton C. Miller, who in 1941 generously bequeathed his collection of flutes and printed material relating to the instrument to the Library of Congress. Without access to that collection, it would have been nearly impossible for me to write this book.

The enormous value of the instruments, the books, the trade catalogs, and the music in the collection is obvious at once, but the factor that adds luster to the gold mine is Miller's personal touch. In the largest sense, this personal touch is apparent in Miller's application of his professional habits of scientific precision to his avocation. But it is most evident in what is perhaps the least used—but to my mind, possibly the most valuable—portion of the collection, Miller's voluminous correspondence.

Those unique files make one pray that letter writing is not a lost art, that use of the telephone, though quick and convenient, will not obliterate written communication, leaving, as Donal Henahan noted recently in *The New York Times*, only the bills as a permanent record. "Instead of belles-lettres," complained Henahan, "we have Ma Bell." Whether Miller's correspondence qualifies as belles-lettres may be debatable; what is certain is its value as a source not only of obscure factual information, but also of direct insight into the thinking of manufacturers, performers, and musicologists.

Of course, the personal perspective that characterizes the

Miller Collection calls for an extra measure of selectivity on the part of the researcher. The manuscript portions of the collection, in particular, must be utilized with careful attention to the intended audience for each item. Thus, in Miller's accession lists, compiled primarily for his own use, the evaluations of mechanisms are blunt and to the point; indeed, the pungency of his observations often provides a welcome infusion of humor. In his letters, however, Miller proved himself a diplomat as well as a scientist, so one must weigh his comments more carefully. For this reason, unmailed first drafts, which, characteristically, Miller retained, can be even more revealing than the final versions.

But these caveats in no way lessen the magnitude of Dayton Miller's contribution. His meticulous scholarship and insistence on quality in forming his collection are a continual inspiration to new avenues of inquiry.

Many other, more personal acknowledgments are also very much in order. My own interest in the history of the flute began almost as soon as I began to play it, but that interest was nurtured in no small way by a wonderful teacher, Arthur Lora. Lessons with that grand old man of the flute were more than technical instruction; they were hours-long explorations of the instrument, its music, and its performance traditions. More recently, he has been of inestimable help during the writing of this book, constantly filling in gaps in my research both from his library and from his own firsthand knowledge of the subject.

Appreciation must also be extended to the following people whose efforts on my behalf made this book possible: Professor Elliot Forbes of Harvard University, for his constant encouragement and careful editorial criticism; Jerry L. Voorhees, for generously contributing most of the mechanical diagrams in the book; Noëlle and George Beatty, for their hospitality during two early research trips to Washington; and my father, Ira N. Toff, for invaluable photographic assistance. I am also grateful to the Wesley Weyman Trust for funding my early research at the Library of Congress.

Peter Fay and David Shorey of the Library of Congress Music

Division were most helpful in allowing me free run of the Dayton C. Miller Flute Collection. The other members of the Music Division staff also tolerated my peregrinations with amazing good humor. Bob Dennis and Mary Lou Little of the Eda Kuhn Loeb Music Library at Harvard were of great assistance in locating materials and arranging numerous interlibrary loans. Cynthia Hoover of the Smithsonian Institution kindly allowed me access to the trade catalogs in the Division of Musical Instruments.

Many flute manufacturers have provided useful information on the current state of the art: Bickford Brannen (Verne Q. Powell Flutes), Lewis J. Deveau (Wm. S. Haynes Flutes), Norman Maloney (Rudall, Carte & Co.), Gary Sigurdson (C. G. Conn), Mark Thomas (W. T. Armstrong Company), and Mel Webster (DeFord Flute Division, King Musical Instruments). Alice Avouris, Robert J. Baasch, Samuel Baron, Philip Bate, Robert Cantrick, Walfrid Kujala, Alexander Murray, James Pellerite, and Leslie Timmons have also generously shared information and expertise. My thanks as well to Eugene Anderson, Susan Bryan, Mary Anne Schwalbe, and James M. Swain for their assistance.

A special vote of thanks goes to Martha Kleinschmidt, who as my next-door neighbor during most of the writing of this book endured daily, if not hourly, progress reports and the seemingly perpetual clacking of my typewriter. She also assisted in the mundane but essential tasks of photocopying, proofreading, and other paperwork when deadlines became imminent. To my other Harvard neighbors and to my colleagues at Time-Life Books, my gratitude for their encouragement and tolerance.

N.T.

Contents

Illustrations

Unless otherwise indicated in the captions, all photographs are by the author. Instruments from the Dayton C. Miller Flute Collection in the Library of Congress are labeled with their DCM numbers. Captions for those instruments are based on Miller's accession books and the *Checklist* of the collection compiled by Laura E. Gilliam and William Lichtenwanger.

Terminology Used in This Book

In general references, notes or keys are referred to by capital letters, but specific octave references are denoted by the following alphabetic notation:

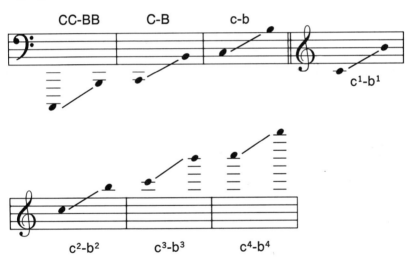

In the text and on the mechanical diagrams, each hole is labeled according to the note that it vents; i.e., the note that sounds when that hole is the lowest one open. Keys are named for the notes that are produced when they are depressed. Closed keys, therefore, have the same names as the holes they cover. The names of open keys, however, differ from the names of the holes they cover; thus, on the Boehm flute, the F hole is covered by the E key. On the diagrams, letters alone refer to holes; keys are always identified by the word "key." Keys that do not directly cover holes are labeled as levers, touches, rollers, or crescents.

Fingers are numbered and labeled as follows:

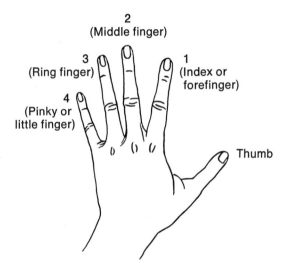

the
DEVELOPMENT
of the
MODERN FLUTE

Introduction

The literature on the history of the flute is huge; in fact, it is overwhelming. Its size is perhaps understandable merely in view of its advanced age, but its true scope is not evident until one considers that the history of a musical instrument is the product of a delicate balance of acoustics, mechanical engineering, aesthetic standards, and the exigencies of musical composition and performance. Thus the literature is scattered, appearing in journals of physics and acoustics as well as in the expected musical sources. The unfortunate result of this dispersion has been a certain narrowness of perspective. Scientific papers and histories of the flute written by inventors and organologists generally take a purely mechanical or acoustical approach. Similarly, studies of flute music and orchestration concentrate primarily on the written notes, with little regard to the instrument which is to play them. But only rarely, if ever, does one encounter a treatise that fully relates the mechanical history of an instrument to the music written for it.

One of the few individuals to recognize this segregation was Dr. Dayton C. Miller, who, as professor of physics at the Case School of Applied Science in Cleveland and an enthusiastic amateur flutist, made what is perhaps the greatest historiographical contribution to organology in modern times. His dual interests led him to assemble a comprehensive collection of material relating to the flute, including instruments, books and other printed matter (patents, catalogs, concert programs, etc.), music, works of art, and photographs of flutes and flutists. In his laboratory at

Case he conducted numerous experiments regarding the acoustical properties of the flute and even tried his hand at flutemaking. He wrote and lectured extensively on both the scientific and musical aspects of the instrument.

The culmination of Miller's efforts was to have been a magnum opus entitled "The Modern Flute: Its History and Construction," begun in 1906, in which he proposed to cover the theory, construction, and musical history of the instrument. Unfortunately, professional commitments and the time involved in the acquisition of his flute collection prevented the completion of the work. Only the outline and a draft of the first chapter survive among his papers, now deposited in the Library of Congress. It is the aim of the present study to continue Miller's much-needed synthesis of the art and science of the flute, paying special attention to the developments of the twentieth century.

Clearly, the histories of music and instrument are inseparable, for the period from roughly 1700 to 1900, which encompasses almost the entire structural and mechanical development of the woodwinds, correlates closely with simultaneous developments in composition and performance practice. In order to analyze this relationship, it is first necessary to define the parameters of each category.

Compositional and performance factors consist of pitch standards, ideals of tone color, the evolution of instrumentation and orchestration, the demands of composers, the role of performers, and the critical expectations of both musicians and the public.

The acoustical and mechanical aspects of flute construction, which provide the central orientation of this study, consist of the following: bore, division and assembly of the instrument, materials of construction, embouchure shape, mechanism, and fingering system. The separation of the last two items may seem surprising, but in fact it is a crucial distinction: the term "mechanism" refers only to the actual mechanical devices—keys, levers, sleeves, etc.—while "fingering system" pertains to the application of fingers to control the mechanism. Fingering systems consider the human element of the instrument; mechanisms do not necessarily do so, and it is that dichotomy that provides the principal criterion for evaluating the multiplicity of flute models of the last few centuries.

The process of invention may be divided into three phases: recognition of need, development of theory and method, and practical implementation. These roles have variously been assumed by three groups: composers, amateur and professional performers, and craftsmen and mechanics. But the correspondence is far from one to one. The problem, then, is to determine both the motivation for and the influence of structural modification of the instrument as represented by the human interactions of these parties.

The influence of purely musical factors on instrument construction was explicitly acknowledged as early as 1851, when Richard Carte, commenting on the achievements of the early part of the nineteenth century, wrote, "This great advance as to the resources of the instrument was necessary, in order to meet the increasing demands of modern scientific music."[1] From the larger perspective of the twentieth century, Curt Sachs has observed, "Great inventions . . . are consciously or subconsciously dictated by musical trends and currents—even when such trends are still remote from maturity."[2] The musical influence may be one of performance practice; for instance, the varying circumstances of solo, chamber, and orchestral performance may mandate different qualities of color and volume. Similarly, pitch levels exert a very direct effect on an instrument by determining its dimensions; in the eighteenth century, in fact, they necessitated versatility within a single instrument in order to adjust to standards that were by no means standard. Composers' demands have been particularly notable with regard to range; consequently, existing instruments have been altered and new ones invented to provide the requisite pitches.

A prime demand of composers and performers alike has been greater technical facility for the flute. By the eighteenth century, when woodwind reform began in earnest, the strings had far outdistanced the winds in technical capability owing to the perfection and standardization of the instruments. Wind players' prestige suffered greatly in comparison. Furthermore, composers were reluctant to write for obviously imperfect instruments. The only way for wind players to equal the technical accomplishment of their string colleagues was to simplify the fingering system.

Perhaps the most obvious musical influence on instruments, yet the most difficult to define, is the element of critical judgment. Quite simply, a rise in the qualitative demands of composers and listeners will effect a corresponding elevation of performers' standards. In order to achieve the requisite competence for musical success, and for the professional musician, financial prosperity, the player is greatly dependent upon the capabilities of his instrument. Indeed, a player's best and most common excuse for technical weakness has always been to blame his instrument, and it is therefore logical that he has turned to the inventor for help.

A variant view is propounded by some historians, who argue that while composers' requirements have been of utmost importance in the improvement of instruments, the players have exerted a negative influence in this regard. Dayton Miller suggests that, in the eighteenth century, such reluctance to change may have been a matter of pride: "Flute players, strangely, resisted the tendency to add more keys for producing the four tones obtained only by fork-fingerings. The suggestion of the need for such keys was considered by eminent performers and teachers as a reflection on their technical ability."[3] Once the concept of keys did become accepted, the conservatism of players regarding changes in their instruments is attributable to several factors, not the least of which is the comfort of tradition. Such apparent complacency does have its practical aspects, however, especially for professional players. Christopher Welch explained the situation in the nineteenth century:

> . . . the cause of this absence of reform may . . . be traced to the want of a sufficiently large number of amateurs to break down by their influence the conservatism of professional players, and to overcome their disinclination to change. A musician who has spent his youth in learning to conceal the defects of an instrument, has but little inclination to give up the vantage he has gained, nor has he

time, amidst the engagements of his professional career, to learn a new system of fingering. Still less can he be expected to place in the hands of a young player, soon, perhaps, to become a rival, an instrument which may be the means of enabling him to come to the front in the race for artistic distinction.[4]

In the late nineteenth century, however, many noted performers, including Welch, became enthusiastic tinkerers, adding countless devices to the keywork to expedite specific passages that gave them difficulty.

Twentieth century flutists have followed two divergent patterns. The first group, echoing the philosophy of the post-Boehm nineteenth century "improvers," may be termed the "gadgeteer school." In extreme cases, such players have complicated the Boehm mechanism monstrously; the moderates, on the other hand, have come up with some eminently workable and useful devices, such as the high C facilitator key, commonly known as the "gizmo." The second school may be termed "purists"; they resist the addition of gadgets, placing primary responsibility on the performer, rather than relying on special mechanical crutches. Significantly, a prime exponent of the latter view was Verne Q. Powell, one of the foremost flutemakers in the United States, and the catalogs of the firm he founded still reflect that view.

Indeed, the position of manufacturers in terms of instrument improvement has been problematical. Though one would expect this group to be a truly progressive force in mechanical development owing to their professional expertise, they have often, for a variety of reasons, played a curiously negative role. In the nineteenth century, professional jealousy was a major factor; much of the time expended in bickering over the credit for and the relative superiority of inventions might better have been spent in substantive research and experimentation. Moreover, gadgets were often added or changes made to the instrument merely for the sake of the inventor's prestige. While the "X" model might indeed project the tinkerer's name into the musical limelight, the new contrivance might well hinder rather than enhance the technical capabilities of the instrument.

Another potent factor affecting manufacturers is inertia; Dayton Miller once wrote sympathetically to the inventor of a new device, "I well know that makers deslike [*sic*] to depart from their routine." The results of such inertia may be seen, for instance, in the shapes of instruments, many of which owe their present designs to the limited capacities of the nineteenth century lathe. The traditional shapes have remained despite the advances in tooling made by modern technology, which might permit more efficient or attractive shapes. The explanation, according to Jack Fedderson, president of H. & A. Selmer, a leading American manufacturer of wind instruments, is economic:

> If there is any field that is more hide-bound by tradition than the music field, I certainly don't know what it is. Tradition is hindering progress in our field. Most manufacturers . . . are reluctant to invest the large amounts of capital required to tool up and introduce such innovations because they know each will be greeted with that old objection from players, teachers, and band directors that decries the least departure from tradition.[5]

This is not to say, however, that contemporary manufacturers have no research programs; witness, for example, Powell's recent introduction of the Cooper Scale and Armstrong's production model Murray flute. But it is true that extreme caution is exercised before modifying regular models in any way that is evident to the player. Thus improvement in intonation through remeasurement and reapportionment of tone holes is more likely to be implemented than any change in the fingering system.

The apparent implication, then, is that the inventor and the manufacturer are merely the slaves of musicians. In this spirit, Curt Sachs has warned, "Musical inventors should be aware that in music a style represents what a country, an age, or some master feels compelled to express, and that inventors serve this urge by providing the means." But, in turn, does the inventor have any influence on musicians? Sachs seems to minimize this role:

> Most people think . . . it suffices to invent a new instrument or to transform those already existing, and the musical world will meekly follow the inventor's lead into a novel age. This is a grave mistake.

New possibilities do not of necessity entail new tastes—not even where less spiritual things are at stake than music. Inventors have provided excellent refrigerators, and yet no British host will serve you iced tea or a cool bottle of ale.[6]

Indeed, the introduction of a new instrument does not and cannot imply instant strides in composition. But the important point here is the time element, for before an instrument can affect composition, it must be accepted by its practitioners as a viable medium for existing music. This crucial preliminary acceptance is hindered, as we have seen, by the conservatism of established professional players. However, once this obstacle has been surmounted, the effect of a worthwhile invention will have several important effects on music.

In the broadest sense, an improved instrument provides more efficiency, accuracy, and versatility. To take two obvious examples, the lengthening of the footjoint and the invention of the piccolo expand the range of notes available to the composer. Improvements on an instrument may also provide special compositional effects, which, in the case of the woodwinds, have been so widely employed that a distinct school of avant-garde woodwind composers has developed. In short, truly progressive invention, though motivated by the most forward-looking elements of the musical community, expands the instrumental resources available to all composers. Over time, we may observe the gradual evolution of new musical possibilities from the status of special effects to that of integral compositional techniques.

Coming full circle in the twentieth century, we find performers confronted with increasingly complex music, some of which puts even the best of instruments to the test. Consequently, performers are turning once again to the manufacturers to devise instruments more appropriate to their expanded musical functions. Paul Giroux has characterized this cycle as follows:

Scientific experimentation, improvements in flute manufacture, and the efforts of . . . flutists to raise the standard of musical performance have led toward a new understanding of music for the flute.

> The relationship of the flute to its music . . . has become symbiotic; the more subjectively responsive instrument demands richer music, and the new musical style requires a flute more immediately responsive to the manipulations of the performer.[7]

Giroux's use of the biological metaphor in a musical essay is perhaps symbolic of the approach of the present study, which rejects the vacuum conceptions of traditional organology whereby technological and compositional achievements have been rigidly isolated. While the ultimate aim of musical invention is, of course, the improvement of musical performance and the expansion of compositional possibilities, it is of the utmost importance, in order to ensure continued progress in the field, to recognize the mutual indebtedness of the scientific and musical communities.

Notes]

1. Richard Carte, *Sketch of the Successive Improvements Made in The Flute*, 3rd ed. (London: Rudall, Rose, Carte & Co. and Keith and Prowse, 1855), p. 11.

2. Curt Sachs, "Music and the Musical Inventor," *Musical America* 74, no. 4 (February 15, 1954): 20.

3. Dayton C. Miller, "The Evolution of the Wood-Wind Instruments," TS, p. 29.

4. Christopher Welch, *History of the Boehm Flute*, 3rd ed. (London: Rudall, Carte & Co.; New York: G. Schirmer, 1896), pp. 6–7.

5. Jack Fedderson, "Tradition and Music Instrument Technology," *The Instrumentalist* 16, no. 10 (June 1962): 35.

6. Sachs, p. 20.

7. Paul H. Giroux, "The History of the Flute and Its Music in the United States," *Journal of Research in Music Education* 1 (Spring 1953): 73.

CHAPTER I

The Flute Before Boehm

The history of the flute naturally divides itself into two distinct, though chronologically overlapping, phases, that of the "German" or "old system" flute and that of the Boehm flute. While the scope of this book lies primarily with the latter, the instrument's prehistory, as it were, is by no means irrelevant, for it was in the earlier period that experimentation on the more primitive instruments produced some of the fundamental mechanical devices and acoustical theories which were later applied and developed with increasing sophistication in the nineteenth and twentieth centuries.

THE MIDDLE AGES AND RENAISSANCE

The transverse flute of the Middle Ages is known not so much from extant specimens, which are, for obvious reasons, extremely rare, but through contemporary iconography— carvings, manuscripts, and pictures. Thus a work such as Jeanne d'Evreux's *Book of Hours*, ca. 1320, though not primarily a musical source, becomes just that for historical purposes. The flute of this period was wood, built in one piece, and just under two feet in length, sounding a primary scale of D major. In the early thirteenth century, this cylindrical flute, or more properly, fife, became associated with a small side drum for use as an infantry march accompaniment. Sebastian Virdung, writing in 1511, referred to this instrument as a *Zwerchpfeiff* and illustrated it as a very narrow tube with six unusually close finger holes (Fig. 1).

With the Renaissance came the emancipation of instrumental from vocal music. Whereas, before 1400, instrumentalists merely accompanied singers, participating in vocal compositions such as dancing songs and later madrigals and motets, they now were provided with new, exclusively instrumental forms. Yet the construction of instruments still followed the vocal model; each type of instrument was made in several sizes, roughly corresponding to the parts of a vocal ensemble. Martin Agricola, whose *Musica instrumentalis deudsch* was published in 1529, showed four flutes called *Schweitzer Pfeiffen* (Fig. 2). These were acoustically in much better proportion than the flutes described and shown by Virdung.

The second half of the sixteenth century saw increasing interest in timbre as an independent entity, which in turn acted as a major stimulus for the design of musical instruments.[1]

> The creation of instrumental music as an unrestrained, self-reliant form of art required the appreciation of the tonal qualities of different types of instruments and the consideration of tone color in connection with melody, harmony, and choral and contrapuntal effects. Instrumentation became an important part of composition, and the modern orchestra came into existence.[2]

Michael Praetorius's *Syntagma Musicum* of 1619–20 was the first work to recognize a family of transverse flutes with self-sufficient musical value, as distinct from the military function of the *Schweitzer Pfeiffen*. His plates show three sizes of flutes, called *Querflötten* or *Querpfeiffen* (Fig. 3), each with a "natural" compass of two octaves and an additional four "falset" notes obtainable only by skilled performers. Their ranges and dimensions are as follows:[3]

	NATURAL COMPASS	FALSET	LENGTH (MOUTH HOLE TO FOOT)
Discant	a^1-a^3	b^3-e^4	14 inches
Alto or tenor	d^1-d^3	e^3-a^3	22 inches
Bass	g -g^2	a^2-d^3	32 inches

These instruments anticipated the "German flute" of the seventeenth through nineteenth centuries in two respects: the alto or

Fig. 1. *SCHWEGEL* AND *ZWERCHPFEIFF*
from Sebastian Virdung, *Musica getuscht und auszgezogen* (1511).

Fig. 2. *SCHWEITZER PFEIFFEN*
from Martin Agricola, *Musica instrumentalis deudsch* (1529).

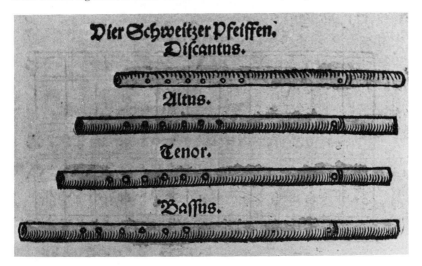

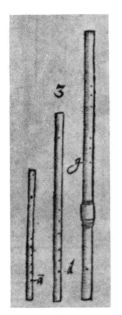

Fig. 3. *QUERFLÖTTEN*
from Michael Praetorius, *Syntagma Musicum* (1619–20).

[13

tenor flute is pitched in D major, a characteristic of all concert flutes prior to Boehm; and the bass flute was the first flute to be divided into two pieces to regulate tuning within an ensemble.

Marin Mersenne, writing in 1636, identified two transverse flutes, called *Flûtes Allemands*, pitched in D and G (Fig. 4). The D flute measured 23½ inches from the end of the stopper above the mouth hole to the end of the foot. Its basic fingering table provided a diatonic D major scale of two octaves (d^1–d^3), composed of fundamentals and octave harmonics. The chart was extended to a^3 by the use of twelfth and double-octave harmonics. This flute had a cylindrical bore, but no keys.[4] Interestingly, Mersenne did call attention to the absence of keys and argued for the further development of the transverse flute as a chromatic instrument, an objective that could be accomplished, he explained, by the addition of keys. He even went so far as to make a sketch showing the form of a key and spring suitable for this purpose.[5]

Fig. 4. *FLÛTE ALLEMAND*
from Marin Mersenne,
Harmonie Universelle (1636).

Nevertheless, it was more than fifty years before the first key was added to the flute.

Notable also in Mersenne's writing is his mention of materials. The common assumption is that flutes were constructed of wood, but this does not prove to have been exclusively the case. Mersenne wrote in his *Harmonicorum* of 1648:

> Flutes are made of plum, cherry, box and other woods which are easy to work. Particularly such woods are chosen as can be stained a beautiful color and which can be polished so as to please the eye as well as to give a satisfactory sound to the ear. Flutes are also made of ebony, glass, and crystal, and even of wax.[6]

Glass flutes had been known a century earlier, in fact; the Inventory of the Wardrobe of Henry VIII, King of England from 1509 to 1547, recorded "3 flutes of glasse." But what is especially important about Mersenne's observations is his recognition of the influence of technology, an obvious yet crucial component of the manufacturing process. Furthermore, Mersenne considered the visual aspect of an instrument to be of importance for the sake of public appeal, the desirability of which is obvious. For this same visual reason, modern instruction books stress regular cleaning of an instrument, not only for hygiene and mechanical maintenance, but also on the theory that a player who takes pride in his instrument will perform better.

THE SEVENTEENTH AND EIGHTEENTH CENTURIES

The evolution of the Baroque period, as symbolized by the music drama's replacement of the lyric madrigal, necessitated improvement of the woodwind instruments. The new expressiveness of the monodic style, effected by contrasts of range and dynamics, required increased instrumental flexibility in order to express the great depth of human feelings. Clearly the recorder was no longer suitable for such a role, and the transverse flute was substituted in view of its more brilliant tone and third octave range. However, even the transverse flute had far to go in order to achieve the requisite expression.

The principal figure in the late seventeenth century remodeling of the flute was Jacques Hotteterre le Romain (ca. 1680–ca. 1761), one of a prominent family of musicians and instrument makers. His major contribution, which is generally dated about 1660, was the construction of the first one-keyed flute (Figs. 5 and 6). The date is established by evidence of the presence of just such an improved flute in Lully's orchestra by 1670.[7] Quantz, writing in 1752, said that the D♯ key was added in France less than one hundred years earlier and that it had been adopted in Germany only fifty or sixty years before.[8] The first tutor for the one-keyed flute, entitled *Principes de la Flûte Traversière, ou Flûte d'Allemagne*, was published by Hotteterre in 1707.

Like the flute depicted by Mersenne, Hotteterre's instrument was based on the D major scale, with d[1] as the fundamental tone.

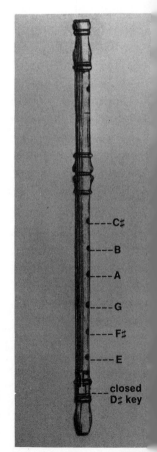

Fig. 5. 1-KEYED FLUTE.
August Grenser, Dresden,
mid-eighteenth century.
Boxwood, with ivory fittings,
1 brass key. Register on lower end.
This flute is said to have belonged
to Frederick the Great. (DCM 140)

C♯

B

A

G

F♯

E

closed
D♯ key

Fig. 6. 1-KEYED FLUTE
from Hotteterre-le-Romain,
*Principes de la Flûte Traversière,
ou Flûte d'Allemagne* (1707).

It was divided into three sections: a head, containing the mouth hole; the middle, with six finger holes; and the foot, which housed the single key. Later, because of discrepancies in pitch, the middle joint was to be divided still further. These sections were fitted together by means of tenon-and-socket joints.

Hotteterre's principal improvement was, of course, the addition of the D♯ key, operated by the fourth finger of the right hand, which controlled a new seventh hole bored just below the E hole. The key itself was of the "shut" or "closed" variety; that is, its rest position was closed, and pressure on the key would open the hole.

Another of Hotteterre's changes in the flute was his construction of the bore. In order to eliminate the fifelike shrillness of earlier instruments, he replaced the cylindrical model with what is generally referred to as conical bore, but which is in fact a combination cylindrical-conical bore. The headjoint retained the cylindrical configuration, measuring just under ¾ inch (between 18 and 19 millimeters) in diameter. A tapering began at the top of the middle joint, continuing to the beginning of the footjoint, where it measured approximately ½ inch in diameter. The footjoint itself varied in shape; most commonly it continued the taper, though there is evidence of both straight and convex feet.[9] In addition to its tonal advantages, the conical bore also had a flattening effect which allowed the finger holes to be placed closer together, thereby reducing an uncomfortable finger stretch.

Hotteterre also reduced the size of the finger holes. Mersenne (1637) cited hole sizes between 7 and 11.3 millimeters; the holes of a Hotteterre model instrument made by Rippert circa 1690 vary from 6.7 to 6.9 millimeters. This reduction was probably suggested by a similar feature of oboes which served to distinguish them from shawms.[10]

A typical flute of the Hotteterre period was constructed of a hardwood such as boxwood, ebony, or cocuswood. Quantz also cited kingwood, lignum sanctum, and grenadilla, but noted that "Boxwood is the most common and durable wood for flutes. Ebony, however, produces the clearest and most beautiful tone."[11] Quantz's reasoning in this regard was quite scientific:

The strength and clarity of tone depend upon the quality of the wood, that is, whether it is dense or compact, hard, and heavy. A thick and masculine tone depends upon the interior diameter of the flute, and upon the proportionate thickness of the wood. A thin, weak tone results from the opposite features: porous and light wood, a narrow interior bore, and thin wood.[12]

Next to wood in popularity was ivory, though its tone tended to be weaker. A frequent expedient was the lining of wood and ivory flutes with metal for durability and tone, though Quantz warned disparagingly, "Anyone who wishes to make the tone of the flute shrill, rude, and disagreeable can have it cased with brass, as some have tried."[13] Still other experimental instruments were constructed of wax, papier-mâché, and Scotch shoemaker leather. Keys were of brass or silver, with ferrule and cap of ivory, bone, or silver. The external appearance of eighteenth century instruments was often highly ornamental, sophisticated craftsmanship being applied to the thickenings left in the wood or ivory to strengthen the sockets.

The compass of Hotteterre's flute, according to his *Principes*, was "two octaves and some notes"; that is, like Mersenne's alto flute, d^1–d^3 plus "forced notes" which took the compass up to g^3.[14] Thus, although Hotteterre's fingering chart ranged from d^1 to g^3, he noted that "The notes above e^3 are forced notes, and cannot enter naturally in any piece. However, as you sometimes find them in Preludes, I will put here those I could discover." Despite this apparent contradiction, Hotteterre did use the upper extremes in his own preludes, and Michel Corrette commented in his method that $g^3\sharp$ and a^3 were used only in "preluding." Hotteterre warned that f^3 "can almost never be done on the flute" (he omitted the note from his chart altogether), that $f^3\sharp$ is easier, g^3 is possible, but above that, the notes are of little use and not worth the trouble.[15] Quantz's *Essay* * of 1752 provided scales ranging from d^1 to a^3. His charts were divided into three sec-

---

*The original German title was *Versuch einer Anweisung die Flöte zu spielen*, which translates as *Essay on Playing the Flute*. The work is always referred to as the *Versuch* or the *Essay*. However, the translator of this edition, Edward R. Reilly, chose the title, *On Playing the Flute*.

tions: a D minor diatonic scale from d^1 to a^3, a "flat" scale from e^1b to a^3b, and a "sharp" scale from $d^1\sharp$ to $g^3\sharp$.[16] Most charts of the period showed this same range, though the earliest ones, like Hotteterre's, were thoroughly chromatic for only two octaves, lacking the high f^3.

In about 1722, some attempts were made to extend the lower range of the flute to c^1, probably to match the oboe. Although Quantz owned such a flute, made by Biglioni of Rome, which had an open-standing key on the foot to produce $c^1\sharp$, he judged the added length to be detrimental to tone and intonation. Quantz's objections notwithstanding, Joseph Majer's *Theatrum Musicum* of 1732 gives a fingering chart with keys for low c^1 and $d^1\sharp$.[17]

The typical flute of the eighteenth century was stopped at its head by an ordinary cork plug. Analogous to the sound post of a violin in terms of tone and intonation, this cork could be pushed or pulled by the performer. To facilitate this operation, the cork was extended by a screw threaded through the cap on the upper end of the headjoint (Fig. 7). Quantz provided the following instructions for the use of the screw stopper:

> . . . if you wish to moderate the tone of the flute and play somewhat more softly, as is required in the Adagio, you must cover the mouth hole with your lips a little more. . . . Since, however, the flute becomes a little lower as a result, you must also have a screw attached to the plug found in the head piece with which you can press the plug the breadth of a good knifeback further into the flute, in order to raise the flute from its normal level. . . . This makes the flute shorter, and thus higher; and in this fashion you can always remain in tune with the other instruments.[18]

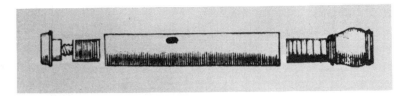

Fig. 7. QUANTZ SCREW STOPPER from Diderot, *Supplément* to *Encyclopédie* (1777).

In performing an entire concerto or sonata with movements of alternating tempi, Quantz advised the player to tune the flute lower for the Allegro, while also rotating the embouchure outward and blowing more strongly. For the Adagio, he instructed the player to push the plug in, restoring it to the original position for the concluding Allegro movement.[19] The projecting part of the screw indicated the position of the inner end of the cork with respect to the mouth hole, and was often marked with numbered rings to facilitate its setting.

Adjustment of the cork, however, did not prove sufficient to compensate for the considerable changes of pitch caused by non-universal pitch standards. Quantz observed that ". . . the pitch to which we tune is so varied that a different tuning or prevailing pitch has been introduced not only in every country, but in almost every province and city, while even at the very same place the harpsichord is tuned high at one time, low at another, by careless tuners."[20] Praetorius had solved this problem by the use of multiple instruments, in his case recorders, with one tuned a semitone lower than the other. Later, a single instrument had been divided into two and then three pieces in order to alter the length at will.

In 1720, these ideas were combined in a rather sophisticated constructive technique known as *corps de réchange* (Fig. 8). This maneuver involved the division of the flute into four joints, whereby the former middle joint or body was now itself divided between the two sets of finger holes, necessitating an additional tenon-and-socket joint. The variable component was the upper middle joint, which was provided, for each instrument, in three to six different lengths. These were designed for tuning to various pitches without disturbing the response of the critical left-hand cross-fingerings. Most common was the provision of three alternate joints, the shortest making the flute a semitone sharper than the longest; later, as the pitch rose, another three were added.

Naturally, the substitution of the *corps de réchange* necessitated adjustment of the cork to correct octave intonation. In turn, the frequent shifts of the cork eventually caused the disappearance of the heavy, ornamental head cap in favor of a smaller and

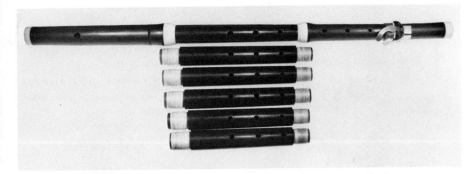

Fig. 8. QUANTZ 2-KEYED FLUTE. Johann Joachim Quantz, Potsdam, ca. 1750. Ebony, with silver keys and ivory rings. 6 upper body joints (*corps de réchange*), numbered with notches on end of each joint. Length 636, 641, 650, 658, 664, or 672 mm. Quantz's tuning slide. This flute was made for Frederick the Great. (DCM 916)

lighter one. For the shortest joint, the cork was screwed out; for the longest, it was screwed in. Quantz's instructions for the use of the *corps de réchange* were nearly identical to those for the use of the screw stopper; the long upper joint, which flattened the pitch, was to be used for Allegro movements, in which the flute must sound over a strong accompaniment; the short joint was to be used for the Adagio movements.[21]

A small tuning device called the register (Fig. 9) appeared shortly after the *corps de réchange*. Designed to regulate the internal tuning of the lower body and footjoint, it consisted of a two-part footjoint, the length of which could be varied by about half an inch by sliding the telescopic metal tubes that lined the internal joint. In his 1752 *Essay*, Quantz decried the register as a cause of false intonation except for the D octave; he concluded that "this invention must be rejected as most harmful and detrimental." Anton Mahaut, however, in his *Nieuwe Manier* of 1759, ascribed its origin to Pierre Gabriel Buffardin, Quantz's teacher, and defended it, as did Johann George Tromlitz in his *Ausführlicher und gründlicher Unterricht* of 1791. The alternative suggested by Quantz was the division of the head into two pieces. The tenon of the lower part would be longer than that of the upper, and when inserted, could be adjusted to improve the intonation. This invention, which Quantz claimed as his own, in time became the modern tuning slide.[22]

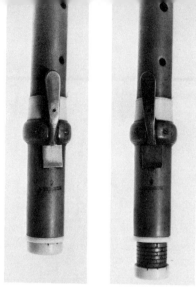

Fig. 9. REGISTER
from 1-keyed flute (Fig. 6).
Register measures 31 mm overall and
has a cork-packing ring to close the
circle airtight. The six numbered ring
graduations are 2.5 mm apart, permitting
a total adjustment of up to 15 mm.

Another device introduced by Quantz was a second footjoint key, this one for E♭ (Figs. 8 and 10). Added in 1726, it was designed to correct "a slight impurity in certain tones" within the mean tone system of tuning. Thus the use of an E♭ as well as a D♯ key supplemented Quantz's elaborate system of cross-fingerings for sharped and flatted notes. The second key, however, did not win popular approbation, and the inventor reported in 1752 that "it still has not been generally accepted."[23] Indeed, it was soon abandoned.

Even Quantz's two-keyed fingering system, however, was not sufficient to ensure accurate intonation; chromatic cross-fingering was never as successful on the flute as it was on the oboe and bassoon. Expert manipulation of the embouchure was an absolute necessity to compensate for the defects of the instrument. Particularly out of tune were b^1♭, g^1♯, g^2♯, f^1, and f^2. As a result,

Fig. 10. QUANTZ 2-KEYED FLUTE from Diderot, *Supplément* to *Encyclopédie* (

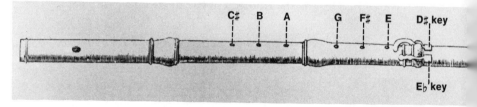

although F♯ was far from perfect (its straight fingering was flat and the cross-fingering too sharp for any but upper register leading tone use), the best keys for the flute were G and D major. Indeed, this tonal limitation provides a useful device for ascertaining whether a piece marked merely "flute" or "flauto" was intended for transverse flute or recorder, as the favorite recorder keys were B♭ and F.[24] Tromlitz wrote, at the end of the eighteenth century, that keys with more than three sharps or flats were "difficult and unsuitable" for the flute. For the most part, composers were appropriately wary of dangerous keys. Mozart, for instance, had an acutely sensitive ear and therefore confined his major flute compositions to the relatively safe keys of D, G, A, and C.* Unfortunately, less enlightened composers did write for transverse flute in some of the less reliable keys. Thus Quantz warned performers that "Pieces set in very difficult keys must be played only before listeners who understand the instrument, and are able to grasp the difficulty of these keys on it; they must not be played before everyone. You cannot produce brilliant and pleasing things with good intonation in every key, as most amateurs demand."[25]

Notwithstanding its poor intonation, the flute of the eighteenth century enjoyed great popularity. "That some of the forked sounds were dull and out of tune seems to have been philosophically accepted as a natural weakness of the instrument which it was the player's duty to conceal by skilful manipulation; the wind-players of that period accepted their instruments as they accepted (we hope) their wives—for better or for worse."[26] A multitude of tutors, beginning with Hotteterre's in 1707, promoted the flute's popularity among amateurs, whose critical faculties may be expected to be less developed than those of professional musicians. Thus Sir John Hawkins, writing in A General History of the Science and Practice of Music in 1776, observed that the flute "still retains some degree of estimation among gentlemen whose

*Quartets for Flute and Strings, K. 285 in D, K. 285a in G, K. 285b in C, K. 298 in A; Concerto for Flute and Harp, K. 299 in C; Concerti for Flute, K. 313 in G, K. 314 in D; Andante, K. 315 in C; Adagio in c and Rondo in C, K. 617 for Glass Harmonica, Flute, Oboe, Viola, and Cello.

ears are not nice enough to inform them that it is never in tune."[27]

~ However, the very popularity of the flute in a sense became its own undoing, at least temporarily, for the eighteenth century was both "the age of its flourishing and the period during which its inherent defects became increasingly irksome."[28] Quite simply, the flute's inadaptability to the requirements of ensemble performance led to its disrepute among composers. Alessandro Scarlatti is reported to have said, "I cannot endure wind-instrument players; they all blow out of tune."[29] Similarly, Luigi Cherubini's caustic comment was that "The only thing worse than one flute is two."[30] What is peculiar, however, is the apparent satisfaction of professionals with their instrument. Like the amateurs, they evidently accepted the idiosyncrasies of the one-keyed flute as calculated risks. The probable explanation is a very natural disinclination to relearn their art in any way that an improved instrument might necessitate.

The tone of the eighteenth century flute was considered its savior by nineteenth century observers: "The mellifluous quality of its tone . . . created so general a desire that it might be rendered more extensively available, that invention had a powerful stimulus to improvement."[31] The mid-century introduction of equal temperament, by eliminating the need for Quantz's numerous chromatic cross-fingerings, implied the possibility of developing a complete chromatic key mechanism for the woodwinds. Thus, in the late eighteenth century "we find the beginning of what we might call a 'mechanical' instead of a purely acoustical approach to the intonation problems of the flute. The obvious notion that the chromatic semitones would be better sounded from their own individual holes, if these could be brought under control of the fingers, began to receive practical attention."[32]

Although chromatic keys had been known on bagpipes as early as the beginning of the seventeenth century, the flute, because of the dubious honor of possessing the worst cross-fingerings, became the first orchestral woodwind to accept additional chromatic keywork. Just before 1760, several London makers—Pietro Florio (ca. 1730–1795), Caleb Gedney (1754–1769), and Richard Potter (1728–1806)—began adding three additional keys to the existing one-key flute (Fig. 11). Two of the new keys were assigned to fingers which previously had no mechanical function. The G♯ key, a closed key lying lengthwise down the side of the flute, controlled the G♯ hole bored below the A hole on the far side of the lower end of the upper middle joint, and was controlled by the little finger of the left hand. A B♭ key, also lying lengthwise on the tube, governed a hole bored on the near side of the tube below the B♮ hole and was played by the left-hand thumb. There was no free finger to play the added F key, so the third finger of the right hand, which already covered the E hole, also operated a closed cross key for F♮ whose hole was bored on the back of the tube between the E and F♯ holes. The touch curved over the top of the flute.

The new keys, which were mounted in small wooden blocks, now made the production of f^3 thoroughly reliable; more importantly, the only remaining chromatic note in the D scale was C♮, but its quality was acceptable. The new freedom of tonality, and therefore of modulation, is evident, for instance, in the sonatas of Haydn, particularly in comparison with the much earlier ones of Mozart. Acceptance of the new keys was not immediate, however, for two quite understandable reasons. The first consideration was mechanical; players were skeptical of the efficiency and reliability of the keys. Made of a sheet of brass with a solid leather pad, they rotated on brass pins attached through ridges in the wood; the hole to be closed was rimless. Thus: "Closure was far from hermetic; the leather was porous, the fall of the action imprecise, and the flat brass spring usually sluggish in action."[33] A second objection was the necessary change in fingering; consequently, the new keys were at first used only for shakes or other awkward ornaments rather than for improving the quality of the forked sounds, the primary purpose for which they were designed. General acceptance may be dated between 1785 and 1790.

Notwithstanding players' objections to the three new keys, in about 1774 the same three innovative London makers who were responsible for those keys resuscitated the earlier eighteenth century idea of the C footjoint (Fig. 12). To implement this concept, the flute was lengthened by two inches. Two holes bored in the footjoint were controlled by open keys operated by the fourth finger of the right hand. Since this finger was now responsible for three different keys, D♯, C, and C♯, the latter two had to be specially contrived because it was necessary to close the C♯ key to sound C. Thus the C♯ finger plate was placed under the C finger plate so that both closed when the C plate was pressed, but the C♯ key projected somewhat to allow it to close independently.

The extension of range and technical facility afforded by the four- and six-keyed flutes had a profound effect on musical composition, which may be seen, for example, in comparison of the works of Haydn and Mozart. Haydn's orchestral use of the flute reflects the transition occurring in orchestral sound during the

Fig. 11. 4-KEYED FLUTE. H. Grenser, Dresden (lower body and foot) and Tuerlinckx, Malines (head and probably upper body), late eighteenth century. Ebony, with silver keys and ivory rings. (DCM 767)

Fig. 12. 6-KEYED FLUTE. Clementi & Co., London, ca. 1802–21. Ivory, with silver ferrules. C foot. (DCM 1406)

Fig. 13. 7-KEYED FLUTE, "C. NICHOLSON'S IMPROVED."
Thomas Prowse, London, ca. 1835. Rosewood, with silver ferrules and keys.
Gold inlaid central ring engraved with floral designs. C foot. Large embouchure
and "Nicholson" large holes. Silver lip plate, with ivory ring bushing at
embouchure, engraved "Presented to / Mr. Nicholson / by / Thos. Prowse." According
to Philip Bate, however, Nicholson used flutes by Potter and Astor. (DCM 1265)

second half of the eighteenth century. In his early symphonies,
the flute, like the trumpet and bassoon, is rarely present; it began
to appear regularly only after 1780. Haydn's range was conservative, being confined largely to the middle register, roughly f^1 to
f^2. In his later symphonies, such as the *Military* (no. 100 in G
major), the range expanded to d^1 to g^3. Haydn's work was indicative of the flute's coming role as an integral member of the orchestra. "[T]he transverse flute seems to lose something of the
specialised emotional association that it had had with Bach, and to
become more of an orchestral voice pure and simple. With him,
especially, in his later years, wind instruments generally began to
have status in the orchestra equal to that of the strings, and he
wrote for them more freely than did any of his predecessors."[34]

In Mozart's late symphonies, the flute became an important
constituent of the instrumental polyphony. His Concerto in G, K.
313, includes frequent g^3s in its rapid scalar passages. Even more
notable is his conscious exploitation of low c^1 and $c^1\sharp$ in the Concerto in C for Flute and Harp, K. 299.

Eighteenth century organological achievement culminated in
the development of the eight-keyed flute, referred to in later
years as the "German," "ordinary," "old system," "simple system," or "Meyer system" flute.* In 1782, Dr. J. H. Ribock began to promote a closed key for $c^2\natural$ to control a hole bored on
the near side of the tube between the B and C$\sharp$ holes (Fig. 13).

*The term "Meyer system" was not coined until the late nineteenth century,
when it was adopted to refer to the simple system instruments manufactured by
J. F. Meyer, Hannover.

Fig. 14. 8-KEYED FLUTE.
Rudall & Rose, London
(No. 2241), ca. 1827–37.
Boxwood, with silver rings, stud,
and keys. Inlaid ivory embouchure
ring. C foot. (DCM 26)

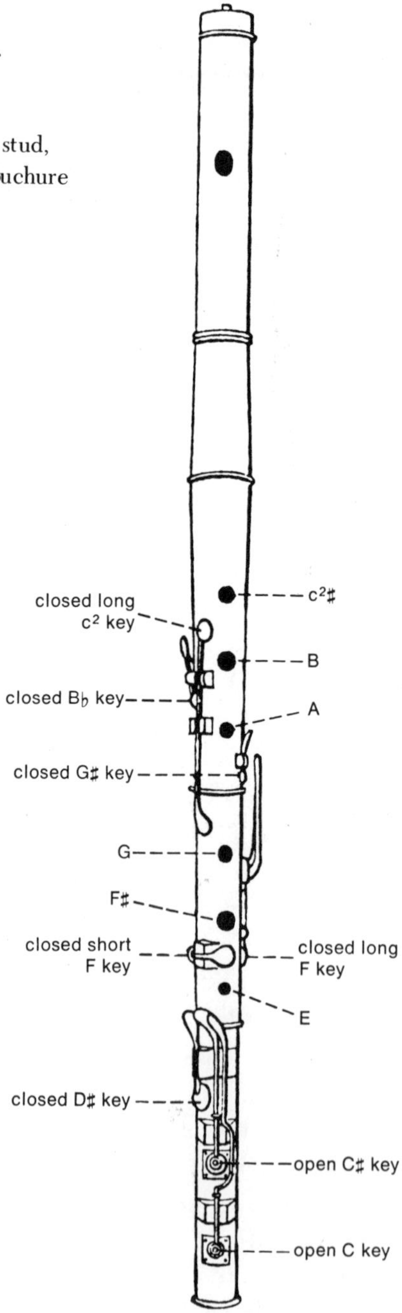

closed long
c² key

closed B♭ key

closed G♯ key

G

F♯

closed short
F key

closed D♯ key

c²♯

B

A

closed long
F key

E

open C♯ key

open C key

Fig. 15. 8-KEYED FLUTE.
Rudall & Rose, London, ca. 1827,
from Rockstro, *Treatise*.

The key was operated by the first finger of the right hand by means of a finger plate connected to the key by a long shank.

Four years later, in 1786, Johann George Tromlitz introduced the duplicate F♮ key (Figs. 14 and 15). On the four- and six-keyed models, it was extremely difficult to move the right-hand third finger sideways from the E hole to the F♮ cross key; thus it was almost impossible to slur from F to D or D♯ or vice versa without involuntarily sounding a "grace note" E between them. Tromlitz's solution was to bore another F♮ hole on the far side of the instrument, covered by a closed key operated by the fourth finger of the left hand. Because of its shape, the new key became known as the "long F."

THE EARLY NINETEENTH CENTURY

Though the eight-key flute is generally considered to be the standard instrument of the late eighteenth and nineteenth centuries, the flute was, in fact, far from standardized. Despite the invention of seven more chromatic keys, the one-keyed flute prospered well into the nineteenth century; several nineteenth century tutors treat the one-key model as the norm, appending supplementary information for "additional" keys. Not the least reason for the survival of the one-key model was the extra cost of additional keys.

At the other extreme, the flute was not limited to eight keys, for the nineteenth century, a period of intense mechanical invention in many fields, witnessed great mechanical elaboration upon the "simple system" flute. Some instruments had as many as seventeen keys and compasses extending to low g. Rockstro provides the following list of the most common optional additions to the eight-keyed flute:[35]

—A lever for the right hand first finger to open the B♭ key (used mostly for shakes)

—A closed key governing a hole above the c^2♯ hole, operated by the right hand first finger (for b^1/c^2♯ and b^2/c^3♯ shakes; also capable of producing poor quality c^2♯/d^2 and c^3♯/d^3 shakes)

—A closed key for another hole above the last-mentioned hole, also for the right hand first finger (for d^3/e^3 shake)

—A third lever for F operated by the left hand thumb (used for sequence d^1, f^1, g^1♯, etc.)

—An extra G♯ key for the left hand thumb

—An open key for b, produced by closing a lateral c^1 hole, operated by the little finger of the left or right hand

—A closed key covering an extra hole above the usual small f♯ hole, controlled by the third finger of the right hand (to raise the pitch of f^1♯ and f^2♯)

—Open keys for b♭, a, a♭, and g

In 1800 Tromlitz, the inventor of the long F key, devised a more practical alternative to his own invention. In order to eliminate the need for the duplicate F♮ hole, thereby reducing the risk of leakage, he devised a lever for the fourth finger of the left hand which raised the head of the original cross key. Tromlitz was also concerned with the double responsibility of the left-hand thumb for the B♭ and C keys, and proposed an additional B♭ lever, constructed on the same principle as the long F. A third scheme of the same inventor was for a keyless flute, which, though seemingly regressive, would eliminate the operational deficiencies of the keys. Although he was not able to devise a suitable keyless instrument, encountering fingering problems similar to those of seventeenth century flutes, "Tromlitz's scheme is of historic importance because it contains the germ of one of the most important concepts of flute-playing theory—that of the 'open-key' system."[36]

The next proposal for improving the flute came in 1803 from a physician, H. W. Pottgiesser, who published an anonymous article outlining his plans in *Allgemeine Musikalische Zeitung*. His design called for a sharper taper to the bore, with a shorter tube and equally spaced holes placed closer together (Fig. 16). Each finger and thumb was assigned its own hole; in addition, the right-hand thumb was to operate the only key. A second key, presumably open-standing, would be allowed only if the player's left-hand fourth finger could not reach the G♯ hole. The body and foot of Pottgiesser's flute were to form a single piece, like the modern piccolo. Rockstro's criticism of the Pottgiesser scheme is fourfold: the absence of the B ♮ hole, the high position and small size of the G ♯ hole, the use of the right-hand thumb for the D ♯ key, and the low position of the D hole. Though Rockstro admitted that this instrument was a definite improvement over the ordinary flute, having only one veiled note, c^2, he correctly judged it to be impractical because of its lack of chromatic keywork. The public, similarly, paid absolutely no practical attention to Pottgiesser's proposal. Pottgiesser's contribution, then, seems to have been one of suggestion rather than mechanical genius, as he himself apparently acknowledged in his article: "It has been my object to further the study of the construction of the flute; to give an impetus to the spirit of invention . . . , and to combat the opinion

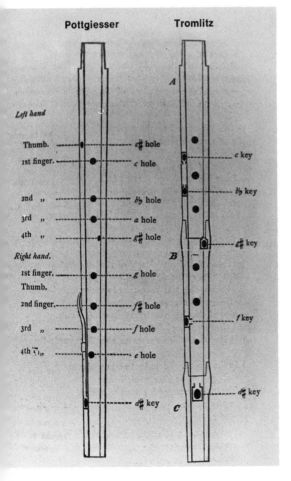

Fig. 16.
FLUTES BY POTTGIESSER
AND TROMLITZ
from H. W. Pottgiesser,
"Ueber die Fehler der bisherigen
Flöten," *Allgemeine Musikalische
Zeitung* (1803).
The body and foot of Pottgiesser's
flute (*left*) were in one piece.
Tromlitz's flute (*right*) was divided
into a middle-piece (*A*),
heart-piece (*B*), and foot-piece (*C*).

that the present flute is capable of no further improvement."[37]

It is evident that nineteenth century flutemakers took Pottgiesser's advice. The first mechanical advance of lasting importance was protected by the French patent of September 10, 1806, issued to Claude Laurent of Paris. The most obvious feature represented by this document was the use of glass for the flute

Fig. 17. 3-KEYED FLUTE. Claude Laurent, Paris, 1809.
Clear white glass, with fine-ground interior and exterior surfaces.
Rose-cut rock crystal cap. 3 silver keys mounted on posts
attached to screwed-on elliptical plates. Bayonet catches for head
and middle body joints. (DCM 719)

Fig. 18. 4-KEYED FLUTE.
Claude Laurent, Paris, 1818.
Crystal glass, with interior surface polished
and exterior surface cut in concave,
diamond-shaped facets. Silver tenons,
sockets, and keys. An amethyst or garnet
is mounted on the upper surface of each
key. Red glass cap. 2 bayonet catches,
wrapped footjoint tenon. (DCM 611)

tube (Figs. 17–20). The advantages claimed were not only sweetness and purity of tone, but, more importantly, constancy of dimensions. And since glass was not affected by humidity, leakage and checking of keys would be eliminated. What is most notable about the patent, however, is not the use of glass per se, but rather, the mechanical contrivances which it necessitated. The

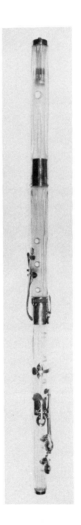

Fig. 19. 7-KEYED FLUTE. Claude Laurent, Paris, 1815. Clear fluted glass with polished exterior surface. Head lined with half-inch-long silver tube where cork rests. Ivory screw cap with flat sheet of pearl on outside and silver edge. Silver mountings and keys. C foot. Miller knew of only one other Laurent glass flute with a cork. This flute was mistakenly dated 1817 in the catalog of the Music Loan Exhibition (1904). (DCM 1400)

Fig. 20. BOEHM FLUTE. Claude Laurent, Paris, 1844. Green "uranium" glass, fluted and polished. Silver mountings and rings, pearl plate on upper end. In place of a cork, a glass disc is cemented in place. (DCM 11)

simplest such device was the use of silver tenons and sockets for the joints; another was the lengthening of the springs, which gave them increased resilience. Most revolutionary was the mounting of the keys. Prior to this time, metal "saddles" were used on the smaller woodwinds; the key rotated on a screw-headed pin held in a metal bearing. Laurent's problem was to attach the keys to a tube of glass; his solution was to mount the keys in silver posts which were then attached to metal plates screwed to the glass tube. This expedient was soon applied to wood flutes as well, in all cases affording greater security of operation by permitting little or no lateral play in the keys.

On May 28, 1808, William Henry Potter (1760–1848), a London flutemaker and son of Richard Potter, took out a patent for sliding keys (Fig. 21), intended to facilitate an interpretive technique known as the "glide." This was a favorite gimmick of the English virtuoso Charles Nicholson (1795–1837), who described it as "one of the most pleasing expressions of which the Instrument is capable,—and which is produced by *sliding* the Finger or Fingers gently off so as to gradually uncover the hole or holes, instead of lifting them up suddenly."[38] Potter's invention called for key levers to have a horizontal action in relation to the flute tube, in place of the normal vertical action of a key plug; the key slid away from, rather than rose from, the hole. Although Potter's design was rapidly consigned to oblivion, it is significant as being the first mechanical alteration to the flute designed to remedy a specific technical fingering problem.

Another variable device was patented by Charles Townley in August 1808. Described as "A Key—causing the Bore—to lengthen or contract at Pleasure," the mechanism consisted of two levers, governed by the left-hand thumb, which acted on the tuning slide. It could be operated during the course of a performance. However, it was seldom manufactured. In November of the same year, Townley took out a second patent, this one concerning a clip-on mouthpiece to assist the direction of the airstream. The patent also included an extra key which covered a small hole designed to sharpen d^1 on flutes with extended footjoints. On such instruments, the d^1 hole was often bored lower

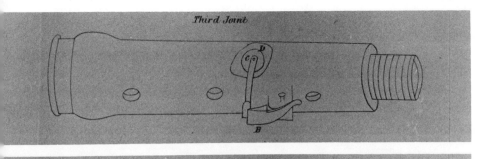

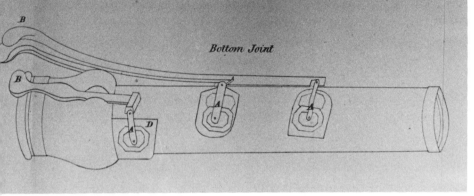

Fig. 21. SLIDING KEYS OF WILLIAM HENRY POTTER.
British Patent No. 3136 (1808).
Pressure on the keys (B) caused the valves (C)
to slide over, by means of springs (A), to stop the holes in the plates (D).

than its acoustically correct position in order to improve the quality of f^3 and other high notes for players who rather stubbornly adhered to the fingering of the one-keyed flute.

In the same month, November 1808, Reverend Frederick Nolan took out a patent for a device designed to effect greater evenness of intonation. It consisted of open-standing keys, either a second order lever or a linked pair of first order levers, whose touchpieces were rings that surrounded the finger holes (Fig. 22). This is the first known contrivance for simultaneously closing both an open key and a regular hole with the same finger, a principle that is fundamental to the highly mechanized instruments developed later in the century. A further application was the possibility of closing the key while the immediate hole remained open; this was done by sliding the finger off the key, but keeping it on the shank. Nolan also proposed a small catch which could deactivate the device at the performer's discretion, but this gadget has been dismissed as merely a complication.

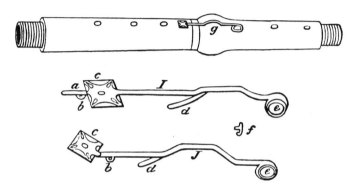

Fig. 22. RING KEYS OF REVEREND FREDERICK NOLAN.
British Patent No. 3183 (1808).
The key was attached to the instrument as at g.
The perforated key (I) was equipped with a touch (e);
a hinge (b) behind a valve (c); springs (d) between the
perforation and the valve; and a projecting tongue (a) behind the
hinge "to prevent the spring from throwing the touch too high."
The catch (f) was placed behind the touch to fasten down the key.
A jointed key (J) could be substituted when there was sufficient
distance between the holes to require a double lever.

A patent registered in 1810 by George Miller, a London flutemaker, concerned the bore and material of the instrument, rather than its mechanism. The specification provided for a cylindrical bore to be fashioned of metal; though intended primarily for the military fife, the patent also made mention of concert flutes. Reaction to Miller's proposals was not good, however. John Clinton, for instance, provided the following critique:

> . . . first, as to its material; this I consider most objectionable—the absence of vocality, richness and body of tone in the metal when compared with wood; its harsh and shrill quality, . . . added to the unpleasantness of its use, and its sensibility to heat and cold, causing

a constant variation in pitch; and secondly, as to the bore—the cylindrical form preventing the possibility of obtaining that gradation requisite for quality of tone.[39]

A letter written by Carl Maria von Weber to *Allgemeine Musikalische Zeitung* in 1811 described a flute attributed to Johann Nepomuk Capeller, a court musician in Munich. Its mechanical innovations included a G♯ key with a second touch for the right hand and an extra shake key for d^2, a feature which has survived on the Boehm flute. Most notable on this instrument was the movable mouthpiece. Attached to an oval plate affixed to the headjoint, both the mouthpiece and the cork could be moved longitudinally by the rotation of a screw, thereby altering the pitch of the instrument without upsetting its internal intonation.

In 1812, Tebaldo Monzani was issued a patent for several features which had already been tried, though not patented. These included cork lapping and metal lining of the sockets, which French makers had used "for some time," according to Fitzgibbon; a combination body and footjoint, used by Capeller and others since at least 1807; and a "nob" on each side of the mouth hole.

In 1814, James Wood of London secured a patent for a flute with three tuning slides. Each joint was comprised of telescopic metal tubes, and each was marked with sharp, natural, and flat calibrations. Although useful at the time they were introduced, the multiple tuning slides became obsolete with the subsequent stabilization of musical pitch.

In 1822, Charles Nicholson had his flutes designed with excavations carved into the tube in strategic places. Intended to afford a thinner feel and better grip, these slight indentations or flattenings of the wood (Nicholson preferred cocus) were frequently lined with sharkskin. One such excavation, for the first joint of the left-hand forefinger, was placed on the front of the tube near the uppermost hole; the other was on the bottom of the flute between the F♯ and G holes for the convenience of the right-hand thumb. Nicholson's most important contribution, however, was his enlargement of the tone holes. This expedient was first employed by Nicholson's father, Charles Nicholson the elder, who, like many English players of the early nineteenth century, was dissatisfied with the rather small tone of the contemporary flute. The younger Nicholson was perhaps extreme in his timbral ideals, writing in his tutor that "the tone ought to be as reedy as possible, as much like that of the hautboy as you can get it,"[40] but his advocacy of larger holes created widespread demand for such increased dimensions. Instruments built according to his designs were manufactured by Thomas Prowse the elder in London and marketed by Clementi & Co. with great success (Fig. 13, page 27).

In 1824, Dr. Pottgiesser announced still another model. He at last succumbed to the necessity of additional keys, including Capeller's d^2 shake, but he retained open holes for the four fingers of each hand. The most important feature of his 1824 flute was the equalization of finger hole diameter at 6.4 millimeters, with the exception of the $c^1\sharp$ and d^1 holes, which measured 7.9 millimeters. His insistence on the proper positioning of the holes rather than on the convenience of the fingers clearly anticipated the acoustical principles propounded by Boehm in the next decade. Another innovation of the Pottgiesser instrument was the use of a ring key with a crescent touchpiece for altering the size of the $c^2\sharp$ hole (Fig. 23). The device consisted of a metal bar lying along the tube. A crescent at the lower end bordered closely on the B♮ hole, and was closed by the same finger. The portion of the bar that crossed the C♯ hole formed a ring, whose bottom was faced with a perforated pad, which reduced the size of the hole when the crescent was pressed. The device functioned as a second

Fig. 23. POTTGIESSER'S RING-AND-CRESCENT KEY
from H. W. Pottgiesser, "Nachtrag zu der Abhandlung 'Ueber die Fehler der Flöte . . .,' " *Allgemeine Musikalische Zeitung* (1824).

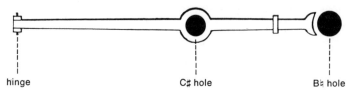

hinge   C♯ hole   B♮ hole

order lever pivoted on a hinge even farther above the C♯ hole. Its effect was to flatten the forked c^2♮ and to sharpen c^2♯. Bate notes that the ring-pad principle has been adopted on many modern woodwinds to adjust hole diameters.[41]

The first three decades of the nineteenth century were marked by a notable extension of the range of the flute in both directions. Improvements in upper register notes are quite evident, for example, in Beethoven's scores. In his Symphony no. 1, written in 1799, he stays almost exclusively within a compass from g^1 to g^3. Realizing the difficulty of g^3♯, he drops the flute an octave in measure 51 of the second movement, but does not change registers when the same melody is repeated a fifth lower in measure 150. In the same movement, one finds in measure 54 a unison flute and violin melody in C major. When this melody is repeated in measure 153 in F major, Beethoven omits the notes above f^3 in the flute part. In the Third Symphony, written in 1803, the flute range remains essentially g^1 to g^3, but more a^3s are present, as in measures 482–486 of the first movement. In Symphony no. 8 of 1814, the flute reaches to b^3♭, as in measures 186–189 of the fourth movement, yet in measures 386–389, Beethoven drops the part an octave to avoid b^3. Upward extension of range is also evident in the instructional materials of the period; Charles Nicholson's *Preceptive Lessons*, published in 1821, provided fingerings for c^4 and d^4, albeit with the qualification that "The Author conceives he is the first who has ever introduced these notes into print. They are, however, so difficult to produce that he has not the least expectation of ever seeing passages written for them. . . ."*[42]

The option of downward extension was very common in the early nineteenth century. Many flutes reached down to b♭ while some by Trexler and Koch of Vienna (circa 1815 and 1820, respectively) and Laurent of Paris (1834) reached to g (Figs. 24 and 25). The latter model, for which Georg Bayr published his *Practische Flöten-Schule* in 1823, required seven keys below the d♯ key; of these, three were operated by the right-hand fourth finger, two

---

*Yet Joseph Francoeur's *Diapason général de tous les instruments à vent* (Paris, 1772) cited the flute range as d^1-c^4.

Fig. 24. 15-KEYED FLUTE.
S. Koch, Vienna,
mid-nineteenth century.
Ebony, with silver rings and keys.
Footjoint and lower middle joint
in one piece because of long keys.
Key for low g, played by
left thumb, is 470 mm long.
(DCM 231)

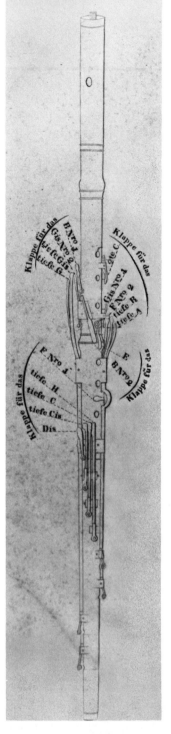

Fig. 25. 15-KEYED FLUTE BY KOCH
from Georg Bayr, *Practische Flöten-Schule* (1823).
The fingering chart for this flute gives a range from g to c⁴.

by the left-hand fourth finger, and two by the left-hand thumb.
All of these keys were fitted with metal plugs. The lower end of
the footjoint was sometimes recurved toward the head at a point
below the b hole, with the reversed section reaching almost up to
the d¹♯ hole (Fig. 26).

Despite the rash of mechanical and inventive activity of the
first third of the nineteenth century, of which the aforementioned
contrivances are only representative, the so-called German flute
was far from perfection. While the addition of chromatic keys was
a marked improvement over the numerous fork fingerings of the
one-keyed flute, fingering was still far from optimal. Cross-fingerings persisted, the F♮ being the most awkward. A commentary of
1831 explained:

> In all passages of Music, . . . where the notes preceding or follow-
> ing the F♮ require either the G♯ key to be opened, or the sixth hole
> to be closed with the third finger of the right hand, there is a
> difficulty on the common Flutes in gliding to or from the F♮ keys
> and a partial unstopping of the intermediate holes, which produces a
> sound between the respective notes. . . .[43]

Moreover, the tone produced by fork fingerings was veiled in
quality and poor in intonation. The problem of intonation was
compounded by the unscientific placement of the tone holes. "In
every flute of the usual manner, the low C♯ and E♭ apertures
are much too low; the E♮, very much too high; the F♮ is also too
high, and the F♯ too low; the G nearly right; the G♯, A♮, and
B♭ much too high, and the topmost aperture much too low."[44]
Though keys were of some help in correcting intonation, the
keys themselves were the source of other problems; insufficient

Fig. 26. 17-KEYED FLUTE. J. Ziegler (?), Vienna, mid-nineteenth century.
Ivory, with silver rings and keys. Recurved footjoint to low g.
Total length 705 mm, recurved section 210 mm from end. (DCM 230)

tension of the springs of the closed keys resulted in a loss of sound as a result of inadequate stoppage. And although the tone of the wooden flute was sweet, it was relatively feeble and not up to the demands of power and brilliance made by its new environment, the modern orchestra.

Notes]

1. Curt Sachs, *The History of Musical Instruments* (New York: W. W. Norton & Co., 1940), pp. 297–98.

2. Dayton C. Miller, "The Evolution of the Wood-Wind Instruments," TS, p. 2. Hereafter cited as Miller, "Evolution."

3. Adam Carse, *Musical Wind Instruments* (1939; reprint ed., New York: Da Capo Press, 1965), pp. 82–83.

4. M[arin] Mersenne, *Harmonicorum Libri XII* (Paris: G. Baudry, 1648).

5. Miller, "Evolution," pp. 10–11.

6. Dayton C. Miller, "Flutes of Glass," *The Flutist* 6 (July 1925): 151. Hereafter cited as Miller, "Glass."

7. Robert J. Baasch, "Modern Flutes and Their Predecessors" (Ed.D. diss., Teacher's College, Columbia University, 1952), p. 17.

8. Johann Joachim Quantz, *On Playing the Flute*, trans. Edward R. Reilly (1752; London: Faber and Faber, 1966), p. 30.

9. Carse, p. 85.

10. Philip Bate, *The Flute* (New York: W. W. Norton & Co., 1969), p. 111.

11. Quantz, pp. 34–35.

12. Ibid., p. 50.

13. Ibid., p. 35.

14. Jacques Hotteterre le Romain, *Principles of the Flute Recorder and Oboe,* trans. and ed. David Lasocki (1707; New York: Praeger Publishers, 1968), p. 39.

15. Ibid., pp. 45–46.

16. Quantz, pp. 42–43.

17. Joseph Majer, *Neu-eröffneter Theoretisch und Prakticher Music-Saal* (Nürnberg: Berlegts Johann Jacob Cremer, 1741), p. 45.

18. Quantz, p. 59.

19. Ibid., p. 197.

20. Ibid., p. 31.

21. Ibid., p. 32.

22. Ibid., pp. 33–34.

23. Ibid., p. 47.

24. Anthony Baines, *Woodwind Instruments and Their History* (New York: W. W. Norton & Co., 1962), p. 291.

25. Quantz, p. 200.

26. Carse, p. 87.

27. Sir John Hawkins, *A General History of the Science and Practice of Music* (1776; London: J. Alfred Novello, 1853; reprint ed., New York: Dover Publications, 1963), 2:739.

28. Bate, p. 90.

29. Richard Shepard Rockstro, *A Treatise on the Construction the History and the Practice of the Flute*, 2nd ed., rev. (1928; reprint ed., London: Musica Rara, 1967), p. 543.

30. H. Macaulay Fitzgibbon, *The Story of the Flute*, 2nd ed., rev. (London: William Reeves Bookseller; New York: Charles Scribner's Sons, 1928), p. 135.

31. *Scale and Description of Boehm's Newly-Invented Patent Flute* (London: Gerock and Wolf, ca. 1831–32), p. 1. Hereafter cited as *Scale and Description*.

32. Bate, p. 95.

33. James A. MacGillivray, "The Woodwind," in *Musical Instruments Through the Ages*, ed. Anthony Baines (London: Faber and Faber, 1961), pp. 228–29.

34. Bate, p. 174.

35. Rockstro, pp. 303–4.

36. Bate, pp. 103–4.

37. Rockstro, pp. 269, 266.

38. Charles Nicholson, *Preceptive Lessons for the Flute* (London: The Author and Clementi & Co., 1821), p. 5. Hereafter cited as Nicholson (1821).

39. John Clinton, *A Treatise upon the Mechanism and General Principles of the Flute* (London: H. Potter, [1852]), pp. 7–8.

40. C[harles] Nicholson, *A School for the Flute* (London and New York: Wm. Hall & Sons, 1836), p. 3.

41. Bate, pp. 109–10.

42. Nicholson (1821), p. 20.

43. *Scale and Description*, p. 2.

44. Cornelius Ward, *The Flute Explained* (London: The Author, 1844), p. 5.

CHAPTER II

The Boehm Flute

The early nineteenth century, it would appear, was a golden age of the flute. For perhaps the only time in history, wind soloists enjoyed status commensurate with that of their string colleagues; virtuosi such as Drouet, Tulou, Berbiguier, Demersseman, and Nicholson toured Europe with enviable success. Amateurs, too, took up the instrument with great enthusiasm. For their benefit, publishers issued several specialized journals, containing flute music, critical notices, and other items of musical interest.*

As a consequence of this popularity, a considerable amount of music was both transcribed and composed for the flute. Whole operas were somehow arranged for one or two flutes, and the *Musical Monthly* complained in 1820 that German flute accompaniments were added to every piece. To the performers, the most important aspect of composition was provision for technical display, an ideal determined in good measure by their competition with violinists for audiences. The most popular musical forms were the *air variée* and the fantasia. The former was described by *Musical Opinion* in 1890 as follows:

Air first, then common chord variation (staccato), 'runs' variation,

---

The Flutonicon: or, Flute Player's Monthly Magazine was published by Sherwood & Co. in London between 1834 and 1850. A similar journal, edited by W. N. James, was variously known as *The Flutist's Magazine; and Musical Miscellany* (1827), *The Harmonist* (1828), and *The Flutist's Magazine, and Piano-Forte Review* (1829). James also published *The German Flute Magazine or Plain Practical Instructions for the Flute, being a complete Guide to the Monthly Work entitled the Flutonicon*, a book, in 1832. The history of these publications is detailed by Dayton C. Miller in his *Catalog*, pp. 53 and 61–62.

slow movement with a turn between every other two notes, and pump handle shakes that wring tears of agony from the flute; then the enormously difficult finale, in which you are up in the air on one note, then drop with a bang, which nearly breaks you, on to low C♮, only to bounce up again, hold on to a note, shake it (wring its neck, in fact), scatter it in all directions and come sailing down triumphantly on a chromatic (legato) with a perfect whirlpool of foaming notes, only to be bumped and pushed about until you are exhausted.[1]

Contrary to the designs of either composers or performers, though, the requisite technical gymnastics taxed the flute to such a degree that the technical defects of the instrument became all too obvious. A contemporary flutist and critic explained that "The imperfections of the instrument are always visible if the performer is too ambitious in playing music of too great execution; he either loses his tone in paying attention to his fingering, or vice versa."[2]

The defects of the flute were also revealed in its growing role in the orchestra. Intonational discrepancies in the context of the full ensemble, and particularly in comparison with the highly flexible strings, were obvious. But even more important were the flute's failings with regard both to quantity and quality of sound. In the course of Europe's transition from an aristocratic to a democratic culture, music shifted from the salon to the concert hall; the chamber orchestra evolved into the full symphony orchestra. Force and power became the expressive outlets of musical composition and performance. Brilliance, of which steadily rising pitch was only one symptom, was the tonal ideal of the era. Closely related to this quantitative development was the demand for a greater variety of timbres. In practice, this development meant not only the introduction and exploitation of new instruments, such as the piccolo, but also greater demands for variety from a single instrument. At this time, orchestration clearly took its place as a "self-sufficient branch of musical composition."[3]

The wooden German flute clearly could not fulfill the requirements of the nineteenth century. Its intonation was uncertain; its tone, though mellow and even beautiful in chamber music, was relatively weak, better designed for tonal blending than for a solo role within the orchestra; and its dynamic capacity was not sufficient to compete with the improved brass section of the Romantic orchestra.

The situation could have reached crisis proportions had it not been for the genius of one (Theobald Boehm)(1794–1881), who made pioneering applications of science to the construction of the flute. Boehm began his study of the flute with Johann Nepomuk Capeller, inventor of the d^2 shake key, in about 1810. Progressing rapidly, Boehm was soon appointed to the orchestra of the Isarthor Theatre in Munich. Meanwhile, he continued to practice his trade as a goldsmith, also making flutes for his own use and that of his friends. In 1818, Boehm was appointed to the service of the Royal Court, at which time he devoted himself entirely to music, entrusting to others the manufacture of his flute designs. In 1828, however, he opened his own flute factory, where he produced simple system instruments with several modifications of his own design, including tuning slides and hardened gold springs. Another advanced feature of Boehm's early flutes was the mounting of the keys on screwed-in pillars. By 1829, he had begun to experiment with longitudinal rod-axles for connecting the keys (Figs. 27 and 28).

In 1831, Boehm presented several concerts in London, where he was well received. But he was critical of his own performance, particularly in comparison with that of Charles Nicholson, whose tone far exceeded Boehm's in both strength and volume of tone. Nicholson's tone was lauded by one of his pupils, W. N. James, as follows: "It is not only clear, metallic and brilliant, but possesses a volume that is almost incredible; and this too, be it observed, in the very lowest notes of the instrument." Indeed Nicholson's goal, as stated in his tutor, was to make his flute tone not only "as reedy as possible," but also "embodying the round mellowness of the clarinet."[4]

Boehm realized that Nicholson's exceptional technique was far above the norm; that, although his enlargement of the finger holes contributed to an increase in tonal capacity, the defects of intonation for which Nicholson's eminently flexible embouchure

Fig. 27. BOEHM'S 1829 FLUTE.
Boehm & Greve, Munich,
ca. 1829–32.
9 keys, Boehm's improved old system.
Cocus, silver keys, rings, and stud.
Keys mounted on short silver pillars.
Flat gold springs. Conical bore.
(DCM 240)

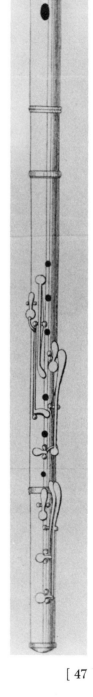

Fig. 28. BOEHM'S 1829 FLUTE
from Theobald Boehm, *Ueber den Flötenbau* (1847).

could compensate were irremediable by the majority of flutists. In short, Boehm, recognizing that the defects of nineteenth century fluteplaying were in large part the fault of the instrument, was inspired by Nicholson to make higher standards of performance accessible to players of only ordinary ability. Boehm explained his motivation in his *Essay on the Construction of Flutes*, first published in German in 1847: "There is no doubt that many artists have carried perfection to its last limits on the old flute, but there are also unavoidable difficulties, originating in the construction of these flutes, which can neither be conquered by talent nor by the most persevering practice."

Boehm was also responding to what he perceived as a new division of labor; one person was no longer required to function as instrument maker, performer, and composer. Though many men, including Boehm, did assume all three roles, these individuals were not the authors of the symphonic repertoire; for the most part they wrote only for flute.

> Thus passages are often met with in music for the orchestra, much more difficult than in any concertos composed by flute players, who, acquainted with the defects of their instruments, are generally prudent enough not to prepare for themselves such stumbling-blocks. Among such defects are to be reckoned all those notes which sound with difficulty or uncertainty; those which cannot be sustained in a crescendo or diminuendo without the risk of the tone 'breaking;' and those that require great management of lip to preserve a pure intonation.

Boehm's major criticism of the German flute of the time was acoustical in nature. A perceptive student of his instrument's history, he traced the origin of contemporary tone hole placement to the makers of keyless instruments:

> The instrument makers of former times, ignorant of key-mechanism, could not do otherwise than place the holes—without regard to acoustical principles—at such distances from each other that the fingers could still reach them. Afterwards a better chromatic scale was obtained by the adoption of keys; but as the position of the holes of the old diatonic D major scale remained the same, their in-

correct position (by which the nodes of vibration were often disturbed) and their insufficient size not only diminished the easy emission and pure intonation of some high notes, but also lessened the clearness and power of the tone throughout the instrument.

He concluded that changes in mechanical details would not be sufficient to remedy the defects of the German flute, and that a total redesign of the fingering system would be necessary. Though he recognized the initial inconvenience of such a scheme, Boehm believed that its advantages would more than compensate both the composer and the performer: "[T]he greater facility of execution has . . . merit, because it is an immense gain to the composer when instruments can be used to the full extent of their compass, without regard to key or difficulty." Additionally, he predicted, with the new flute "the artist [would be able to] execute passages which were impracticable in former times."[5]

Though his mechanism was to be new, Boehm drew upon the inventions of others in designing it. Most notable of these borrowings were three items: the use of large finger-holes placed according to acoustical principles rather than digital convenience, as Nicholson had done; covering the holes with keys to enable the fingers to control distant holes; and the use of ring keys like those of Nolan. Thus, although Boehm did make several mechanical innovations, his major contribution was the adaptation of preexistent devices to newly discovered acoustical principles.

One further predecessor must be mentioned before turning to the details of Boehm's work—namely, a Captain Gordon. Boehm met Gordon, a military man and amateur flutist, in London in 1831.* Like Boehm, Gordon aspired to improve the flute and in 1826 had constructed an instrument based on an open-keyed system. While visiting London in 1831, he had flutes constructed according to his designs both by Rudall & Rose and by Cornelius Ward (Figs. 29 and 30), and in 1833 he published a prospectus entitled *Tablature of the diatonic flute manufactured in the work-*

---

*A detailed biographical sketch of Gordon is contained in P. R. Kirby's "Captain Gordon, Flute Maker," *Music and Letters* 38 (July 1957): 250–59.

shops of Boehm, which described a slightly different model (Figs. 31 and 32).

The open-keyed construction, coupled with the use of cres-

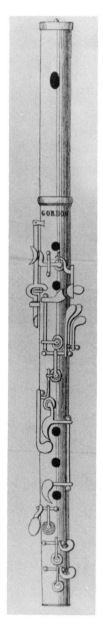

Fig. 29. GORDON'S FLUTE, ca. 1831.
This diagram was first published in
John Clinton's *School for the Boehm Flute* (1846).
Boehm reprinted the picture in his
Ueber den Flötenbau (1847).

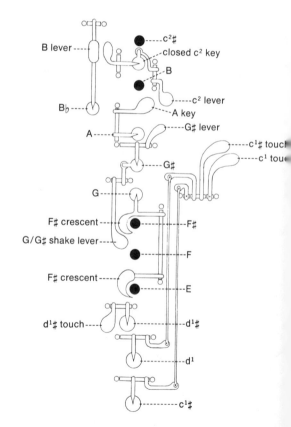

Fig. 30. GORDON'S FLUTE, ca. 1831.
(Diagram by Jerry L. Voorhees)

cent-shaped touchpieces to control distant holes (a feature which Pottgiesser had introduced in 1803), provided the basis for the modern flute. Gordon's mechanism itself, however, was distin-

Fig. 31. GORDON'S 1833 "DIATONIC FLUTE."
This diagram was originally published in Gordon's *Tablature* (1833). It was reprinted in Coche's *Méthode* and *Examen Critique* (1838).

Fig. 32. GORDON'S 1833 "DIATONIC FLUTE."
(Diagram by Jerry L. Voorhees)

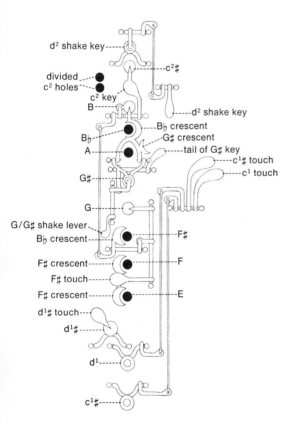

guished only by its rather remarkable complexity. A series of angular levers and wires was used to pull the keys closed. Reversing the fingerings of the old system, F♮ was produced by the first finger of the right hand (which also operated the B♭ key); F♯ was produced by the third finger. The F/F♯ mechanism was carried by a rod running parallel to the flute tube, a feature that also appeared on Boehm's flutes. An open D♯ key made the instrument difficult to hold; two small holes were provided under the left thumb for c^2 and c^3, and a wooden thumb rest helped to support the instrument. A closed D key above the thumb was governed by a lever on the front of the tube. Typical of the mechanical complexity of this flute was the G♯ arrangement. The G♯ key was of the open form, to be closed by the third finger of the left hand by means of a small crescent attached to a V-shaped contrivance that was hinged in the middle. The little finger opened the key in the usual manner while the third finger closed the A hole, thereby producing G♯.

The clumsiness of Gordon's mechanism would have consigned his flute to oblivion were it not for the jealousy of still other inventors, who, in order to discredit Boehm, accused him of stealing ideas from Gordon. Indeed, the use of rods was an early feature of Boehm's work, his experiments with that device being evident as early as 1829. Additionally, Boehm's fingerings for F and F♯ were identical to Gordon's, and Boehm also adopted an open-keyed system. But closer study reveals that these similarities are only superficial. Boehm's 1847 *Essay*, in fact, contains a description of Gordon's instrument that concludes with the following critical statement: "He also had on his flute a number of keys and levers, some of which were ingeniously devised; but they were much too complicated, and of no use, as the instrument wanted throughout a correct acoustical basis."[6] To summarize a long and tangled tale, the attributions of Boehm's flute to Captain Gordon were clearly the fabrications of rival manufacturers, for the accusations cannot hold up under the scrutiny of Boehm's careful records of his work. The so-called Boehm-Gordon controversy, which Adam Carse so aptly characterized as a "display of rather childish vituperation,"[7] is therefore of little importance in evaluating the history of the flute except as an example of mid-nineteenth century professional competitiveness and as a caveat regarding the extensive critical literature of the period.*

BOEHM'S 1831 "PATENT FLUTE"

We may now turn with a clear conscience to the work of Theobald Boehm. Shortly after hearing Nicholson, Boehm made some slight alterations in the design of the German flute and constructed such an instrument in the London shop of Gerock and Wolf, who then issued a descriptive pamphlet entitled *Boehm's Newly-Invented Patent Flute* (Figs. 33 and 34). The announcement to the contrary notwithstanding, the 1831 flute was not patented, for Boehm did not consider it enough of an improvement to warrant such protection. It is likely, in fact, that the 1831 model was never produced commercially.[8]

The claims of the Gerock and Wolf prospectus were extravagant. From the new flute, it said, the following results could be expected:

> FIRMNESS, EQUALITY, and RICHNESS of tone, which have never been altogether combined in any other description of Flute.
> SIMPLICITY of mechanism as regards the FINGERING.
> Facility in FILLING; producing sweetness and freedom up to the highest C; and unexampled capabilities for the more delicate graces of expression which belong to a finished style of execution.

In truth, the new flute represented only two major changes from the ordinary flute of the time. Left-hand fingering remained the same, but the A hole was brought down to its acoustically correct position and an open key mechanism used to reach it. This key

---

*Chief among such publications are the violently anti-Boehm, pro-Gordon *Treatise on . . . the Flute* by Richard S. Rockstro (1890) and Christopher Welch's indignant retort, *History of the Boehm Flute* (1896). Philip Bate gives a concise account of the controversy in Appendix I of *The Flute* (New York: W. W. Norton, 1969), pp. 328–41.

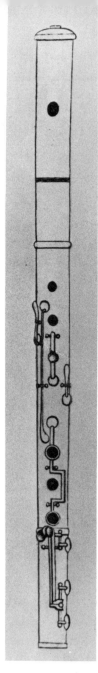

Fig. 33. BOEHM'S 1831 FLUTE
from Gerock and Wolf, *Scale and Description of
Boehm's Newly-Invented Patent Flute* (ca. 1831).

Fig. 34. BOEHM'S 1831 FLUTE.
(Diagram by Jerry L. Voorhees)

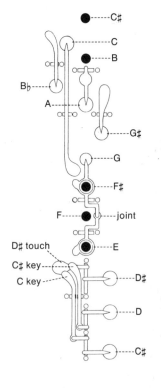

was controlled by an open-standing second order lever with a
touchplate for the third finger of the left hand.

For the right hand, the E, F, F♯, and G keys were respaced
farther down the tube, a procedure that Pottgiesser had in-

troduced in 1803. Boehm's innovation was the use of double-jointed ring keys that allowed the first finger of the right hand to stop two holes, rather than just one, thereby producing F♮ rather than F♯, as on the ordinary flute. The F♯ was now produced by the third finger of the right hand by means of another ring key. The mechanical basis of this arrangement was a linked pair of first order levers, the lower member of which ended in a ring surrounding the E hole and the upper in a ring around the F♯ hole. A padded cup at the far upper end covered the G hole. The acoustical result of this maneuver was to eliminate the infamous "forked" F of the ordinary flute; the new F♯, though technically forked, kept the F hole open at the same time, thereby avoiding any damaging veiling of the tone.[9] In a sense, the new F/F♯ device, by destroying the primary D major scale of simple system flutes, represented the first phase of modern construction.

BOEHM'S 1832 FLUTE

In 1832, Boehm conducted a series of experiments to determine the proportions of tone hole measurements for a totally new fingering system. He determined the distance between the holes by progressively cutting the end off a wooden tube to find the proper length for each pitch; the measurements were then transferred to a second tube into which holes were bored. The notes thus produced were flat, however, because the holes were necessarily smaller than the diameter of the tube, so on a third tube, the holes were all shifted up toward the embouchure. Now, using equal-sized holes, the first and second octaves were in tune, but the third octave was incorrect because for those notes it was necessary to open not only the hole of the fundamental note, but also the fifth hole above it as a vent hole. Boehm's solution was to move six of the upper holes, also modifying their size, in order to correct the tuning.[10]

Following the example of Nicholson, Boehm made the tone holes as large as possible, outlining his reasoning in the following manner:

1. Free and therefore powerful tones can be obtained only from large holes which are placed as nearly as possible in their acoustically correct positions.

2. If the holes are small and are considerably removed from their proper places, the formation of the nodes of vibration is disturbed and rendered uncertain; the tone is produced with difficulty, and often breaks into other tones corresponding to the other aliquot parts of the air column [harmonics].

3. The smaller the holes, the more distorted become the tone waves, rendering the tone dull and of poor quality.

4. The pure intonation of the third octave depends particularly upon the correct position of the holes.

   From accurate investigations it is shown that the disadvantages just mentioned, become imperceptible only when the size of the holes is at least three-fourths of the diameter of the tube.[11]

The logical extension of large holes was the open-key system, which would allow full venting of the holes. Boehm explained that "It is necessary, for obtaining a clear and strong tone, that the holes immediately below the one sounding should remain open, for the air confined in the lower end of the tube tends to flatten the notes, and renders them less free."[12]

The open-key system required some rearrangement of the holes (Figs. 35 and 36). The closed C of the old flute, a side key for the first finger of the right hand, was replaced by a pair of small open holes at the rear of the tube, so that closing the first hole (left-hand first finger) would produce C rather than B. The same two C holes were responsible for venting open C♯ and were closed by the left-hand thumb to produce B. B, in turn, was vented by an open hole on the front, replacing the old closed B♭ key at the rear; this hole was closed by the right-hand first finger ring key to give B♭ and by the left-hand second finger ring key to give A. A in turn had the open G♯ for its vent, thereby reversing the action of the heretofore closed G♯ key, and so on down the scale of the flute.

In order to control the fourteen holes of his flute with only nine fingers (the right-hand thumb was used only to support the instrument), Boehm employed two devices, the ring keys of

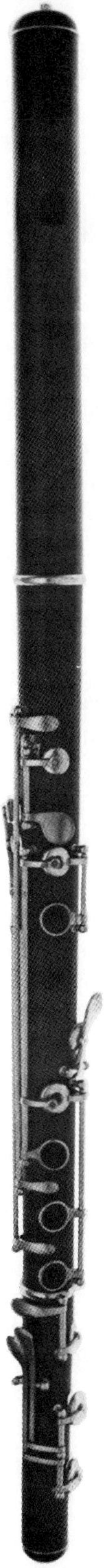

Fig. 35. BOEHM'S 1832 FLUTE. Th. Boehm, Munich.
Cocus with silver rings, stud, and keys. Conical bore. Key cups
fastened to levers with screws. Fingers with adjustable screws in
place of clutches. Open G♯. D trill only. Thumb key
with double hole. (DCM 974)

Fig. 36. BOEHM'S 1832 FLUTE.
(Diagram by Jerry L. Voorhees)

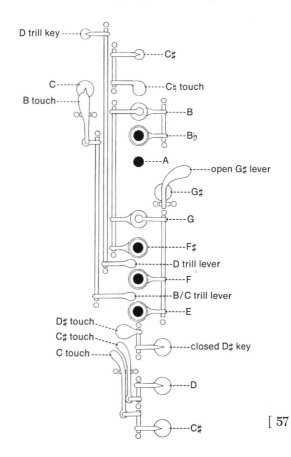

Nolan (though without the catch) and horizontal rod-axles of his own invention. It was this mechanism, not his acoustical achievements, which gained Boehm his earliest recognition. Using the ring keys and axles, Boehm established a fingering system "by which the fingers do not move out of their natural position from the lower D up to the highest B, with the exception of the little finger of the right hand, to which I left the management of the foot-keys, in order to retain as much as possible of the old fingering. There is now no more gliding from one key to another, or to a finger-hole. . . ."*[13]

The three footjoint keys, for c^1, $c^1\sharp$, and $d^1\sharp$, were controlled by the fourth finger of the right hand; of the three, only D$\sharp$ was a closed key. This apparent contradiction of the open-key theory was actually quite logical; because the D$\sharp$ hole must almost always be open, the constant pressure of the fourth finger on that key served to balance the flute.

On the body of the flute, the E, F, and F$\sharp$ holes were controlled by the third, second, and first fingers of the right hand, respectively. There remained no finger on the right hand for the G hole, however, so it was covered with a padded cup attached to a horizontal axle. Ring keys for the E and F holes projected from this axle, so the G hole could be closed by either the second or third finger of the right hand (or both). A ring key over the F$\sharp$ hole was attached to the end of another axle which extended up to the B hole; an arm projected from that axle over the G hole-cover so that the G hole would also be closed when the F$\sharp$ ring was pressed down. Thus three fingers of the right hand controlled four holes. An incidental result of this contrivance was that its connection of the left- and right-hand mechanisms necessitated the elimination of the bipartite body.

On the left hand, the fourth finger controlled the open G$\sharp$

---

*The only exception to this principle involves the two trill keys for the right hand. Boehm apparently took this factor into account when he wrote *The Flute and Flute-Playing;* since the trill keys are used to finger $b^3\flat$ and b^3, he revised his statement to read: ". . . the very troublesome sliding from keys and tone-holes which is required on the old flute is entirely done away with, and one can certainly and easily play all possible tone combinations from low d^1 to a^3" (pp. 61–62).

key, with the third and second fingers covering the A and B♭ holes. A ring key over the B♭ hole and a key cover for the B hole were attached to a common axle so that depressing the former would also close the latter. In addition, the B cup was connected by a lateral arm to the long axle which carried the F♯ ring, so that the B hole could also be closed by the first finger of the right hand; otherwise, opening the B♭ hole would sound B♮. The C♯ hole was positioned too high to be reached by the first finger of the left hand, so it was covered by a padded cup and controlled by means of a finger plate attached to a short axle. The left-hand thumb controlled an open key for the C hole on the near side of the flute.[14]

One or two shake keys were also provided. The first, whose finger plate was operated by the third finger of the right hand, was connected by a long axle to the C key. Its purpose was to facilitate trills which would be awkward for the left-hand thumb. The second shake key, modeled on Capeller's invention, facilitated the c^2♯/d^2 trill. The mechanism consisted of a small d^2 hole bored above the c^2♯ hole and controlled by a finger plate for the second finger of the right hand via another long axle and covered key. A projection from the d^2♯ key appears to be a touchpiece, though it is far above the grasp of the left hand. In fact, the projection was merely an extension of the key shank which was necessary to carry the leaf spring, a flat contrivance typical of early Boehm instruments.[15]

A unique aspect of Boehm's 1832 model was the elimination of the usual tuning slide between the head and body. He did so "on account of the unequal and disturbed vibration which arises from the close combination of the wood, producing, to my ear, a disagreeable hardness of tone." In place of the tuning slide, he inserted several silver rings to fill up the space in the joint which resulted from lengthening the flute to lower its pitch.

An interesting nonmoving part used by Boehm was the crutch for the left-hand thumb (Fig. 37). Made of wood, this device permitted the entire weight of the instrument to rest in the cavity between the thumb and index finger of the left hand, the aim being to "obtain a steady hold of the instrument, and a free and easy movement of the left hand."[16] The crutch was attached to the underside of the flute tube near the C hole by a short pillar; the other end was fitted with a small crosspiece to accommodate the hand. The length of the crutch could be regulated by the player by means of a screw.

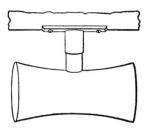

Fig. 37. BOEHM'S CRUTCH
from Rockstro, *Treatise*.

At this time, all of Boehm's flutes were made of hardwood; specifically, he wrote:

> I usually employ either the so-called cocus wood, or the grenadilla wood of South America. The first, of dark or red-brown color, is especially desirable because of its brilliant tone, notwithstanding that this wood contains a resin, which, in very rare cases, induces an inflammation of the skin of the lip. To obviate this difficulty, as well as to secure a very pleasant ringing quality of tone in the high notes, many will prefer black grenadilla wood.

Grenadilla, also known as African blackwood or Mozambique ebony, was not only highly resonant but also easily turned on the lathe. Boehm dismissed ebony and boxwood as "now used only for the cheaper grades of instruments:"[17] Boxwood in particular had a tendency to warp badly, which, with the complicated mechanism of the Boehm flute, would cause the keys to bind.

Boehm introduced his new flute in public performances in Munich on November 1, 1832, and April 25, 1833. The instrument was described in *Der Bazar* of April 25, 1833, and the article was reprinted in *The Harmonicon* the following August. Boehm visited Paris and London in May 1833, where he played the flute several times; he returned to London in July of 1834, remaining for a year. By 1835, however, Boehm had sold only one flute in London. He explained his apparent failure as follows:

> Many flute players and instrument makers examined it, but most of them were discouraged by the new system of fingering. Flautists of old standing decided against it because they could not resolve upon studying an entirely new instrument; and possibly, they sometimes saw with displeasure that young artists, by adopting it, acquired an accession of means for producing greater effects in their performance. Most of the instrument makers were against it, because they found it inconvenient or unprofitable to imitate a sort of key-mechanism quite new to them.[18]

Boehm submitted his design to the Paris Academy of Sciences for consideration, but the professional jealousy of Victor Coche, a professor at the Conservatoire, interfered with the evaluation. Acceptance was slow in Germany, as well, where, Philip Bate concludes, "its admittedly more 'open' tone was compared unfavourably with that of the older instrument, and probably proved more of an obstacle than the changes of fingering involved."[19] In 1834, a lone note in the *Leipsic Gazette Musicale* mentioned that certain French and German players had adopted the new Boehm instrument.

In 1837, Paul Hippolyte Camus, first flutist of the Opera Italien, introduced the Boehm flute to Paris, though here, too, objection was made to the revised fingering system. The next year, however, the efforts of three of Camus's colleagues helped to win the Boehm flute favor in their country.

THE MODIFICATIONS OF BUFFET, COCHE, AND DORUS

The most important of these men was Auguste Buffet, a Paris instrument maker. Like many other flutemakers, he objected to Boehm's placement of axles on both sides of the flute tube, and he decided to move them all to the inner side. But in so doing, he would have crowded the rod which connected the F♯ ring with the G and B hole-covers. His solution was to attach the rings for E and F and the cup for G to a single axle, with the F♯ ring

A B C

Fig. 38. BUFFET'S CLUTCH from Rockstro, *Treatise.*
The sleeve carrying the B♭ ring, B cup, and C♯ cup and touch is attached
to lug A. The axle carrying the G cup and E and F rings is pinned
to lug B. The loose sleeve carrying the F♯ ring is attached to lug C.

mounted in a loose sleeve through which the axle passed (Fig. 38). A lug was soldered to the sleeve; a similar lug was pinned to the axle above the sleeve. On the left-hand portion of the tube, the B♭ ring/B cup mechanism and the C♯ cup and touchpiece were attached to loose sleeves threaded on a fixed rod. The B/B♭ sleeve carried a third lug which lay on top of the other two, together forming a "clutch." Thus Boehm's original key functions were maintained, but the mechanism was constructed with greater elegance. The rod and sleeve device was also applied to the foot-joint keys, thereby avoiding possible complications at the point where Boehm's c^1 and c^1♯ levers passed under the key tails. Closely allied to the introduction of the sleeve and clutch were rotary action needle springs, whose delicacy made them more appropriate than the flat leaf springs.[20]

Flutist Victor Coche, working in collaboration with Buffet, suggested several further changes to Boehm's design that were incorporated into Buffet's patent of January 22, 1839 (Figs. 39 and 40). Perhaps the most controversial aspect of Boehm's 1832 model was the open G♯ key, which was one of the most difficult features for players to become accustomed to. The acoustical advantage claimed by Boehm was that of full venting; moreover, he explained, the configuration was mechanically logical. With the open key, G♯ could be obtained by raising the little finger, just as A was sounded by raising the third finger. When the two fingers were raised separately for halftones (as in the sequence G, G♯, A, A♯) or together for whole tones (as in the sequence G, A, B), the digital motion would be similar, instead of contrary as with the closed G♯. To many players, however, conve-

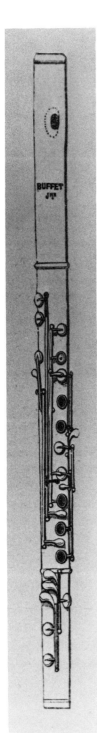

Fig. 39.
FLUTE OF COCHE AND BUFFET
(1838) from Victor Coche, *Méthode* (1838)
and *Examen Critique* (1838).

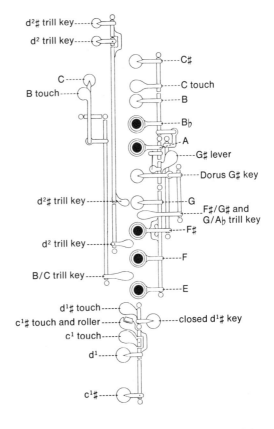

d²♯ trill key ----
d² trill key ----
---- C♯
C ----
B touch ----
---- C touch
---- B
---- B♭
---- A
---- G♯ lever
---- Dorus G♯ key
d²♯ trill key ----
---- G
---- F♯/G♯ and G/A♭ trill key
---- F♯
d² trill key ----
---- F
B/C trill key ----
---- E
d¹♯ touch ----
c¹♯ touch and roller ----
---- closed d¹♯ key
c¹ touch ----
d¹ ----
c¹♯ ----

Fig. 40. FLUTE OF COCHE AND BUFFET.
(Diagram by Jerry L. Voorhees)

nience was more important than either acoustics or logic. For this reason, Coche reinstituted the closed G♯ mechanism of the old flute. Because he made no provision for adequate venting, however, his regressive idea did not survive. His placement of a ring around the A hole for closing the B♭ hole likewise enjoyed little success. Coche's great contribution, however, was a trill key for C♯/D♯ in the second and third octaves. Operated by the third finger of the right hand, the trill key governed a small hole above the d² hole at the top of the flute. Buffet combined Coche's D♯ trill key and Boehm's D trill key in a common sleeve.

Vincent Dorus, a professor at the Paris Conservatoire and solo flutist of the Opera, responded to the widespread objections to the open G♯ key by devising a new type of closed key for that note (Fig. 41). Its intention was both to maintain the old fingering and to avoid veiling the tone of the A, which had been the defect of the old closed G♯ mechanism. Dorus's arrangement added a ring key to the A hole, attaching it to the open G♯ key with a divided sleeve and clutch. The G♯ key was closed when the ring key was depressed, but it could be opened independently by a lever for the little finger that was attached to the part of the sleeve that supported the G♯ key. Thus the G♯ hole was automatically closed until opened by the little finger to produce G♯ by the traditional fingering.

The chief defect of Dorus's contrivance was its dependence on two opposing springs, one of which was stronger than the other. The unavoidable strength of the more powerful spring made the G♯/A trill difficult. Combinations of G♯ with F♯, F, E, D♯, or D in the lower and middle octaves made either a cross-fingering

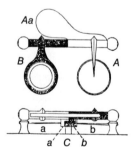

Fig. 41. DORUS G♯ KEY
from Rockstro, *Treatise*.
The G♯ hole (A) was controlled by touch Aa.
A ring surrounding the A hole (B) was connected by a tube with clutch b. Weak spring a acted on stop a; strong spring b acted on clutch b. A projection from the flute (C) served as a stop for the clutches.

or a veiled note unavoidable. On wooden flutes, moreover, the outer axle of the device sometimes interfered with the action of the third finger of the left hand because of the thickness of the tube. Nevertheless, Dorus's retrograde fingering was successful because it did maintain the old fingering, and it may be considered a positive invention because of its role in easing the transition to the Boehm flute.

The improvements of Buffet, Coche, and Dorus attracted sufficient attention to Boehm's flute that in 1838 the new French version was examined by the French Academy of Fine Arts and introduced to the Paris Conservatoire. Boehm's design not having been patented, Coche and Buffet formed a partnership to manufacture the instrument. Their promotional literature contained diagrams of three flutes labeled "Invention GORDON," "Modification BOEHM," and "Perfectionnement V. COCHE."[21] Boehm, meanwhile, having become increasingly involved in the steel industry, closed his own factory in 1839. In the same year, the London flutists Cornelius Ward and Signor Folz adopted the Boehm flute, probably as a result of hearing Dorus's and Camus's London performances on it. At the same time, Ward, who favored the Dorus G♯, became the first manufacturer in London to make Boehm flutes. John Clinton, professor of flute at the Royal Academy of Music, claimed to have adopted the Boehm flute in 1841; Richard Carte and George Rudall did so two years later, at which time Boehm made official arrangements for his instrument to be manufactured by Rudall & Rose in London and Clair Godfroy, ainé in Paris.[22]

BOEHM'S 1847 FLUTE

In 1846 and 1847, Boehm studied classical acoustics under Dr. Carl von Schafhäutl at the University of Munich in preparation for further work on the bore of his flute. For his experiments, he made several cylindrical wooden tubes of varying lengths and diameters in order to determine the modifications in tone effected by those variables. The wood tubes proved to be unstable, however, and Boehm was forced to replace them with thin, hard-drawn brass tubes for greater consistency and reliability. Boehm began with the following hypothesis:

> I was always at a loss to understand why the flute alone should be played at the wide end, while all other wind instruments of conical proportions are played at the narrower end, especially as the latter method seems more in accordance with Nature; for while the section of the air-column decreases in length as the pitch rises, so they also decrease in diameter. The reverse of this is the case with the conical flute, in which the cone is continued beyond the lower holes.

The experiments confirmed Boehm's doubts regarding the conical bore, and he was able to formulate these fundamental principles:

1. That the strength, as well as the full and clear tone of the fundamental notes, is proportional to the volume of air put in motion.
2. That simple vibrations can be most perfectly excited in large tubes having a contraction at the embouchure.
3. That every modification in diameter or length of this contraction has a great influence on the emission and intonation of the aliquot parts.
4. That this contraction must not be made in straight lines, but in curves.
5. That, moreover, the divisions of the columns of air into aliquot parts, or the formation of vibrational nodes—in short, all phenomena which appear in a vibrating column of air—are exhibited in a cylindrical tube in the most perfect and easy manner; consequently that a cylindrical tube is that best adapted for the construction of a flute.
6. That cylindrical tubes with the cone, as applied by me, at the upper end may be considered as entirely cylindrical; since the influence of the cone on the pitch is so insignificant, that in a tube with the fundamental note C it scarcely occasions a difference in length of 0.00492 ft.[23]

Boehm's flute of 1847 (Figs. 42 and 43) was constructed in accordance with these principles. The body of the tube was cylindrical, with an internal diameter of 19 millimeters. The original specifications had called for a diameter of 20 millimeters, but because this dimension made production of the third octave difficult, Boehm accepted the compromise figure of 19 millimeters. The bore of the headjoint gradually decreased in diameter, measuring only 17 millimeters at the cork. The exact curve of the headjoint was a matter of great importance: "The free speech of the tone and the correct tuning of the higher octaves depend upon the particular form of this curvilinear reduction in the diameter."[24] Boehm described the curve as "parabolic," though Dayton Miller's careful measurements of many of Boehm's flutes revealed that the actual curve bore little mathematical resemblance to that geometric figure despite the similarity in general shape.[25]

Another deviation in theory was necessitated by the impossibility of making the distance from the center of the embouchure proportional to the lengths of the undulations of the air within the tube. Such a goal could only be accomplished, Boehm found, by additional mechanism, the construction and use of which would present "almost insuperable difficulty." As a result, Boehm was forced to find a compromise position.

For the same reason that he adopted the cylindrical bore—namely, to increase the volume of air in the tube—Boehm was concerned with the shape and size of the embouchure.

Fig. 42. BOEHM'S 1847 FLUTE. Th. Boehm, Munich [No. 14], 1848. Silver. Open G♯. This instrument was sold to Richard Carte in 1848. (DCM 1237)

Fig. 43. BOEHM'S 1847 FLUTE
from Theobald Boehm, *Die Flöte und das Flötenspiel* (1871).

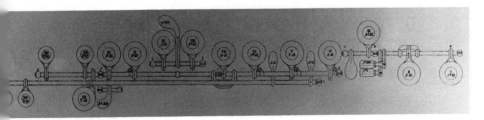

. . . as the aperture between the lips through which the air passes into the embouchure is in the form of a slit, a long-shaped quadrangular embouchure, with rounded corners, which presents a wide edge to the broad pencil of air, must be better adapted to take in a large quantity of breath than an oval or round hole of equal size. For the same reason a larger embouchure will produce a stronger tone than a smaller one.[26]

An allied feature of the embouchure, an excavation on the side where the lip rests, was designed to assist in the direction of the breath. The resultant concentration of the airstream eliminated the hissing common to the old embouchure and minimized the retention of water vapor deposited by the breath in the interior of the flute.[27]

Boehm's initial plan was gradually to increase the size of the tone holes from the bottom to the top of the flute. Indeed, he reported in 1862, he had made and played on such an instrument for a time. Its smallest hole, for the c^2 thumb key, was 12 millimeters in diameter; the largest, for $c^1\sharp$, was 15 millimeters, with a constant intermediate gradation of a quarter of a millimeter. Boehm's eventual conclusion, however, was that "The graduated holes are in my opinion the best, but the difference is scarcely appreciable. I have discontinued making them on account of the greater difficulty in the manufacture." Boehm aimed to make the holes as large as possible, preferably not less than three-quarters of the bore, which for his 19.0-millimeter flute would imply a hole size of 14.25 millimeters. Such dimensions were difficult to execute, however, particularly on wood instruments, so he compromised at figures of 13.5 and 13.0 millimeters for silver and wood, respectively. Dayton Miller's measurements of many Boehm and Mendler flutes discovered uniform diameters of 12.8 millimeters.* A notable exception was the so-called Macauley flute, made in 1877, now No. 161 of the Miller collection (Fig. 50, page 75). The nine holes on its body measured 13.2 millimeters, while the four holes on the B footjoint were 14.5 millimeters in

---

*Carl Mendler, who had worked in Boehm's shop since 1854, was made a partner in 1867. Though Boehm died in 1881, the firm was known as Th. Boehm & Mendler until 1895.

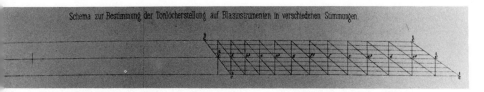

з. 44. BOEHM'S *SCHEMA* from Theobald Boehm,
e Flöte und das Flötenspiel (1871).
e Schema was first published in Boehm's *Ueber die Bestimmung der Tonlöcherstellung* (1868).

diameter. Miller reported that while the enlargement of the foot-joint holes was unusual for Boehm, it is common in modern manufacture, as is the use of two or three different sizes for the principal holes of the body.

Certain adjustments in the sizes and positions of tone holes were necessitated by the narrowing of the tube to 19 millimeters. The intention of the reduction was to improve the third octave, but in so doing, the quality of the second octave, and especially of d^2 and d^2♯, was altered. Ideally, therefore, the flute should have had three additional large holes for c^2♯, d^2, and d^2♯; the latter two would also serve as vent holes for the twelfths of those notes, g^3♯ and a^3. The problem was that only one finger was available, and it had to be used for c^2♯. Once again, Boehm was forced to compromise: ". . . as I was unwilling to make my key system more complicated, the c^2♯ hole must be so placed that it may serve at the same time as a so-called vent hole for the tone, d^2, d^2♯, d^3, g^3♯, and a^3." Thus the theoretical position of the c^2♯ hole was abandoned and, along with the d^2 and d^2♯ holes operated by the two trill keys, it was placed considerably above its true position and made correspondingly smaller.[28]

Once the final proportions of the bore and the tone holes had been determined, Boehm recorded them in a geometrical diagram called a *Schema* (Fig. 44). These dimensions could be read off the diagram for a flute of whatever length was necessary to conform to the prevailing pitch standard. The *Schema* was submitted to the Paris Exposition of 1868 for consideration, but the judges ruled themselves unqualified to evaluate it, and it was consequently ignored except for its publication by the Bavarian Polytechnic Society in its *Kunst und Gewerblatt* of October 1886.

The use of large tone holes, while acoustically advantageous, did create a practical dilemma in that they could not be closed directly by the fingers. Padded covers for the holes, similar to those already used for the G and B holes on Boehm's 1832 model, therefore took the place both of ring keys and open holes. Each of these keys had to open independently yet be attached to other keys in accordance with Boehm's fingering system. To construct the requisite mechanism, Boehm adopted the sleeves and rods of Buffet, attaching each key cover to its own sleeve and springing each one open with a light needle spring. Interconnected keys were linked by clutches (overlapping lugs or pins) whose relative vertical positions could be adjusted by means of set screws. In order to ensure proper stoppage of the holes, which had been a problem on the early simple system flutes, Boehm was quite explicit as to the construction of the pads:

> The pads are made from a strong cloth-like stuff of fine wool [felt]. In order that the pads may close the holes air tight, these felt disks are covered with a fine membrane (skin); this membrane is usually doubled, so that any accidental injury to the pad shall not become troublesome all at once.
>
> The pads are covered over on the back side with little sheets of card and a hole is punched through the center, so that they may be screwed fast in the key cups.
>
> The pads are held by screws, the nuts being soldered to the key cups, and under the heads of the little screws there are silver washers. [29]

Another crucial feature of the 1847 flute was the choice of material for the body. As always, there was a scientific basis for Boehm's concern:

> That the tones of a flute may not only be easily produced, but shall also possess a brilliant and sonorous quality, it is necessary that the molecules of the flute tube shall be set into vibration at the same time as the air column, and that these shall, as it were, mutually assist one another. The material must possess this requisite vibration ability, which is either a natural property of the body, for example as in bell-metal, glass and various kinds of wood, or has been artificially produced, as in the case of hardened steel springs and hard-drawn

metal wire. . . . Any variation in the hardness or brittleness of the material has a very great effect upon the timbre or quality of tone.*[30]

In 1846, Boehm began to experiment with metal flutes—specifically, of brass, silver, and German silver—and was pleased with the results. He observed that metals with the least elasticity gave the softest and weakest tone, whereas the very hard German silver yielded a "clear but shrill tone." In every respect, Boehm finally concluded, silver and brass tubes produced the best tone. Furthermore, he found that thin and hard-drawn tubes, by increasing the metal's capacity for vibration, produced a more resonant tone.

Boehm was also concerned with the amount of energy necessary to sound the instrument. He ascertained that the requisite expenditure of energy was directly proportional to the mass of the material; thus a lighter tube would require less strength of breath. A thin, hard-drawn silver tube, weighing only half of the thinnest possible wood tube, would therefore be far less fatiguing for the player to blow. Boehm ultimately concluded that

> The superior excellence in regard to tone and intonation of my flute, made entirely of silver, when compared even with my newly constructed one of 1832, was so striking that it was remarked by every one immediately. These metal flutes are not subject to splitting, they cannot vary in the bore, and require neither to be oiled nor to be frequently played, but they always sound equally well. And even temperature affects them less than wooden flutes, because the metal, being an excellent conductor of heat, reaches its highest possible temperature in a few seconds, so that the pitch cannot rise any higher.[31]

He maintained that "The silver flute is preferable for playing in

*Dayton Miller, in his 1922 edition of Boehm's *The Flute and Flute-Playing*, made the following assessment of this statement: "Undoubtedly the material of which a wind instrument is made sometimes affects the tone quality, but the manner in which this influence is exerted has not been explained; it is doubtful whether it is correct to ascribe it to the molecular vibrations of the material" (p. 53). Details of Miller's own research into this problem (1909) as well as more recent efforts are described infra, Chapter 4.

very large rooms because of its greater ability for tone modulation, and for the unsurpassed brilliancy and sonorousness of its tone."[32] Moreover, he stated, "I could produce effects on my silver flute, which I could never afterwards produce on wooden flutes."[33]

But Boehm's recommendation was not without qualification, for he was just as aware of human as of mechanical limitations. The silver flute, he wrote, "on account of its unusually easy tone-production, very often . . . is overblown, causing the tone to become hard and shrill; hence its advantages are fully realized only through a very good embouchure and diligent tone-practice. For this reason, wooden flutes on my system are also made, which are better adapted to the embouchures of most flute players. . . ."[34] Indeed, once Boehm had lost some of his front teeth, he reverted to a wood instrument for his personal use, reasoning that ". . . quality, not quantity, is the first consideration for me as an artist," and "I was no more sure of a round sonorous quality in the metal flutes."[35]

In 1847, Boehm sold the rights to his latest model to Rudall & Rose of London, who, on September 6 of that year, took out a patent in the name of John Mitchell Rose for the metal tube and cylindrical bore with parabolic headjoint. The patent for France was sold to Clair Godfroy (ca. 1814–1878) and his son-in-law, Louis Lot. At first, both firms constructed their Boehm flutes of metal; in 1848, however, Godfroy and Lot manufactured some cocoawood instruments at the suggestion of Dorus. The Frenchmen also reintroduced the perforated keys of Nolan and Pottgiesser, opening the center of the A, G, F♯, E, and D keys, which are played directly by the fingers, to allow increased venting. This model subsequently became known as the "open hole" or "French" model (Fig. 45).

Fig. 45. BOEHM FLUTE. Louis Lot, Paris (No. 163), late nineteenth century. Silver with gold lip plate. 5 perforated keys. Closed G♯. (DCM 219)

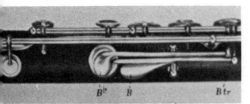

Fig. 46. BRICCIALDI
B♭ THUMB LEVER from
Dayton C. Miller's edition of Boehm's
The Flute and Flute-Playing (1908).

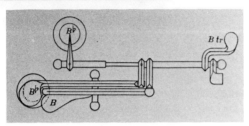

Fig. 47. BRICCIALDI
B♭ THUMB LEVER.
(Diagram by
Dayton C. Miller)

The only mechanical alteration to the 1847 Boehm flute that permanently affected the fingering system was made two years later by Giulio Briccialdi (1818–1881), an Italian flutist living in London.* In Boehm's original design, there was only one thumb lever, which governed an open key for B. B♭ was produced by adding the first finger of the right hand. Briccialdi's aim was to provide an alternate fingering for B♭ using the left-hand thumb, an arrangement which would be more convenient in flat keys (Figs. 46 and 47). The mechanism consisted of a second thumb lever, placed above that for B, which was sprung so that pressing it would also close the B hole. Thus B♭ could be fingered simply by the first finger and thumb of the left hand; only in passages where B and B♭ occur in succession was the original fingering necessary. Briccialdi's new lever was first applied by Rudall & Rose, at his request, to a cocuswood flute built by Godfroy.

Boehm later devised his own B♭ thumb device (Figs. 48 and 49), which he considered logically superior, in that the B♭ lever was below the B lever. On the Briccialdi version, in contrast, the thumb moved upwards to produce the lower tone. Briccialdi's design nevertheless prevailed.

* Other keys have since been added to the Boehm flute, but they have supplemented rather than changed the fingering system. The duplicate-hole closed G♯ mechanism introduced later in the century, though apparently a fingering modification, was merely a mechanical improvement of the principle established by Dorus in 1838.

[73

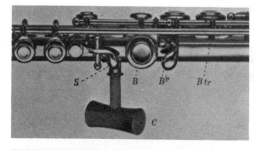

Fig. 48.
BOEHM'S B♭ THUMB KEY from
Dayton C. Miller's edition of Boehm's
The Flute and Flute-Playing (1908).
This instrument also features
a crutch (*C*) and *Schleifklappe*
or octave key (*S*).

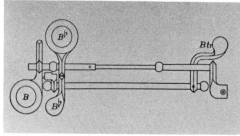

Fig. 49.
BOEHM'S B♭ THUMB KEY.
(Diagram by Dayton C. Miller)

Another Boehm modification was the addition of a *Schleif-klappe* or octave key (Fig. 48). In 1854, while working on the *Alt-Flöte* in G (commonly but incorrectly referred to as a bass flute), Boehm found that the upper register harmonics did not "speak" easily and that their tone lacked purity. Accordingly, he devised the octave key, now standard equipment on reed instruments, to assist in the formation of an antinode in the sound wave and to prevent the formation of a node at the point where the hole was located. The *Schleifklappe* was a small closed key with a touch-piece just above the left-hand thumb keys that could be opened by a small rolling motion of that thumb. The corresponding hole was placed about 7 millimeters above the C♯ hole. Boehm, impressed by the effect of the vent key on the G flute, then applied it to his C instrument.[36] He later wrote, "I find this little key very useful if the player wishes always to be in perfect tune in the following notes: d²♯(e²♭), d³, d³♯(e³♭), f³. These tones always have a tendency to get a little flat if played pianissimo, while if you open the little octave key they are not only perfectly correct, but also sound very easily." Dayton Miller's evaluation, however, reflects the view of the twentieth century: "For several of the notes mentioned in the supplementary tables of fingerings, the influence of

74]

the key cannot even be detected, while for the other notes its effect is very small, so small as to be entirely negligible. This no doubt accounts for the fact that the octave key has not been generally adopted."[37]

The only other device invented by Boehm was a closed G♯ key (Figs. 50 and 51). Despite his long-standing objection to this arrangement, Boehm was willing to sacrifice his principles for special customers such as General Daniel Macauley, former mayor of Indianapolis. He refused, however, to employ the Dorus G♯, as Godfroy and Lot had done. The alternative that he devised closely resembled his regular open G♯ model, but the key was sprung closed and the lever attached to it was divided in the middle and given an extra fulcrum to reverse its effect. In order to compensate for the flattening of the A which resulted from closing the G♯ hole directly below it, Boehm shifted the A hole 1.2 millimeters above its theoretical position as indicated in the *Schema*. Philip Bate judges this device to be "probably the best type of closed G♯ ever designed but it does not seem to have been copied by any other maker. No doubt Boehm did little to publicize it."[38]

Fig. 50. BOEHM FLUTE. Th. Boehm & Mendler, Munich, 1877.
Silver with gold embouchure, springs, ferrules, and plates on all keys.
Boehm's special closed G♯ key. *Schleif* key. B foot.
Made for General Daniel Macauley, former mayor of Indianapolis. (DCM 161)

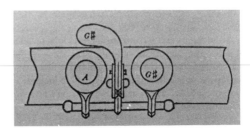

Fig. 51.
BOEHM'S CLOSED G♯ KEY.
(Diagram by Philip Bate)

PUBLIC REACTION AND MUSICAL IMPLICATIONS

The Boehm flute quickly became popular with professional players in both France and England. The Paris Conservatoire had adopted the 1832 model in 1838; shortly afterward, Jules A. E. Demersseman (1833–1866) was refused a teaching appointment at the Conservatoire because of his adherence to the old flute.[39] In the United States, acceptance was also rapid; having been imported to New York by two prominent teachers, John A. Kyle and Philip Ernst, it was first manufactured in the United States by Larribee in 1847. In 1851, the Boehm flute took first prize in the Industrial Exhibition of All Nations held in London, where it was demonstrated by Benjamin Wells (1826–1899), the president of the London Flute Society. Sir Henry Bishop's report found that "Mr. Boehm has acquired not only a perfection in the tone and tuning never before attained but also a facility in playing those keys which were hitherto difficult and defective in sonorousness and intonation." Another juror was surprised and pleased to find "*all* the notes equally fine."[40] In 1855, the Boehm flute took the gold medal at the Paris Exhibition.

In the same year, the new instrument was also awarded first prize at the General German Industrial Exhibition in Munich. Nevertheless, acceptance in Boehm's native country was, rather ironically, very slow. W. S. Broadwood attributed this apparent conservatism to aesthetic principles:

> . . . certain German conductors appear to have considered that the Boehm flute does not take its proper place in that gradation of 'wood' instruments, which, commencing with the bassoon, culminates in the piccolo. In power and breadth of tone, sometimes also in quality, it approaches too near the clarinet to give the balance of tone, which writers—like, for instance, Mozart (whose minute appreciation of the characteristics of each instrument is very striking)— would seem to have aimed at.[41]

Arthur Brooke, however, credited slow German acceptance to a lack of qualified teachers in the early years after the instrument's introduction. "The untimely death of Hans Heindl, Boehm's best pupil on the new flute and an artist of great promise, and the departure of Martin Heindl and Carl Wehner for the United States, were serious setbacks to the adoption of the Boehm flute. . . ."[42] Even by 1906, Dayton Miller reported, the Boehm system had not become common in Germany, Italy, or Russia;[43] in 1914 Fitzgibbon observed that some German conductors still banned the Boehm flute from their orchestras.[44] Players objected to the sharp tendency of the upper octave, but most of all to the new system of fingering.

Even in England, objections to the new fingering slowed the adoption of the Boehm flute by a large proportion of flutists. W. N. James, for instance, attacked the new instrument as containing "clumsy (though ingenious) complicities, the remedy being actually worse than the disease."[45] Moreover, an 1870 article in *The English Mechanic* reported, "[I]t was pertinently objected that what had already been so changed and complicated would in all probability undergo further mutation at no distant period."*[46] The result of the older players' unwillingness to relearn their fingering, coupled with the high prices of the complex Boehm flutes, was that many such older players abandoned the instrument in the face of competition from younger players who knew only the superior new system. For the same reason, the number of professional players also decreased temporarily. The serious decline in the number of amateur players effectively diminished the flute's role as a drawing room instrument; the new generation of professionals who did adopt the Boehm flute introduced it primarily into orchestral and concert work, where its powerful tone was not only necessary but also considered more appropriate than for *Hausmusik*.

Eventually, then, the Boehm flute became a valuable resource for nineteenth century orchestral composers, fulfilling Coche's optimistic 1838 prediction that "the music already written for the instrument will be infinitely better executed, and that henceforth the field is open for all kinds of new developments. . . ."[47] The

*This prediction was temporarily correct, many different fingering systems being introduced during the second half of the nineteenth century, but the Boehm system ultimately prevailed.

new compositional possibilities were particularly evident in the matter of range. In 1878, for example, Brahms wrote a b^3 for the flute in the second movement of his Symphony no. 2. This note could be produced only with great difficulty on the old flute. In his Fourth Symphony of 1886, Brahms scored c^{4}s for the flute in the first movement. Richard Strauss, in the following decade, was even more adventurous; c^4♯ appears in the flute part of *Till Eulenspiegel* (1895), while d^4 is used in *Also sprach Zarathustra* and *Ein Heldenleben* (1899). At the opposite extreme, nineteenth century composers began to exploit the newly powerful lower register of the Boehm flute. Tchaikovsky, for example, required the second flute to play low b in the third movement of his Sixth Symphony (1893).

A new technique made possible by the Boehm flute was the use of natural harmonics. As early as 1843, John Clinton recommended this device for simplifying difficult passages in the third octave, noting that the procedure had been unacceptable on the old flute because of the obvious intrusion of the fundamental tones, which had produced the effect of parallel fifths. Among the compositions which Clinton used to demonstrate the effectiveness of harmonic fingerings were Rossini's Overture to *La Gazza Ladra*, Méhul's Overture to *Les Deux Aveugles de Tolède*, Cherubini's Overture to *Anacréon*, and Kuhlau's Duos, Op. 39 and 81.[48] Performers also learned to use harmonics to vary tone color and expression; subsequently, several composers, such as Terschak and Doppler, introduced "flageletto" notes into their works.

In general, however, the solo compositions of the mid-nineteenth century were of little substance. As in the pre-Boehm era, the majority of solo flute pieces were virtuosic showpieces written by rather second-rate composers. Boehm, it must be admitted, was as guilty as the rest of his contemporaries, if not more so; most of his compositions were designed to exhibit the technical capabilities of his invention.* Some, it is alleged, were consciously written so as to be almost impossible on the old system

*A complete list of Boehm's compositions appears in Miller's edition of Boehm's *The Flute and Flute-Playing*, pp. 181–88.

flute.[49] The great composers of the century, possibly discouraged by the performers' enthusiasm for merely impressive pieces, were not inclined to waste their creative efforts on the flute. Louis Fleury, reflecting despairingly on the lack of Romantic solo literature, charged that the virtuosi thereby "did more harm to their instrument, in spite of their undoubted mastery of it, than the clumsiest amateur could have done."[50] The trend was only reversed in the twentieth century, when audiences, having tired of the "fireworks" genre, demanded better, and the solo flute experienced a renaissance.

Notes]

1. H. Macaulay Fitzgibbon, *The Story of the Flute*, 2nd ed., rev. (London: William Reeves Bookseller; New York: Charles Scribner's Sons, 1928), p. 110.

2. W. N. James, "Essay No. 1," in *Six Essays on Fingering the Flute*, supplement to *Flutonicon* 13 (1846): 1.

3. Curt Sachs, *The History of Musical Instruments* (New York: W. W. Norton & Co., 1940), pp. 388–90.

4. C[harles] Nicholson, *A School for the Flute* (London and New York: Wm. Hall & Sons, 1836), p. 3.

5. Theobald Boehm, *An Essay on the Construction of Flutes*, ed. W. S. Broadwood (London: Rudall, Carte & Co., 1882), pp. 17–18. Hereafter cited as Boehm, *Essay*.

6. Ibid., p. 12.

7. Adam Carse, *Musical Wind Instruments* (1939; reprint ed., New York: Da Capo Press, 1965), p. 98.

8. Philip Bate, *The Flute* (New York: W. W. Norton & Co., 1969), pp. 117–18.

9. Ibid., p. 118.

10. Boehm, *Essay*, p. 19.

11. Theobald Boehm, *The Flute and Flute-Playing*, trans. and ed. Dayton C. Miller, 2nd ed., rev. (1922; reprint ed., New York: Dover Publications, 1964), pp. 26–27. Hereafter cited as Boehm, *Flute*.

12. Boehm, *Essay*, p. 20.

13. Ibid.

14. Carse, pp. 95–96.

15. Bate, pp. 121–22.

16. Boehm, *Essay*, p. 23.

17. Boehm, *Flute*, p. 55.

18. Boehm, *Essay*, p. 13.

19. Bate, p. 121.

20. Ibid., p. 122.

21. Victor Coche, *Examen Critique de la Flûte Ordinaire comparée à la Flûte de Boehm* (Paris: The Author, 1838), p. 31.

22. Dayton C. Miller, "The Modern Flute: Its History and Construction," TS (1906), pp. 55–56.

23. Boehm, *Essay*, pp. 34–36.

24. Boehm, *Flute*, p. 14.

25. Ibid., pp. 17–19.

26. Boehm, *Essay*, pp. 36–38.

27. Victor Coche, *Examen Critique de la Flûte Ordinaire comparée à la Flûte de Boehm*, trans. Edith E. Miller, TS, p. 22. Hereafter cited as Coche-Miller.

28. Boehm, *Flute*, pp. 27–30.

29. Ibid., p. 104.

30. Ibid., pp. 53–54.

31. Boehm, *Essay*, p. 45.

32. Boehm, *Flute*, p. 54.

33. Boehm, *Essay*, p. 61.

34. Boehm, *Flute*, pp. 54–55.

35. Boehm, *Essay*, pp. 48–49.

36. Boehm, *Flute*, pp. 84–86.

37. Ibid., p. 88.

38. Bate, p. 129.

39. Fitzgibbon, p. 202.

40. Ibid., p. 57.

41. W. S. Broadwood, Preface to Boehm, *Essay*, pp. vii–viii.

42. Wm. S. Haynes Co., *The Modern Boehm Flute* (Boston, ca. 1902), p. 5.

43. Miller, p. 69.

44. Fitzgibbon, p. 57.

45. W. N. James, "Essay No. 6," in *Six Essays on Fingering the Flute*, supplement to *Flutonicon* 13 (1846): 1.

46. Sable [pseud.], "The Flute and Its Vicissitudes," *The English Mechanic* 11 (1870): 13.

47. Coche-Miller, p. 25.

48. John Clinton, *A Theoretical & Practical Essay, on the Boehm Flute*, 2nd ed. (London: R. Cocks & Co., ca. 1843–46), pp. 49–51.

49. Fitzgibbon, p. 58.

50. Louis Fleury, "The Flute and Its Powers of Expression," trans. A.H.F.S., *Music and Letters* 3 (October 1922): 383.

Contemporaries and Critics of Boehm

The history of the nineteenth century flute is an extremely complicated one. The mathematician could not represent the succession of mechanisms or fingering systems on a continuous line graph. Instead, he would have to be content with a highly overlapping bar graph that reflects the indecision and professional competitiveness of the period (Appendix I). In part, the diversity of flute models may be attributed to a lack of communication between some player-inventors, who maintained a steadfast policy of intellectual isolationism as a matter of pride. The inevitable result was a multitude of parallel but mutually unknown developments which, from a historical perspective, were simply a waste of time. On the other hand, would-be inventors were frequently spurred to "creativity" by jealousy of others' originality and the egotistical desire to have their own names emblazoned on an instrument. The situation was complicated by strong national musical allegiance as evidenced by the varying rates of adoption of the Boehm flute.

The latter two-thirds of the nineteenth century may best be divided into three categories that correspond in large measure, though not exclusively, to these national allegiances. Work on the old system cone flute was continued primarily in Germany, though also in other areas of Continental Europe. Completely new designs and modifications of and additions to the cylinder Boehm flute were executed, for the most part, in England.

OLD SYSTEM CONE FLUTES

As we have already seen, acceptance of the Boehm flute was far from instantaneous, particularly in the inventor's native country of Germany. Primarily, this reluctance to change may be attributed to a lack of either the time or the inclination to learn new fingerings, and accordingly, many players remained loyal to the old system of fingering. Moreover, the simple system flute was often considered quite satisfactory for the performance of literature of the Baroque and Classical periods; it was, after all, the instrument for which that music was written. The old system cone flute was also judged to have a tone more "subtle and interesting in character, though less telling than that of the cylindrical Boehm," such qualities being thought preferable for the earlier literature.[1]

Numerous variations were made on the simple system flute which, though they rendered it less simple, nevertheless preserved both the tonal characteristics of the conical bore and the original scheme of fingering. Many individuals designed distinctive models, with varying numbers and arrangements of keys, to

Fig. 52. TAYLOR'S APPROVED FLUTE. C. Peloubet, New York, ca. 1829–35.
Ivory, with silver rings, stud, and embouchure band.
8 silver keys in ivory lugs. C foot. Large holes. (DCM 73)

Fig. 53. MONZANI'S 9-KEYED FLUTE.
Monzani & Co., London (No. 1227), ca. 1814–20.
Cocus, with silver keys and fittings. Monzani's patent (1812) joints, with silver-lined sockets and cork-covered pin. Lower body and foot in one piece. (DCM 394)

which they then affixed their names. The Dayton C. Miller Collection contains a generous sampling of these varieties, including Richardson's Improved Flute, Taylor's Approved Flute (Fig. 52), Monzani's nine-keyed flute (Fig. 53), Cloos's ten-keyed flute, Luvoni's thirteen-keyed flute, and Rampone's seventeen-keyed flute.

One of the best publicized simple system modifications was made by Jean Louis Tulou (1786–1865), who submitted to the Great Exhibition of 1851 in London a cone flute with small holes, both long and cross F keys, and c^2♯ and d^2 trill keys (Figs. 54–56). To supplement the C key operated by the right-hand forefinger, Tulou added a duplicate C, with its own hole, for the third finger of the left hand. A unique feature of this flute was a longitudinal F♯ vent key for the third finger of the right hand. Tulou did draw on Boehm's mechanism for axles, on which most of the longer keys were mounted, but his footjoint resembled Boehm's 1832 model. Tulou was also credited with the design of thumb keys for C and B♭.

A frequent addition to the old flute was known in Germany as the *Brille* ("spectacles"). Consisting of two rings and a vent on the upper joint that were designed to improve the intonation of c^2 and c^2♯, this device was later adopted in the manufacture of Rudall & Rose.

By the late part of the nineteenth century, the cone flute had evolved, in Germany, into what was labeled by its manufacturers as the "reform flute." The first version was designed in about 1885 by Maximilian Schwedler, a Leipzig flutist, and it was produced in conjunction with manufacturer Friedrich Wilhelm Kruspe of Leipzig and later in partnership with his son, known as Carl Kruspe, Jr. The "Schwedler-Kruspe" flute was patented in 1895 and won the gold medal at the 1897 Leipzig Exhibition.

The footjoint of this flute, as of many of its German predecessors, was built on axles. Along with the usual cross and long Fs and the side C key, this model featured a side trill key near the head for such shakes as d^3/e^3. The younger Kruspe made several mechanical improvements to the instrument, including an F♯ correcting mechanism patented in 1921. Depressing the cover of the

Fig. 54. TULOU FLUTE.
Tulou, Paris (No. 1809), ca. 1860.
Grenadilla, with polished surface. 12 silver
keys. Small holes. (DCM 188)

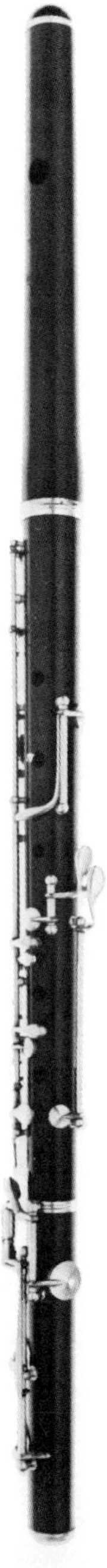

Fig. 55. TULOU FLUTE.
Fernand Chapelain & Cie., Paris, ca. 1878.
Rosewood, German silver rings and keys.
12 keys on posts. Steel needle springs.
Small holes. (DCM 376)

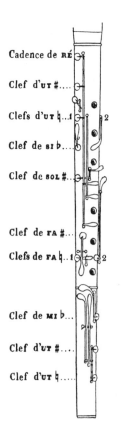

Cadence de RÉ

Clef d'UT #....

Clefs d'UT ♮...1   2

Clef de SI ♭....

Clef de SOL #..

Clef de FA #...

Clefs de FA ♮..1   2

Clef de MI ♭...

Clef d'UT #....

Clef d'UT ♮.....

Fig. 56. TULOU'S OLD SYSTEM FLUTE
from Tulou, *Méthode de Flúte* (1835).

F♯ hole produced F♯; adding the supplementary roller (a feature typical of German manufacture) provided a simple transition to F♮. Connected to the C♯ brille at the upper end of the instrument, the device could be deactivated to produce a properly tuned c³♯.

The reform flute was further mechanized by the Mönnig family of Leipzig, who installed plates over some holes and rings for certain automated devices. The Moritz Max Mönnig catalog of about 1930 lists, in addition to ten-keyed and eleven-keyed wood *Meyerflöten, Schwedlerflöten* (with a choice of C or B footjoint) (Fig. 57) and six basic varieties of *Reformflöten* (Figs. 58–60)—the last category with all holes covered. Both *Schwedlerflöten* and *Reformflöten* had wood bodies and silver heads. Wilhelm Heckel, famed woodwind manufacturer of Biebrich, also contributed to the mechanization of the reform flute. Similar models were brought out by A. E. Fischer of Bremen and F. O. Uebel of Leipzig.

The most striking innovation of the reform flute was not in the keywork, however, but in the construction of the embouchure,

Fig. 57. *SCHWEDLERFLÖTE* from
1930 catalog of Moritz Max Mönnig, Leipzig.
Grenadilla. Metal head with Schwedler mouthhole.
12 keys. C♯- and F♯ brille. A♯-B, high D-E,
high G-A, and G♯-A, C-D, and C♯-D trills.
Left-hand touches for F and B.

Fig. 58. SCHWEDLER REFORM FLUTE.
Moritz Max Mönnig, Leipzig, ca. 1925.
German silver, silver-plated. Keys on posts
and rods. 8 rollers. Conical bore. B foot.
This is the only Schwedler reform flute
entirely of metal. It was made for
Maximilian Schwedler by Moritz Max Mönnig
as a mark of gratitude. Schwedler did not
approve of the metal flute, however, and
replaced it with a wooden one. (DCM 1026)

Fig. 59. SCHWEDLER REFORM FLUTE.
(Diagram by Jerry L. Voorhees from DCM 1026)

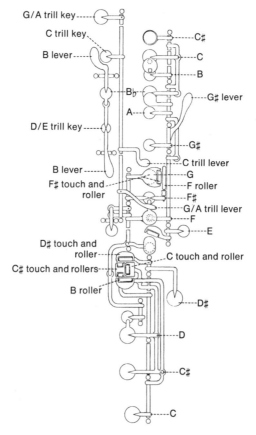

Fig. 60.
SCHWEDLER REFORM FLUTE.
Moritz Max Mönnig, Leipzig, ca. 1930.
Ebony, with silver head and fittings. B foot.
These materials were the usual ones for
reform flutes. (DCM 1584)

Fig. 61. REFORM HEADJOINTS from 1931 catalog of Otto Mönnig, Leipzig.
Four versions of the reform mouthhole, originally designed for reform flutes,
but still offered by Otto Mönnig in 1931 for Boehm flutes.

which had raised bosses or cusps both above and below the
mouth hole (Fig. 61). Many players preferred this design because
they believed that it expedited the control of the airstream. Similar concerns led to much investigation of the depth of the mouth
hole on Boehm flutes, as well. Thus a small piece of curved ebonite (a compound of India rubber, lead, and sulfur, which was first
used for flutes in about 1850) was often attached by English
makers to the wall of the tube. A metal ring, called a chimney,
was soldered to the tube, and a perforated lip plate, curved like
the head itself, soldered in turn to the chimney. In the late part
of the century, the lip plate was mounted in a barrel which fully
encircled the tube; thus Rudall, Carte offered a choice between
barrel and oval lip plates. Ambitious craftsmen frequently applied
their decorative skills to the elaborate ornamentation of such lip
plates and barrels, but these were eventually eliminated because
of their excessive weight, which tended to unbalance the flute.[2]

NEW DESIGNS

Other flutists rejected both the old system and Boehm's (some
did not wait for Boehm's 1847 perfections, having summarily rejected his 1832 model), and consequently sought to devise their
own systems. One observer remarked that "This invention mania
became so-to-speak, infectious";[3] another referred sarcastically to
the enthusiastic inventors as "The Noble Army of Patentees."[4]

Cornelius Ward may perhaps be considered the "General" of
that army, having secured in 1842 a patent for seven different

conical flutes, each with its own fingering system. All seven models featured a device that Ward called the "Terminator and Indicator" (Figs. 62 and 63), a graduated metal tuning slide coordinated with a silver head stopper. An eccentric disc inside the headjoint was connected by means of a tiny rod to a small regulating lever on the exterior of the tube. The player was instructed to "place the ring of the Index shown at N, to a number (on either side of the circle) corresponding to that which shows itself at the top of the slide, at M, after the flute has been drawn out to any required pitch."[5]

The final Ward model (Figs. 64–66) was on the open-keyed system with silver ring keys, as on Boehm's flute, controlled by wires and cranks similar to those of Gordon. This was the first English flute to employ needle springs. Thus, although Ward's aim was to afford greater mechanical facility than had Boehm, Gordon, or Coche and Buffet, his flute was actually a composite of their designs and those of Dorus.

Fig. 62.
WARD'S TERMINATOR
AND INDICATOR
from Ward flute (Fig. 65).

Fig. 63.
WARD'S TERMINATO.
AND INDICATOR
from Cornelius Ward,
The Flute Explained (18-

Fig. 64. WARD FLUTE.
Cornelius Ward, London, ca. 1842–60.
Cocus, with silver rings, cap, and keys. A foot.
Patented "bell-crank" action (1842). (DCM 44)

Fig. 65. WARD FLUTE.
Cornelius Ward, London, ca. 1842–60.
Silver. Conical bore. "Bell-crank" action
for low C♯. C♮ for left thumb. Embouchure
nearly square. Small bell on lower end.
Elaborate engraving. (DCM 1260)

Fig. 66. WARD FLUTE
from Cornelius Ward,
The Flute Explained (1844).

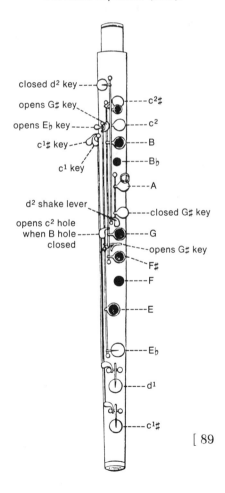

closed d² key ---
opens G♯ key ---
opens E♭ key ---
c¹♯ key ---
c¹ key ---
d² shake lever ---
opens c² hole
when B hole ---
closed

--- c²♯
--- c²
--- B
--- B♭
--- A
---closed G♯ key
--- G
---opens G♯ key
--- F♯
--- F
--- E
--- E♭
--- d¹
--- c¹♯

On the right hand, each finger was assigned its own hole, which it operated directly. There was also a d^2 shake key for the right forefinger. On the left hand, the first three fingers also controlled their own holes directly, with the fourth finger responsible for both the G♯ and A holes by means of a Dorus G♯-like device. An interesting feature was the arrangement for C♯, whereby two holes of different size closed together; the hole covered directly by the left forefinger had a ring key, while its mate had a padded hole-cover. Bate dismisses this scheme as having absolutely no merit. Another Dorus principle that Ward "borrowed" was the mechanism for D♯, which was closed by the ring on the E hole and released by a touchpiece for the left-hand thumb. In all, that thumb was required to operate five keys, three of which controlled foot keys.[6] Several were duplicate keys used for slurs and other difficult passages. A critic for *The English Mechanic* judged Ward's system to be a poor compromise, however, for, though the inventor claimed to have abolished cross-fingerings, "all departures from the old mode of fingering (which is decidedly the best because based upon simple and natural laws) is *practically* a back or cross fingering." The result of his attempted compromise between old and new systems was that "neither the old or the new were accomplished well; this flute was to dazzle all the orchestras in Europe, but its fame was circumscribed, its existence brief, and it is scarcely remembered."[7]

Another new design was the work of John Clinton, a professor at the Royal Academy of Music in London, who had been one of the earliest British proponents of the Boehm flute, having adopted it in 1843 and defended it in his *Theoretical & Practical Essay, on the Boehm Flute,* first published in the same year. In 1848, Clinton patented two devices (Fig. 67) which, though judged by Rockstro to be useless, reflected his growing disenchantment with the open-keyed system on which the Boehm flute was based. On the upper body, he substituted a single bar for the three rings that normally closed the G hole. More importantly, he devised a mechanism which, by covering the B♭ and G♯ holes with the original form of closed keys, allowed c^2 to be fingered as in the old system.

In his *Treatise upon the Mechanism and General Principles of the Flute*, written in 1852, Clinton outlined the following objections to the Boehm flute: (1) A complete change in fingering required "patience and application." (2) As Coche had written earlier, keys and scales which were easiest on the old flute were now the most difficult on the Boehm, and vice versa. (3) The Boehm flute had back- or cross-fingerings in the first and second octaves, as for F♯ in the D scale or B♭ in the F scale. (Clinton complained of intervening Gs in the first instance, which were probably due to his inexperience with the new fingering. In the second case, he obviously was not yet familiar with the Briccialdi B♭ thumb lever invented three years earlier.) (4) Passage from c^2 to d^2 was difficult, and there were many cross-fingerings in the third octave. (5) The open-keyed system caused the tone, "although considered more equal, [to be] not so brilliant or vibratory as the best notes on the ordinary flute." (6) The four lowest notes had a feeble tone quality. (7) The third octave was thin, and too sharp. (8) The mechanism was complicated and too expensive for most players to be able to afford.[8]

Fig. 67. CLINTON 1848 PATENT. British Patent No. 12,378.
An open key (*b*) over the duplicate C♯ hole was linked with the cover
of the A hole (*c*) by bar c^1. When the A hole was open, the duplicate C♯ hole
was shut by a small arm (*d*) falling on the C♯ key. A touch or "dumb key" (*e*) shut
the duplicate C♯ hole and the C♮ hole just below the touch. A long C key
on the far side of the flute was controlled by the right forefinger and was mounted
on the same rod as the G♯ key. A bar (*a*) connected to the G key (a^1) lay adjacent
to three holes; closing any of the holes closed the key.

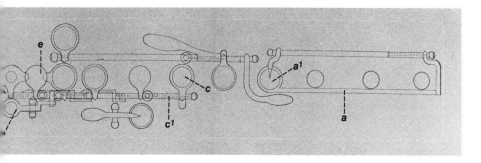

Clinton therefore set out to design a new flute with the dual aims of retaining the old fingering and maintaining equality of tone and correct intonation throughout the compass. In 1855, he published *A few practical Hints to Flute Players upon the subject of Modern Flutes* in which he presented a description of a new "Equisonant Flute" (Figs. 68 and 69). A few features of the mechanism may be cited as representative. On the left hand, the ring on the B hole also closed a circular open key over the C♯ hole, which reduced the size of the latter hole, thereby tuning it. The A♮ hole was moved farther down the tube than on the German flute in order to improve its intonation. However, this vent hole, in turn, made the A too sharp, so Clinton placed an open key over the vent hole, which was operated by action of the left-hand first finger on the ring over the C♯ hole.

On the right hand, the E hole was moved much lower than usual, but in order to avoid using an open key operated by the third finger, as on the Gerock and Wolf flute of Boehm (1831), Clinton shifted the entire right hand downward. Thus the E hole was operated directly by the third finger, and the G and F♯ holes were covered by open keys and controlled by ring keys for the first and second fingers, respectively.[9] As one may expect from such complications, the result was far from successful. Rockstro recounts the question of a staunch Boehm partisan, who asked, "What is the meaning of 'equisonant,' Mr. Clinton, does it mean equally bad all over?" Rockstro offered his own typically sardonic reply: "Unfortunately, the flute had not even that negative merit, for it was unequally bad."[10]

By 1862, Clinton had reverted to the manufacture of Boehm flutes, whose patent protection had expired, despite his own opposition to them. Presumably he was a better businessman than acoustician. On March 31, 1862, he was granted a patent for graduating the holes of cylinder flutes, with the size decreasing toward the head. Boehm disputed the originality of the patent, having used graduated holes himself for six years. Clinton's final flute patent, issued in 1863, covered a lever level with and contiguous to the right-hand first finger key and operated by the same finger for obtaining F♮ with the Boehm fingering without

Fig. 68. CLINTON EQUISONANT FLUTE.
Clinton & Co., London, ca. 1863–71.
Cocus with silver keys. 4 rings.
Conical bore. Head and barrel are marked
with Siccama No. 1409. (DCM 379)

Fig. 69. CLINTON EQUISONANT FLUTE.
(Diagram by Jerry L. Voorhees from DCM 710,
which has mechanism identical to DCM 379)

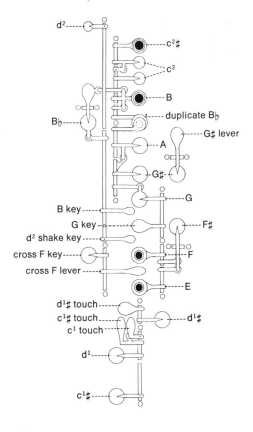

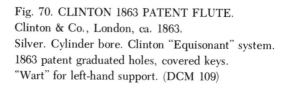

Fig. 70. CLINTON 1863 PATENT FLUTE.
Clinton & Co., London, ca. 1863.
Silver. Cylinder bore. Clinton "Equisonant" system.
1863 patent graduated holes, covered keys.
"Wart" for left-hand support. (DCM 109)

Fig. 71. CLINTON 1863 PATENT FLUTE.
The instrument on which this diagram is based is
identical to DCM 109 except that this one has the
closed G♯ action and hole on the inner side of the tube.
(Diagram by Jerry L. Voorhees from DCM 1284)

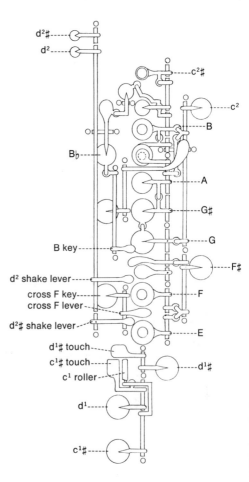

losing the old F♯ fingering. This flute retained the closed F♮, G♮, and B♭ keys of the German flute, with the additional complication of a duplicate open counterpart for each (Figs. 70 and 71).

PROPOSALS FOR KEYLESS FLUTES

In reaction to the trend of mechanical complication of the flute, beginning with the German flute and continuing through Boehm, Ward, Clinton, and many more, several men proposed schemes for keyless flutes. The absence of keys, it was hoped, would obviate the inevitable competition of manufacturers and the confusion of players regarding the abundant rival key systems.

One such experimenter was a Dr. Burghley of Camden Town, London, whose flutes Dayton Miller dated as circa 1845 (Figs. 72–75). The simplest Burghley instruments had holes in simple chromatic sequence for all ten fingers and thumbs. The left-hand thumb covered the uppermost hole, which in fact consisted of two contiguous oval slots. Many Burghley instruments had one open

Fig. 72. BURGHLEY FLUTE.
Dr. Burghley, Camden Town, London, ca. 1845.
Mahogany, with ivory rings. 8 open finger holes, 2 black
wood spring keys. 1 perforation on thumb key. D foot.
Holes of nearly uniform large size, nearly equal spacing.
Straight head. 3 joints. (DCM 1092)

Fig. 73. BURGHLEY FLUTE.
Dr. Burghley, Camden Town, London, ca. 1845.
Mahogany, with ivory and wood rings. 10 open finger holes, 1 black wood
spring key. Left thumb operated double open hole, rather than
perforated key. D foot. Jointed swivel head, which allowed various
embouchure angles, in 2 planes, to body tube. 5 joints. (DCM 1093)

Fig. 74. BURGHLEY FLUTE.
Dr. Burghley, Camden Town, London, ca. 1845.
Mahogany, with ivory rings and screw stud. 10 open finger holes,
1 black wood spring key. 2 open foot-holes with black bushings.
D♯ foot key perforated, with ivory bushing. C♯ foot. Bent head
cut from solid wood. 3 pieces. (DCM 1094)

Fig. 75. BURGHLEY FLUTE.
Dr. Burghley, Camden Town, London, ca. 1845.
Alto flute in G. Mahogany with black rings. 7 open finger holes, 6 black wood
spring keys. 2 open foot-holes with black bushings. Body keys for high
C♯, C♮, G♯; foot keys for D♯, D♮, C♯. D♯ key provided with curious ivory screw
arrangement. C foot extended by oboe-like bell. Angular head. (DCM 1095)

foot key to extend the lower range to d¹. The rather mysterious
Burghley left no account of his work, nor did any contemporary
chronicler,* but Miller provided his own explanation of the principles involved:

> This 'Chromatic System' uses all *ten* fingers and thumbs, lifted suc-
> cessively. The left thumb does double duty, opening perforation in
> key and then opening key. This gives (with bottom open end and its
> octave) all the tones of the chromatic scale (two keys only needed!).
> A special support, or crutch, for *right* hand is used (this crutch is
> lost, not being complete on any of the seven specimens [in the
> Miller collection]). Some of the flutes have lower foot-keys for C♯
> and C♮ operated by right little finger as on ordinary flute.[11]

*In his *Treatise* (p. 367), Rockstro refers to Burghley as "an intimate friend of
mine," but does not discuss his work.

Burghley also experimented with various configurations of head-joints, some being angular, others having jointed swivel heads.

Another partisan of the keyless flute was Abel Siccama, a London language teacher and amateur flutist. Siccama's ideal was simplicity of construction, and to this end he began constructing flutes in 1842. A prototype of one such instrument was brought by Alfred Chittenden to Rudall, Carte in that year, but rejected for their manufacture. On March 13, 1845, Siccama obtained a patent for four flutes, three of which reached only the model stage. In 1846, he published *Observations on Correctness of Tune applied to the Flute*, a pamphlet describing the fourth of these instruments, known as the "Chromatic Flute" (Fig. 76). It had one key, a closed C key for the right-hand forefinger, and was as close as Siccama ever was able to come to the keyless ideal. The instrument was a failure, however, owing to the assignment of the G hole to the right-hand thumb, which could no longer fulfill its usual and vital function of supporting the flute.

Fig. 76. SICCAMA CHROMATIC FLUTE.

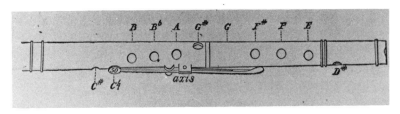

Another flute mentioned in Siccama's 1846 pamphlet and fully described in another publication the following year was inaccurately labeled by its inventor as the "Diatonic Flute." (The correct term would have been "Enharmonic.") It is this instrument that has subsequently taken the appellation of "Siccama flute" (Figs. 77 and 78).

Conical in bore, with large tone holes of equal size, the Diatonic Flute reverted entirely to the old system of fingering with the exception of the high E, F, G, and A. Because the A and E

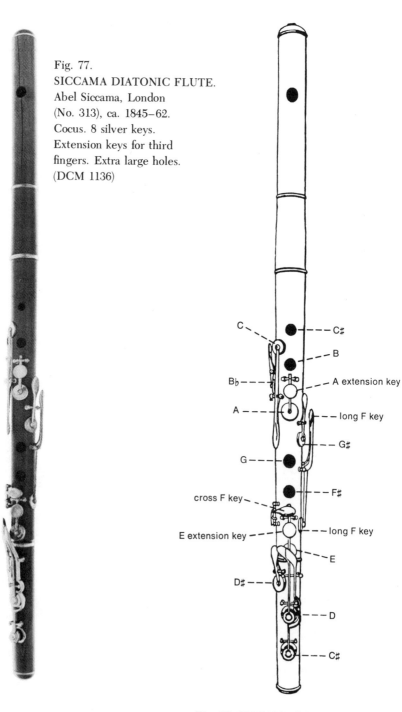

Fig. 77.
SICCAMA DIATONIC FLUTE.
Abel Siccama, London
(No. 313), ca. 1845–62.
Cocus. 8 silver keys.
Extension keys for third
fingers. Extra large holes.
(DCM 1136)

C — C♯

B

B♭ — A extension key

A — long F key

G♯

G —

cross F key — F♯

E extension key — long F key

E

D♯ —

D

C♯

Fig. 78. SICCAMA DIATONIC FLUTE
from Christopher Welch,
History of the Boehm Flute (1896).

holes were placed beyond the reach of the third fingers of the left and right hands, respectively, third order levers controlled open keys with touchplates for those fingers in the middle of the shanks. Bate notes that a quite incidental advantage of this feature was that the touches could be adjusted to the individual player's hands without affecting the mechanism. In line with his ideal of simplicity, Siccama included only one duplicate key, that for F♮.

At first, Siccama manufactured his own flutes, but the "diatonic" model was soon adopted by numerous other makers. These included the firm of Mahillon & Co. of Brussels and London, which added a vent key with two rings over the upper two finger holes in order to improve the intonation of c^2 and c^2♯. The Siccama flute was adopted by two leading English players, Joseph Richardson (1814–1862), who used it until his death, and for a short time by Robert Sydney Pratten (1824–1868). Richardson demonstrated it with great success at the Great Exhibition of 1851. An "improved Siccama flute" (Fig. 79) was offered by Boosey & Co. as late as 1902. Essentially identical to the original model, this instrument had all its holes except the two highest covered with open, axle-mounted keys, and was probably designed by Pratten. It also had the c^2/c^2♯ vent of organologist Victor Mahillon.[12] Rudall, Carte & Co. offered a Siccama model as late as 1904.

Fig. 79. IMPROVED SICCAMA FLUTE
from catalog of Boosey & Co., London, ca. 1900.
C♯ brille. Covered keys.

A more exotic attempt at simplicity by means of keyless construction was made by Carlo T. Giorgi in 1888 and patented in 1897 (Figs. 80 and 81). The instrument was made of ebonite. It had eleven finger holes, one for each semitone from d^1 to d^2; each

Fig. 80.
GIORGI KEYLESS FLUTE.
Joseph Wallis & Son, Ltd.,
London, ca. 1888.
Ebonite cylindrical tube, with
German silver rings, metal slide
at mouthpiece. 11 finger holes.
Lowest pitch d¹. 2 joints.
(DCM 112)

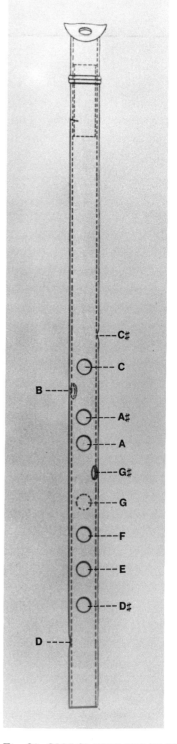

Fig. 81. GIORGI KEYLESS FLUT
U.S. Patent No. 594,735 (1897).

finger and thumb was responsible for stopping one hole with its tip and another with its upper joint. The inventor claimed that his instrument was based on Boehm's acoustical principles in terms of the division of the tube into semitones, but he claimed superiority to Boehm by his abolition of cross-fingering. The descriptive literature issued by Joseph Wallis & Son, the instrument's London manufacturer, made the following comparison:

> . . . in Boehm's flute the production of the harmonics depends on appropriate positions suggested by the laws of harmony, whereas in the Giorgi Flute, after the first twelve chromatic grades are obtained by means of the principal positions, and also the second series of twelve chromatic grades in the octave above, the notes from 'D' to 'G♯' above the line are obtained even without the aid of keys, but simply by the position of the notes on the 12th minor. Special positions are only required for the notes above 'G♯.'[13]

In addition to the simplicity of fingering, because of which the Giorgi flute was highly recommended to students, other advantages claimed were lightness and low cost, ". . . there being no mechanism to get out of order, and, should any portion of it become damaged in any way, the parts can be replaced at a small cost in comparison with the cost of repairs of expensive flutes at present in use."[14]

It is instructive to note, however, that Giorgi did envision the possibility of adding keys to his instrument. The patent specification thus includes modifications with keys for use in producing supplementary upper register notes. The Miller collection contains two Wallis instruments, dated circa 1888, with three keys (Fig. 82), and another by Maino & Orsi of Milan, circa 1900, with four keys (Fig. 83). The Adam Carse Collection includes a Wallis one-keyed flute, circa 1890, a Maino & Orsi model of the same year with two keys, and a contemporaneous anonymous flute with eleven open keys.

A rather unique feature of the Giorgi flute was its vertically blown mouthpiece (Fig. 84). As described in *Scientific American*, "This flute has a mouthpiece curved in direction of the length of the flute, with a mouth hole on its top and a resounding chamber extending below the line of communication between the mouth-

Fig. 82. GIORGI FLUTE.
Joseph Wallis & Son, Ltd., London, ca. 1888.
Ebonite cylindrical tube. German silver slide
and rings. 8 open finger holes. 3 German silver
keys (D♯, G♯, high C♯). Lowest pitch d¹.
(DCM 481A)

Fig. 83. GIORGI FLUTE.
Maino & Orsi, Milan, ca. 1900.
Ebonite cylindrical tube, with German silver
rings. 10 open finger holes. 4 German silver key
(C, C♯, D♯, high D♯ trill).
C foot. (DCM 223)

Fig. 84. SIGNOR GIORGI demonstrating
the Giorgi flute, from Joseph Wallis & Son,
The Giorgi Patent Flute (1896).

piece and the body of the flute."[15] It was "disposed for blowing directly instead of transversely to avoid the dispersion of wind and so that the harmonics of the twelfth are got in perfect intonation, and no special fingering is required for the production of the third octave." Attributes claimed by Wallis & Son included "unexceptionable intonation," "greater hygienic advantages," surer and more natural tone production, and excellence of tone.[16] Speaking before the Royal Musical Association, H. Standish made the following assertions:

> The claim of the inventor for his flute is, firstly, that a far superior, clearer, and purer tone is gained by the adoption of his mouthpiece; secondly, the necessary position for the player to assume in playing on his mouthpiece accords to the player a greater capacity of lung, and, in consequence, wind power; also, it gives him an easier position to play in, as it does away with the necessity of having the arms and hands raised nearly level with the chin, which position all flute players will admit is very tiring during a long performance; and consequently the neck of the player is not twisted, but the head is kept in a straight position.[17]

Because of its durability and the advantages of the vertical position, Wallis & Son recommended the Giorgi flute for military use as well as for regular orchestras. The instrument won the Grand Prix of the Bologna International Musical Exposition of 1888 as well as medals at the Paris Exposition of 1889 and the Chicago Exposition of 1893. It has ultimately been viewed, however, merely as a curiosity, but this fate is characteristic of most of the new inventions of the nineteenth century.

COMPROMISE AND COMBINATION MODELS

A major criticism of the Boehm flute was the necessity of constant pressure on the thumb and little finger of the left hand to close their respective keys, which would otherwise be held open by their springs. The result, it was alleged, was a cramping of the fingers of the left hand which was especially bothersome in the upper octave, where cross-fingerings predominated. Another objection involved the cross-fingerings for F♯ and B♭, and still another concerned Boehm's compromise C♯ vent hole, which was adopted in place of three separate vents for C♯, D, and D♯, as dictated by theory. The result was a C♯ of relatively poor quality and intonation. Yet the open-keyed system advocated by Boehm was recognized to be superior in terms of tone quality, and so various schemes were contrived to combine the best of the old and new systems in a single instrument.[18]

An instrument which would appear to be the perfect example was the so-called "Meyer-Boehm" flute, manufactured by Köhler and Son of London and imported to Boston by J. B. Claus of the New England Conservatory circa 1890. A broadside (Fig. 85) distributed to prospective customers described the flute as "made after a 'genuine Meyer' pattern, in exact measurement and conical bore, with application of the Boehm system of fingering, combining the beauties of tone of the old instrument, enhanced by the perfect equality and purity of intonation of the new system." In fact, there is no way of determining from the advertisement any difference between Boehm's conical bore of 1832 and that of the Meyer flute. Moreover, there certainly was no standard dimension for the Meyer flute, which was not a single model, but a generic term referring to any simple system flute. So it seems likely that Köhler's ostensible hybrid was more of a psychological than a mechanical compromise, designed to appeal to new converts to the Boehm system who nevertheless maintained a sentimental allegiance to the older instrument.

A more instructive and quite frequent phenomenon in the mid-nineteenth century was the adaptation of a single feature of the Boehm flute to the old system conical flute. Just as Ward "borrowed" from Boehm, Gordon, Coche, and Dorus, so William Card copied the right-hand mechanism of Boehm (Fig. 86). Basically, he was unwilling to change fingering systems, but he did recognize the superiority of Boehm's nonforked F. Card, who was an active player in London between 1825 and 1861, had his instruments built by Whitaker, a former employee of Rudall & Rose. Card's fingering was identical to that of the old German flute except for the F♯ key, which was open-standing and closed

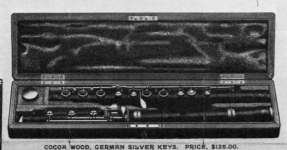

Fig. 85. 1890 FLYER for an allegedly hybrid instrument that was actually indistinguishable from the Boehm 1832 model except for what appears to be a Briccialdi B♭ thumb key.

Fig. 86. CARD SYSTEM FLUTE.
Card & Co., London, ca. 1861–76.
Rosewood, with silver ferrules, keys and rings
inset around 5 open finger holes. 9 keys on short posts.
Unique silver slide, moved by rack and pinion,
halfway between barrel and embouchure. (DCM 1230)

by rings for the first and second fingers of the right hand only. The flute also had a d^2 shake and a B♮ shake for the right-hand forefinger.[19]

In 1850, Richard Carte set out to free the little finger and thumb of the left hand and restore the old F♯ fingering, while retaining the cylindrical bore, the principle of open keys, and the large, equally spaced holes of Boehm (Figs. 87 and 88). To do so, Carte added an additional hole for d^2 and d^3, which eliminated the imperfect C♯ hole and reduced both the number of cross-fingerings and the requisite motion of the left-hand thumb and little finger. In his *Sketch of the Successive Improvements Made in The Flute*, Carte provided the following statistics:

	NO. CROSS-FINGERINGS	NO. TIMES LITTLE FINGER MOVES	NO. TIMES THUMB MOVES
Ordinary flute	176	51	37
Boehm flute	127	71	54
Carte flute	55	22	28

According to the inventor, by decreasing the number of cross-fingerings he thereby removed "a certain ruggedness or abruptness in the utterance of the notes" which resulted from the gap between notes and possible intervening tones. Carte retained the open keys for the little finger and left thumb, but allowed them to be closed not only by those two fingers, but by others as well; the thumb key also by the second finger of the left hand and the first and third fingers of the right hand, and the little finger key also by the first finger of the right hand.[20] Carte's decision to retain the old system of fingering unfortunately implied the necessity of retaining the closed key system. So, in order to counteract the negative acoustical effects of the closed keys, he constructed duplicate holes for venting F♮, B♭, and G♮. Carte also instituted duplicate holes to improve C♮ and C♯.[21] Additionally, he employed a device for closing the F♯ hole by means of rings on the E and F holes, which was merely a one-hole downward shift of the usual mechanism for closing the G hole. This device, prob-

Fig. 87. CARTE 1851 SYSTEM FLUTE.
Rudall, Rose, Carte & Co., London, ca. 1857–71.
Silver. Barrel mouthpiece. (DCM 43)

Fig. 88. CARTE 1851 SYSTEM FLUTE.
(Diagram by Jerry L. Voorhees from DCM 43)

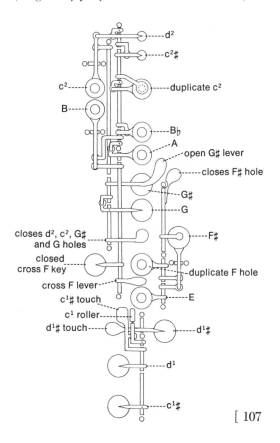

ably the invention of William Forde, was also adopted by Briccialdi and Clinton on their flutes.

In 1852, Richard S. Rockstro brought out a conical adaptation
of the Boehm flute; indeed, except for the lowest four notes,
which were fingered according to the old system, the fingering
was identical to Boehm's. The G♯ key was open-standing, and the
flute had Coche's d²♯ trill key, which was given a "crescentic"
touch to facilitate the c¹♯/d¹♯ slur.

Like Carte, Rockstro was concerned with the F♯ cross-fingering of the Boehm flute. He claimed to have become accustomed
to pressing the ring of the E hole without covering the hole in
passages where F♯ was preceded by either E or E♯, in order to
avoid cross-fingering and veiled notes. He rejected the reversal of
the ring position as tending to decrease leverage, so he shifted
the position of the B/C shake lever so that it was operated by the
first rather than the third finger. In its original position, he inserted a simple lever to close the G hole (Fig. 99, see page 119).
The touch of the d²♯ trill key, however, was not moved. The extra
F♯ lever thus removed any objections to the right-hand fingering
of the Boehm flute.

Rockstro's 1852 design also called for a rearrangement of the
tone holes to improve intonation, for he asserted that ". . . the
intonation of the open-keyed flutes was as false as that of the
eight-keyed flute, but that instead of erring in an irregular manner, like that of the old flute, it became steadily and persistently
more and more false as the finger-holes approached the mouthhole." Rockstro therefore decided to employ five uncovered holes
with rings, keys being uncertain in their behavior. These five
holes were to be equal in size. The G, G♯, B, and c² holes, in contrast, were to be covered; they were to be equal to each other in
size but larger than the uncovered holes in order to compensate
for the flattening influence of their overhanging keys. The holes of
the footjoint were the largest on the instrument. Rockstro's claims
for his alignment of the holes were extravagant; he stated in his
Treatise that "This I believe to have been the first attempt to ar-
range the positions of the holes of a wind-instrument on any rational system." His anti-Boehm prejudice was quite evident.[22] What

is most curious about Rockstro's claims, however, are his successive statements that the pattern was obsolete, the specifications
having been lost, and that, on the other hand, his hole positions
had been adopted by Rose to replace permanently Boehm's dimensions in his manufacture.

In the same year, 1852, Robert Sydney Pratten introduced his
"Perfected Flute" (Figs. 89 and 90). This model was a redesign of
the old system flute using a revised bore and finger plate mechanism. Pratten expanded the lower portion of the bore significantly, allowing him to use larger holes for the lower notes than
had previously been possible. With the inventor's permission, he
copied Rockstro's specifications for the size and position of the
finger holes, and also adopted his crescent-shaped $d^2\sharp$ lever. Pratten covered all the finger holes with keys, perforating some in
order to improve the third octave. The key plates activated a
mechanism for raising the pitch of $c^1\sharp$ and $f^1\sharp$ without interfering
with the cross-fingered d^2 and the forked f^1. The mechanism remained the same as the traditional old system flute except for the
reintroduction of the $c^2\natural$ key for the left-hand thumb.[23]

In 1856, Boosey & Co. began to manufacture Pratten's model;
in 1857, Pratten himself made further attempts at improvement
by increasing the size of the finger holes and adding as many as
seventeen keys. He eventually adapted the cylinder flute to the
old fingering, having recognized the merits of Boehm's theory but
not being willing to change fingering again, having already
switched from the old system to Siccama and back. Boosey & Co.
began manufacturing all its old system flutes on Pratten's model
(Fig. 91); at the turn of the twentieth century, its catalog listed
Pratten cone flutes with eight, ten, twelve, fourteen, or seventeen keys, and Pratten cylinder flutes with ten, twelve, fourteen,
or seventeen keys.

In 1858, Rockstro introduced a new cylindrical flute whose
covered holes made the 1852 F$\sharp$ lever especially useful. For this
device to work, it was necessary that the lever and the key of the
G hole be attached to their own rod, so the three open keys for
the fingers of the right hand were placed on tubes with clutches.
Secondly, Rockstro placed the open G$\sharp$ key and the A key on a

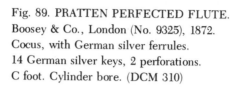

Fig. 89. PRATTEN PERFECTED FLUTE.
Boosey & Co., London (No. 9325), 1872.
Cocus, with German silver ferrules.
14 German silver keys, 2 perforations.
C foot. Cylinder bore. (DCM 310)

Fig. 90. PRATTEN PERFECTED FLUTE.
(Diagram by Jerry L. Voorhees
from Bate Collection No. x127)

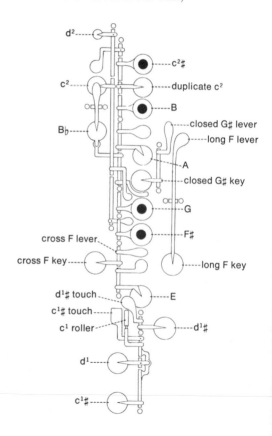

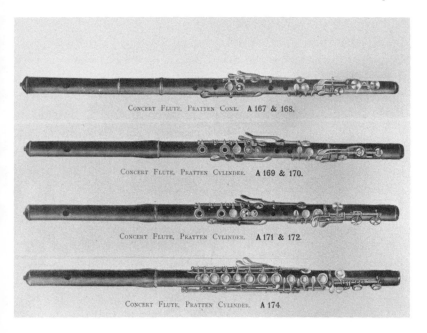

CONCERT FLUTE, PRATTEN CONE. A 167 & 168.

CONCERT FLUTE, PRATTEN CYLINDER. A 169 & 170.

CONCERT FLUTE, PRATTEN CYLINDER. A 171 & 172.

CONCERT FLUTE, PRATTEN CYLINDER. A 174.

Fig. 91. PRATTEN FLUTES from catalog of Boosey & Co., London, ca. 1900.

single rod on the near side of the flute to facilitate the motion of the third and fourth fingers of the left hand. Rockstro also added the Briccialdi B♭ lever to this flute. Only two of the keys were perforated, the F♯ key for the f^3/g^3 shake and the B♭ key for alternations of e^{3}♯ and f^{3}♯. All note holes from c^{1}♯ to c^{2}♮, inclusive, were of uniform size except for the F♯ and B holes, which were slightly reduced in order to compensate for their perforations. Finally, Rockstro slightly decreased the distance between the c^{1}♯ and c^{2}♮ holes.[24]

In 1864, Rockstro made several more modifications to his flute so as to improve the intonation, quality, and power of the third octave and to alleviate certain digital problems. The acoustical proportions of the 1858 flute were maintained, though the tone hole diameter was increased to 0.64 inch. Four modifications were made in the mechanism to expedite fingering. First, Rockstro gave the G♯ key a separate lever; previously, the lever had formed part of the key, and its consequently unprotected position had made it prone to accidental bending. Secondly, he enlarged the bearing surfaces of all stops and clutches and moved the parts of contact farther from the axles. All such surfaces were supplied with corks to ensure silent key action. The combined result of these changes was more reliable leverage of the key mechanism. Rockstro's third improvement was to increase the length of all the key shanks except that of the B♭ thumb key to allow the keys to open more widely without rising higher in front. He also altered the shape of the footjoint key touches for c^1♯ and d^1 in order to facilitate slurs such as c^1/c^1♯, c^1♯$/d^1$, and c^1♯$/d^1$♯.

In 1873, Rockstro added a new lever for B♮, which would allow that note to be fingered by the left-hand forefinger alone. A♯ could then be fingered with the thumb on the Briccialdi B♭ lever; B♮ and f^3♯ could be obtained by placing the left forefinger on the B lever without the assistance of the thumb. By this expedient, Rockstro hoped to facilitate keys with many sharps.[25]

Rockstro's final model (Figs. 92 and 93), introduced in 1877, had three new features. The first was a large hole with a closed key which was connected with the regular c^2/d^2 shake key, its purpose being to improve alternations of B♭, B, C, or C♯ with D or D♯ and also to improve the g^3/a^3 shake. Rockstro also added a lever by means of which the second finger of the left hand partially closed the c^2 hole. Its effect was to flatten g^3, which had a tendency to be too sharp. Third, Rockstro constructed a small vent hole connected with the upper C♯ key. This hole had the triple purpose of preventing d^2♯ from cracking when the flute was flattened, improving a^3, and tuning d^3, which was usually flat.[26] This final version became known as the "Rockstro System" and was offered under that appellation for many years by Rudall, Carte & Co. Among its proponents were Robert Murchie and Gareth Morris.

Another major flute system was patented on December 5, 1866 by Richard Carte as the "Carte and Boehm Systems Combined." It subsequently became known as the "Carte 1867" system (Figs. 94 and 95). By combining certain features of Carte's 1850 flute with the Boehm system, the inventor aimed to facilitate the fingering of B♭, F♮, and F♯. Thus, on the right hand,

Fig. 92. ROCKSTRO SYSTEM FLUTE.
Dayton C. Miller, Cleveland, Ohio, 1904.
Body 22-karat gold, one piece, seamless;
mechanism 18-karat gold. Open G♯. B♭ foot.
Original scale, to Miller's design, with
large (15-mm) holes. (DCM 10)

Fig. 93. ROCKSTRO SYSTEM FLUTE.
(Diagram by Jerry L. Voorhees from DCM 10)

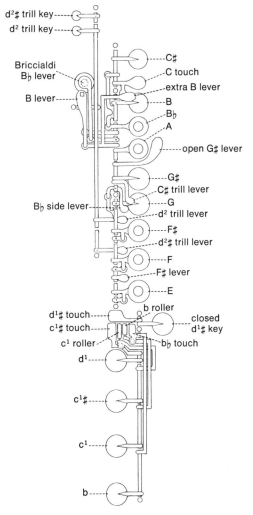

d²♯ trill key
d² trill key
Briccialdi B♭ lever
B lever
B♭ side lever
d¹♯ touch
c¹♯ touch
c¹ roller
d¹
c¹♯
c¹
b

C♯
C touch
extra B lever
B
B♭
A
open G♯ lever
G♯
C♯ trill lever
G
d² trill lever
F♯
d²♯ trill lever
F
F♯ lever
E
b roller
closed d¹♯ key
b♭ touch

Fig. 94. CARTE 1867 SYSTEM FLUTE.
Rudall, Rose, Carte & Co., London, ca. 1867.
Silver. Cylinder bore, extra-thin tube.
Open G♯. (DCM 14)

Fig. 95. CARTE 1867 SYSTEM FLUTE.
(Diagram by Jerry L. Voorhees from DCM 14)

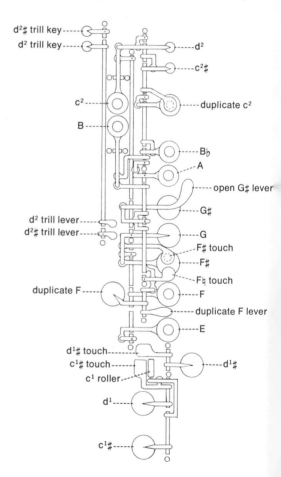

d²♯ trill key
d² trill key
d²
c²♯
c²
duplicate c²
B
B♭
A
open G♯ lever
G♯
d² trill lever
d²♯ trill lever
G
F♯ touch
F♯
F♮ touch
duplicate F
F
duplicate F lever
E
d¹♯ touch
c¹♯ touch
d¹♯
c¹ roller
d¹
c¹♯

Carte reinstated the old, short, closed F♮ key, to be operated by the second or third finger. He also added a second touchpiece for the first finger; the upper produced F♯, as on the old flute, and the lower, F♮, as on the Boehm. The top plate also closed the open G♯ key so that the F♯/G♯ trill could be made with the right forefinger alone. (On the "Guards' Model," however, the G♯ key was closed.) On the left hand, there were two holes for the thumb keys. If, with the forefinger down, the thumb was pressed on the upper plate, B♮ resulted; with the thumb on the lower plate, B♭ was heard, both as in Boehm's system. With the forefinger up, in contrast, placing the thumb on the upper hole gave C♯. Raising the thumb gave "open" D♮, as in the simple system.

The great virtue of the Carte 1867 system was its provision of alternate fingerings, yet this advantage necessarily implied a lack of simplicity. Dayton Miller objected to it for this reason as well as for its duplication of the F and C holes. Nevertheless, Adam Carse considered the system to be the "only important and lasting modification of the Boehm flute."[27] Indeed, its British popularity has continued well into the twentieth century. Anthony Baines reported in 1962 that

> . . . its present devotees in England must run into several hun-
> dreds, both amateur and professional, and Rudall, Carte will still
> supply the instrument, normally in wood, though also in metal if
> desired. It is an excellent design, in some ways technically superior
> to the Boehm, and the mechanism, though it is complex, is positive
> in action throughout and never goes wrong.[28]

A slight modification of the Carte 1867 system was made by William Lewis Barrett with the aim of simplifying the fingerings of c^2♯ and c^3♯ (Fig. 96). On both of Carte's models, the open d^2 had resulted in a cross-fingering between the first and third fingers of the left hand for C♯ and D. Barrett eliminated this cross-fingering by applying the principle of the Dorus G♯ key to the c^2♯ and d^2 holes, thereby restoring the simple system c^2♯ fingering while preserving the acoustical advantages of the open d^2. By pressing the c^2/d^2 trill lever, the mechanism for the open d^2 was activated; releasing the lever produced C♯.[29]

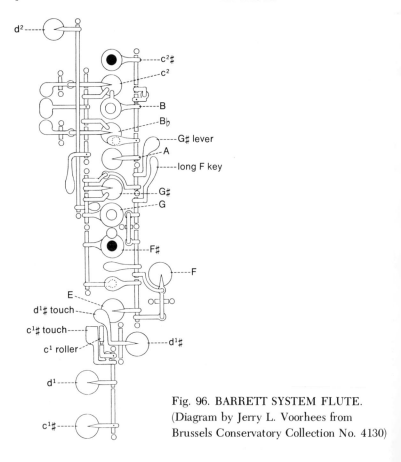

Fig. 96. BARRETT SYSTEM FLUTE.
(Diagram by Jerry L. Voorhees from
Brussels Conservatory Collection No. 4130)

Still another attempt to reconcile Boehm's arrangement of the tone holes with the old system of fingering was made in 1870 by John R. Radcliff, who wrote:

I am aware that there are still many Flute Players trembling on the verge of a transition from the old to the new class of Flutes, desiring, but hesitating whether or not to take this step. Convinced as they are of the superiority of the tone and tuning of the New Flutes, but knowing well their old Flutes, and having perhaps in some measure succeeded in managing them, so as partially to conceal their defects, they fear to take a leap in the dark as to the altered fingerings. To all such I may perhaps not be considered presumptuous if I hold out my hand and say, follow me. I have gone through all your experience, have stepped over the stream before you, and have now planned a bridge by which you may pass over still more easily.[30]

Though Radcliff's attitude now seems patronizing, his efforts were greatly appreciated at the time.

The Radcliff flute was, in fact, a simplification of the Carte 1851 model, and was based almost entirely on simple system fingering (Figs. 97 and 98). The only changes from the old system were for B♭ and C. Like the Boehm flute, its open note was C♯, for which the left thumb could be kept down if the player wished. G♯ was closed and provided with a mechanism similar to the Boehm flute's "split E." In all other respects, the left hand resembled the Carte 1867 flute. On the right hand, F♯ was fingered in the old system manner; F♮ could be produced either with a cross F key, with fork fingering, or with the F♯ fingering and the long F key, which was operated by the left-hand little finger. The third alternative was provided by shifting the tone hole for F♯ to the far side of the flute so that the touch for the right forefinger did not directly close the hole. The repositioned F♯ hole could be closed either by the long F key, for F, or by the second and third fingers of the right hand, as well, for the lower notes. The key did not have to be released for notes below E, thus facilitating passages where F was contiguous with either E♭ or D.

The Radcliff model was praised by Dayton Miller as the most successful approach to adapting the old fingering to modern hole distribution.[31] Anthony Baines, similarly, judged it to be "An excellent design on which nothing is impossible while some high passages are simpler than on the Boehm."[32] Among its partisans was John Amadio.

Two other minor inventions may be mentioned as characteristic of the mid-nineteenth century. The first, the work of Jean Firmin Brossa (b. 1839), was an extra F♯ device similar to those of Carte and Rockstro (Fig. 99) and was perhaps even more common than the other two as an optional attachment. It consisted of a small touch for the third finger of the right hand which duplicated the F♯ action of that finger's regular key. Its advantage was evi-

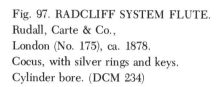

Fig. 97. RADCLIFF SYSTEM FLUTE.
Rudall, Carte & Co.,
London (No. 175), ca. 1878.
Cocus, with silver rings and keys.
Cylinder bore. (DCM 234)

Fig. 98. RADCLIFF SYSTEM FLUTE.
(Diagram by Jerry L. Voorhees from DCM 234)

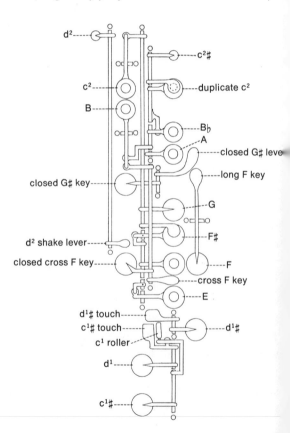

Fig. 99. ROCKSTRO AND BROSSA F♯ KEYS.
(Diagram by Philip Bate after Anthony Baines)

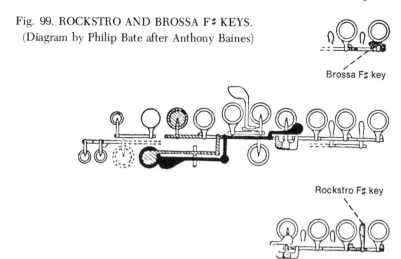

Brossa F♯ key

Rockstro F♯ key

dent in movement between E and F♯, for the extra touch, unlike the F♯ key, could be kept down for E without covering the E hole.

The second invention, contrived by Christopher Welch, consisted of a modification of the closed key reversions of Carte (for F), Buffet (for B♭), and Radcliff (for G♯). In order to retain the advantages of Boehm's open-keyed system, of which he was an ardent defender, Welch added duplicate vent holes (Fig. 100). This modification, he wrote, offered

> very great facilities for fingering, and two new and important shakes in the high octave; at the same time the fingering of the old flute is retained for all the notes except one (C♮). Moreover, by the introduction of a piece of new mechanism, each of the upper notes from D to G, inclusive, is made with only one, and that in every case the correct vent-hole (the fifth below the fundamental note). . . .[33]

Fig. 100. WELCH MODEL FLUTE. Rudall, Carte & Co., London (No. 1181), 1883. Ebonite, with silver fittings. Thinned head. Cylinder bore, large holes. (DCM 342)

MECHANICAL MODIFICATIONS

The remainder of the nineteenth century was characterized by a few minor modifications in mechanism which required no conscious adaptation by the player. Though they were, of course, designed for the ultimate benefit of the player, they were of concern primarily to the maker, and represent a shift in emphasis that would be continued in the twentieth century.

A typical patent was issued on April 7, 1868, to Theodore Berteling, a New York and Boston wind instrument maker, for four improvements (Fig. 101). These consisted of: (1) adjustable regulating screws for "regulating the throw or lift of the keys," which could be adjusted by the performer, (2) mounting the keys on independent shafts to allow the fingers to slide easily from one key to another, (3) a new arrangement of the key springs whereby the ends of the springs were "placed in a groove in the sides of a lug on the posts of the shaft of the keys," and (4) an improvement in the seating of the tone holes to provide a better cushion or set for the keys.

Fig. 101. BERTELING 1868 PATENT. U.S. Patent No. 76,389.
On the second section of a Boehm flute (A), adjustable regulating screws (CC) regulate the throw of the keys (BB). The footjoint (I) shows the mounting of keys (F, F', G, G') on independent shafts (ff' and gg'). The surfaces (hh) of flute mate at the vents or openings of the flute (HH) are made flat for a short distance around the openings to give the cushions of the keys a firm seat for better closure.

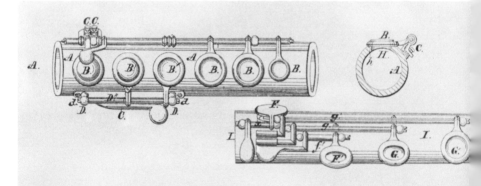

Another mechanical patent was issued on February 28, 1888, to C. G. Conn of Elkhart, Indiana, and was applicable to flutes and reed instruments (Fig. 102). The purpose of the invention was to remedy the unevenness of the bore which resulted from the relation of the holes and keys. Specifically, Conn explained,

Fig. 102. CONN 1888 PATENT.
U.S. Patent No. 378,771.
The illustration is of a clarinet, but is applicable to all wind instruments with similar holes and keys. The tube (1) has holes (2) covered by keys (3) padded as at 4. The holes are countersunk as at 5.

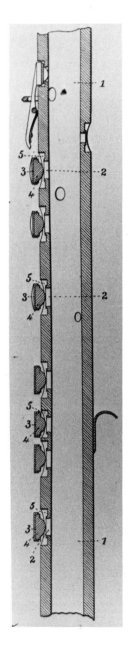

> In the old style of flutes and reed-instruments the holes which are covered with fingers or padded keys are so made that said fingers or keys rest on the outer surface of the instrument, thus creating, when one or more of the fingers or padded keys are covering the holes, one or more breaks in the continuity of the wind-passage equal to the thickness of the material of which the instrument is constructed, preventing to a corresponding extent the instantaneous egress of the wind forced into the instrument to produce the desired tone.

Conn's solution was to countersink the holes almost to the inside bore of the instrument, thus creating a smooth internal bore. The result was a more efficient utilization of the airstream blown into the instrument which in turn produced a larger and freer tone with less wind power from the player.

SUMMARY

If one were asked to apply a one-word description to the history of the flute in the nineteenth century, it would almost certainly be "confused." In 1851, while serving as a judge of musical instruments at the Great Exhibition in London, Berlioz dismissed the eight-keyed flute as "only fit to be played at a fair," and predicted the eventual supremacy of Boehm's design.[34] Yet, as we have seen, the Germans tended to ignore Boehm's invention, the French, to adopt it almost universally, and the English, to complicate it. Rockstro was forced to admit that "In justice to the consistency of our Continental neighbors, it should be mentioned that . . . we have been too prone to vacillation between the old, the new, and the pseudo-old systems. . . ."[35]

Criticism of the Boehm flute centered on the tonal characteristics of the cylinder bore and on the revised fingering system based on open keys. Modification, compromise, and ostensible improvements were rampant, but the verdict of time and experience was that the old fingering was incompatible with Boehm's scientifically determined proportions. The dilemma was aptly summarized by Richard Carte: "If one [flute] realized the object

of greater facility of execution than Boehm, it gave up the principle of open keys, and consequently left some notes weaker than
others, and disarranged the holes. If another retained the open
keys, it was by means of a mechanism which upon trial was found
unfit for action."[36] In evaluating the Siccama flute, which was the
first instrument to evidence such a compromise, Rockstro
branded the attempted reconciliation of the two systems as

> . . . an unphilosophical and unnatural combination of two incompat-
> ible things which necessarily resulted in the loss of the best points of
> both. The old flute, with eight keys and upwards, possesses certain
> facilities in the fingering of the third octave which are not afforded
> by any flutes on the open-keyed system, but the facilities afforded
> by the latter in the first and second octaves far outweigh the slight
> disadvantages in the third. . . . [O]n all . . . flutes in which the old
> fingering is attempted to be combined with the new system of holes,
> there is but one note above $d^3\sharp$ which can be fingered, with even a
> tolerable result, in the same manner as on the eight-keyed flute.[37]

Notwithstanding the logic of Carte's and Rockstro's argu-
ments, the numerous rival key systems (their own included) prospered well into the twentieth century. The confusion was reflected in the catalogs of Rudall, Carte & Co., the foremost
British flute manufacturer since the early nineteenth century. In
what is clearly an understatement, Rockstro noted that the firm
"never restricted their efforts by constructing only one pattern of
flutes; on the contrary, they made variety a special feature of their
manufacture."[38] The company's 1895 catalog, for instance, offered
flutes with eight different fingering systems:

—Cylinder Flute, with Parabolic Head Joint, Carte and Boehm Sys-
   tems combined (1867 Patent)
—Cylinder Flute, with Parabolic Head Joint, Improved Old System,
   Radcliff's Model
—Cylinder Flute, with Parabolic Head Joint, Old System [covered
   keys]
—Cylinder Flute, with Parabolic Head Joint, Boehm's System, Either
   with Open or Shut G$\sharp$
—Cylinder Flute, with Parabolic Head Joint, Boehm's System,
   Rockstro's Model

—Clinton System
—Concert Flutes [simple system]
—Siccama Flutes

The selection was further complicated by the choice of materials: cocuswood, ebonite, sterling silver, or gold tube; German silver, sterling silver, or gold keys; gold springs; and lip plates and extra headjoints of different materials from the body. Other options included a B♮ or B♭ footjoint and the addition of various special keys. Thus, even excluding extra key options from the calculations, some rudimentary arithmetic reveals that in 1895 Rudall, Carte offered 118 possible varieties of flutes.

The effect of such variety, while allowing the player a most democratic choice, was ultimately negative from the musical standpoint. We have already seen that the virtuosic antics of the leading professional flutists discouraged top-quality composition for the instrument. The situation was exacerbated, in terms of the solo literature, by the mechanical competition of the manufacturers and players. The first step in the decline affected performers, who became confused as to the merits of the various systems. James Browne, writing in the *Monthly Musical Record* in 1910, pessimistically observed the result: ". . . the days of the flute are numbered, there can be no doubt as to its decline in popularity. Between 1821 and 1846 twenty-one flute solos were played at the Philharmonic concerts by the best performers of the time, whereas since the latter date I can only find one (by Svendson) given at these concerts." The consequent second step in the flute's decline involved composers; Browne wrote that "No composer of any reputation writes for the instrument except as an important factor in the orchestra."[39] Louis Fleury's desperation was similar: "I have searched libraries and catalogues in vain for an interesting British work by a nineteenth century British composer of some note."

Fleury, in a generous gesture, added that "It must be admitted that the same state of things prevailed elsewhere."[40] Fortunately, however, the end of the nineteenth century saw considerable improvement, particularly in France. The key figure in this renaissance was Paul Taffanel (1844–1908), professor of flute at the Paris Conservatoire, who founded the Société d'Instruments à Vent, a woodwind chamber music organization, in 1879. Taffanel, insisting on high standards of performance and composition, revived classical works such as the Bach sonatas and Mozart concerti as alternatives to the trash of his own century. His own consummate musicianship inspired compositions by Huë, Godard, Widor, and Saint-Saëns, among others. Moreover, his efforts both as performer and teacher fostered a new generation of superior woodwind players with similarly good taste.

Taffanel's successor as the leader of the so-called "French school" of fluteplaying was Georges Barrère (1876–1944), who in 1895 established the Paris Société Moderne des Instruments à Vent, of which Richard Cameron wrote in *Etude* in 1931: "Probably no other organization has done so much toward enriching the woodwind repertoire."[41] Barrère emigrated to the United States in 1905, where he taught at the Institute of Musical Art in New York, thereby transmitting the French style to generations of American flutists, and in 1910 he founded the Barrère Ensemble of Wind Instruments. He later served as the first president of the New York Flute Club, which was founded in 1920. The ultimate importance of all of these organizations was due not only to their direct commissions, but also to their role in inspiring a certain sense of competition among composers to provide music of a quality commensurate with the increasingly high level of musicianship of twentieth century flutists.

Manufacturers, meanwhile, recognized that the only further work on the flute which could have any permanent significance was in the improvement of manufacturing detail. The foresight of men like Berteling and Conn reflects both a practical shift to purely mechanical improvement and a geographical shift of the highest quality flute manufacture to the United States which paralleled the movement of the finest players.*

---

*The two principal manufacturers of professional grade instruments today are the Wm. S. Haynes Company (established 1888) and Verne Q. Powell Flutes (established 1927 by Haynes's former foreman), both in Boston.

Notes]

1. Anthony Baines, *Woodwind Instruments and Their History* (New York: W. W. Norton & Co., 1962), p. 70.

2. Philip Bate, *The Flute* (New York: W. W. Norton & Co., 1969), p. 9.

3. D. Ehrlich, *The History of the Flute from Ancient Times to Boehm's Invention* (New York: D. Ehrlich, 1921), p. 27.

4. Henry Clay Wysham, *The Evolution of the Boehm Flute* (New York: C. G. Conn, 1898), p. 9.

5. Cornelius Ward, *The Flute Explained* (London: The Author, 1844), p. 25.

6. Bate, p. 134.

7. Sable [pseud.], "The Flute and Its Vicissitudes," *The English Mechanic* 11 (1870): 14.

8. John Clinton, *A Treatise upon the Mechanism and General Principles of the Flute* (London: H. Potter, [1852]), pp. 21–23.

9. Ibid., pp. 30–31.

10. Richard Shepard Rockstro, *A Treatise on the Construction the History and the Practice of the Flute*, 2nd ed., rev. (1928; reprint ed., London: Musica Rara, 1967), p. 390. Hereafter cited as Rockstro, *Treatise*.

11. Dayton C. Miller, Accession List of Flutes in the Dayton C. Miller Collection, MS, IV, no. 1092.

12. Bate, pp. 137–38.

13. *Prof. Giorgi's Patent Flute* (London: Joseph Wallis & Son, n.d.), p. 6. Hereafter cited as *Prof. Giorgi*.

14. H. Standish, "The Giorgi Flute," *Proceedings of the Musical Assn.* 24 (1898): 58.

15. "Recently Patented Inventions," *Scientific American* 77 (December 18, 1897): 396.

16. *Prof. Giorgi*, p. 7.

17. Standish, pp. 57–58.

18. Richard Carte, *Sketch of the Successive Improvements Made in The Flute*, 3rd ed. (London: Rudall, Rose, Carte & Co. and Keith and Prowse, 1855), pp. 26–27, 30.

19. Bate, p. 136.

20. Carte, pp. 30–32.

21. Ibid., pp. 34–35.

22. Rockstro, *Treatise*, pp. 384–86.

23. Ibid., p. 386.

24. Ibid., pp. 387–88.

25. Ibid., pp. 393–94.

26. Richard S. Rockstro, *A Description of the "Rockstro-Model" Flute* (London: Keith, Prowse & Co. and Rudall, Carte & Co., 1884), pp. 8–9.

27. Adam Carse, *Musical Wind Instruments* (1939; reprint ed., New York: Da Capo Press, 1965), p. 100.

28. Baines, p. 67.

29. Rockstro, *Treatise*, pp. 398–99.

30. John Radcliff, Preliminary Remarks to *School for the Flute, A Practical Instruction Book by Charles Nicholson* . . . (London: Rudall, Carte & Co., 1873), p. ii.

31. Dayton C. Miller, "The Modern Flute," TS, p. 70.

32. Baines, p. 69.

33. Christopher Welch, *History of the Boehm Flute*, 3rd ed. (London: Rudall, Carte & Co.; New York: G. Schirmer, 1896), p. 12.

34. Jacques Barzun, *Berlioz and the Romantic Century*, 3rd ed. (New York: Columbia University Press, 1969), 2:33.

35. Rockstro, *Treatise*, p. 379.

36. Carte, p. 26.

37. Rockstro, *Treatise*, pp. 372–73.

38. Ibid., p. 287.

39. James A. Browne, "The Fate of the Flute," *Monthly Musical Record* 40 (September 1, 1910): 199.

40. Louis Fleury, "The Flute and British Composers," Part II, *Chesterian*, n.s. no. 4 (January 1920): 115.

41. Richard Cameron, "The Flute—Its Story and Practice," *Etude Music Magazine* 49 (October 1931): 862.

CHAPTER IV

The Twentieth Century

In comparison with the mechanical histrionics of the nineteenth century, the flute of the twentieth century has enjoyed a "Calm Sea and Prosperous Voyage." Experiments with new fingering systems have been relatively infrequent, and even these few have been confined to partial modifications of the Boehm system. Essentially, flutists and flutemakers have become satisfied with the status quo: by 1900, half a century having passed since the introduction of Boehm's final model, that instrument was well on its way to becoming standard.

This trend is clearly reflected in the trade catalogs of the early part of the century. Throughout the nineteenth century, Clair Godfroy, Boehm's French patent assignee, and his successor, Louis Lot, had listed old system instruments ("flûtes ordinaires") in their catalogs. But by 1928, only Boehm system flutes were advertised. Even more revealing are the catalogs of Rudall, Carte & Co. of London. Though a slightly modified version of the Carte 1867 patent, a closed-G♯ instrument known as the Guards' Model, was introduced in 1907, the Siccama flute disappeared from the listing after 1904 and the Clinton model after 1911. And in 1922, *The Flutist* magazine, displaying a typical bit of literary pretension, published a cartoon with the caption, "Breathes there a man with soul so low / Who in preference to a Boehm a Meyer would blow?"[1]

The major determinant of the stability of the flute mechanism was the escalating internationalization of both cultural and industrial ideas. In the case of the flute, this trend was manifested in the dissemination of the French school of fluteplaying and manufacture, for the French had already been recognized for half a century as the premier woodwind players. France, of course, was a bastion of Boehm supporters, and the emigration to the United States of some of its most noted performers, of whom Barrère and Laurent are the most important, served to unite French traditions of performance and manufacture with Yankee industrial ingenuity.

Moreover, the same industrial revolution that improved the technology of communications, thereby facilitating international cultural exchange, also had a more direct stabilizing influence on flute manufacture. Quite simply, the advent of mass production obviated the variety permitted by handcraftsmanship, and a certain standardization of the instrument became a necessity.

This is not to say, however, that the twentieth century imposed absolute uniformity upon the flute. On the contrary, as the trade catalogs also demonstrate, flutists continued to have a fairly wide choice of instruments. The crucial distinction is that twentieth century makers have provided a selection of constructive techniques, materials, and a few supplementary keys, all for Boehm system instruments, whereas their nineteenth century forebears offered a multiplicity of fingering systems.

This change of emphasis in the flutemaking profession is logical from a business perspective, as well; once the makers became convinced of the permanence of the Boehm flute, and therefore, of its commercial viability, they could then shift their attention to mechanical and acoustical perfection. And increasingly they were forced to consider more economical production. Consequently, they began to draw increasingly on modern science and technology in their research and their craft. As E. A. K. Ridley put it alliteratively, makers turned their efforts to "materials, manufacturing methods, and micro-dimensions."[2]

The evolution of twentieth century flutemaking also correlates in an interesting manner with the development of the recording industry, itself a product of the scientific and technological revolution. In the early days of recording, if a take was not perfect, it had to be repeated in its entirety, so that the technical reliability of the musical instruments employed was of paramount importance. On the flute, the demand for technical perfection—getting all the notes right—was manifested in layer upon layer of mechanical complexity, in the form of auxiliary keys, to assist the player in difficult passages of any imaginable sort. As the recording industry became more sophisticated, the wonders of tape splicing obviated the need for technically perfect performance, and thus for the special keys. Some of these have endured, but many more have been abandoned as just so much hardware. But at the same time, modern recording microphones are enormously more sensitive to all kinds of sound, both music and noise, and therefore, for purposes of modern recording, the convenient, but often noisy auxiliary mechanisms were shed in favor of more efficient, and more importantly, quieter instruments. Furthermore, increased demands for timbral reliability and control as well as intonational accuracy, also due to increased microphone sensitivity, have exerted a strong influence on musical instrument manufacture.

Another major factor affecting instrument design in this century has been the broadening of the music curricula of American public schools to include instrumental as well as vocal music. This development created a demand for large quantities of inexpensive, yet reliable and durable instruments. At first, retailers were forced to tap foreign sources to supply the student market. In 1928, for instance, buyers for Carl Fischer, Inc., settled on flutes by A. E. Fischer, of Bremen, Germany, because they "were the only ones that compared favorably with the highest priced flutes on the market and at the same time could be sold for about a third less."[3] But the production of student flutes soon became a major industry in the United States, centered primarily in Elkhart, Indiana. Durability of construction and economies of scale continue to be the watchwords of the highly competitive band instrument industry.

Today, even the two foremost makers of handmade flutes, Haynes and Powell, have become sufficiently big business to attract the attention of *The Wall Street Journal*. In 1977, the *Jour-*

nal announced, those two companies were planning large increases in production in order to meet another wave of foreign competition, this time from the Japanese. Haynes, the newspaper reported, plans to increase production by one-third, from 750 to 1000 flutes a year, by 1982; Powell projects a sixty percent increase, from 250 to 400 per annum, by 1980. Larger ambitions, both companies agree, would inevitably result in a decline in quality.[4]

MODIFIED BOEHM SYSTEMS

The first quarter of the twentieth century was a period of transition; though the Boehm system was well on its way to universal acceptance, several inventors worked on fairly extensive modifications of it. But the nineteenth century spirit of mechanical elaboration was balanced by a progressive change in motivation, for the aim of twentieth century inventors has been to improve the Boehm system rather than to destroy it. While there are so-called "named systems" of recent origin, they are almost all, in reality, modified Boehm systems. With the exception of the Murray flute, which is still evolving and therefore not eligible for final evaluation, none of these systems has survived in toto, though individual mechanical components have endured as optional features.

Research culminating in the "Borne-Julliot System" was begun as early as 1889 by French manufacturer Djalma Julliot, working in conjunction with customer-turned-collaborator François Borne, a professor at the Toulouse Conservatory. Their innovations were protected by two French patents in Julliot's name, dated 1895 and 1901, and by an American patent of 1908 that was assigned by Julliot to Jean Mignolet, an amateur flutist and the Belgian consul in Denver, Colorado.* However, the clearest and most comprehensive account of the Borne-Julliot flute was published by the inventors in book form in 1903.

* Mignolet's correspondence with Dayton C. Miller implies that the new devices were his own inventions. None of the Borne-Julliot literature, however, makes any mention of Mignolet. The relationship thus remains somewhat of a mystery, but in the long run, it is unimportant.

Their philosophy is indicative of the trend that would dominate the twentieth century: the affirmation of the basic principles and configuration of the Boehm system, with the qualification, specifically stated in their treatise, that Boehm left the job incomplete. The Borne-Julliot flute entailed no modification of the basic fingering table; the keywork additions were supplements rather than substitutes. "Our constant preoccupation," the inventors wrote, "was to change neither the fingering nor the bore."[5]

Julliot's analysis of the Boehm flute led him to conclude that its defects were due to the series of compromises inherent in Boehm's scheme for the mechanism and the placement of the tone holes. The resultant inequities made certain notes flat in the first two octaves and sharp in the third. Julliot believed that the addition of several supplementary devices to the Boehm mechanism could remedy those inequities, and, in addition, overcome certain inconveniences in the fingering. Thus the "Borne-Julliot System" was, in reality, not a new system at all, but, in the truest sense of the term, a modified Boehm system.

Julliot's first concern was the third octave E, which, on closed G♯ instruments, had a tendency to be extremely sharp as well as difficult to produce. Since e^3 is produced as the fourth harmonic of e^1, its vent is the A hole, covered by the third finger of the left hand. However, when that finger is raised, the G♯ hole just below it is automatically uncovered as well, thus making the e^3 more difficult than it might be. The inspiration for Julliot's improvement came from Paul Taffanel, who pointed out to him that the defect was nonexistent on Boehm's original open-G♯ flute, on which the G♯ hole remained open when the A hole was closed. The problem, then, was to duplicate the action of the open-G♯ flute on the closed-G♯ instrument.

Julliot's first solution was to add a new lever for the third finger of the right hand, behind and to the right of the lower trill key, which would close the A hole exclusively, thereby making e^3 the exact octave of e^2. During 1902, he experimented with a similar supplementary lever for the right forefinger. However, since both keys involved a modification of the regular fingering, they were not totally satisfactory. Eventually, both were abandoned in favor of activating the cover of the A hole from one of the regular right-hand keys. Julliot settled on the E key, operated by the middle finger, because, he observed, when it was depressed, the A hole was always closed as well. With his new "split E" arrangement (Figs. 103–105), which linked the E key to the cover of the G♯ hole, the A and G♯ plates moved separately. Thus the lower plate could be closed by the right-hand second finger, as well as by the left-hand third finger, so that an excellent e^3 was produced by depressing the first and second fingers of both hands—in other words, the regular Boehm fingering.[6]

Julliot also sought to eliminate another defect of the closed G♯, the contrary motion that it necessitated. He observed that G♯

Fig. 103. BORNE-JULLIOT SYSTEM FLUTE. Djalma Julliot, La Couture Boussey, 1900. Silver with gold springs. 4 perforations. C foot. An early version of the Borne-Julliot system. Split E, left-hand F♯ key, C♯ trill key. Upper side key (right forefinger) opened near side large G♯ hole; lower side key closed C hole under left thumb. Near side levers adjacent to trill levers: upper closed B♭, B, and G holes; lower closed top G♯ hole. Rest for left hand. (DCM 193)

could be produced on an open-holed flute, without any mechanical alteration, by depressing only the rim of the G key with the third finger. His first step was to replace this digital subtlety with an additional lever for the left thumb, placed to the right of the C hole. When this lever was acted on by a smooth sliding motion of the thumb, G♯ could be produced by the usual A fingering. In the 1895 patent, Julliot transferred this function to the right forefinger side lever, which had often been used for B♭ trills. Because of the new independence of the third and fourth fingers of the left hand, trills involving G♯ or A♭ became much simpler since they could be executed by the middle finger, instead of the little finger, of the left hand.[7]

Ultimately, however, both the thumb and right hand G♯ levers were found unsatisfactory because of the delicacy of their mechanisms, the fact that they were impossible to attach to preexistent Boehm flutes, and, most importantly, because the half-hole closure of the A hole by either of the levers was not acoustically just. Julliot's solution was to add a second G♯ lever for the left-hand pinky, to the right of the usual one, with its own G♯ hole on the far side of the flute (Figs. 104 and 105). In all passages involving rapid alternations with G♯ (or A♭), the pinky was to remain on the new lever, thereby obviating contrary motion between the right and left hands. The new key required no change in the fingering chart because, by means of a special combination of springs and levers, action on any of the three right-hand hole covers closed the cover of the new G♯ hole as well.[8]

Julliot acknowledged that the new G♯ lever would be incompatible with the "double F♯" lever for the left-hand pinky (Fig. 103), which had been patented in 1895. This feature duplicated the action of the right-hand ring finger on the F♯ key, eliminating the contrary motion in passages embodying frequent alternations with F♯ or G♭ in the first and second octaves. In such passages, the F♯ lever would be kept depressed by the left pinky, and the passage executed as if the G♭ were G♮. But, on balance, Julliot considered the G♯ lever of greater utility than the F♯ lever.

Julliot's next major objective was to abolish the fork fingering of the F/A and F♯/A trills in the third octave. The contrary motion

Fig. 104. BORNE-JULLIOT SYSTEM FLUTE.
Clement Masson, La Couture Boussey, 1922.
Silver-plated metal.
Borne-Julliot System Model No. 10.
4 perforations. Long foot tenon,
split E, C♯ trill, supplementary F♯ key,
left-hand double G♯ key. (DCM 308)

Fig. 105. BORNE-JULLIOT SYSTEM FLUTE.
(Diagram by Jerry L. Voorhees from DCM 308)

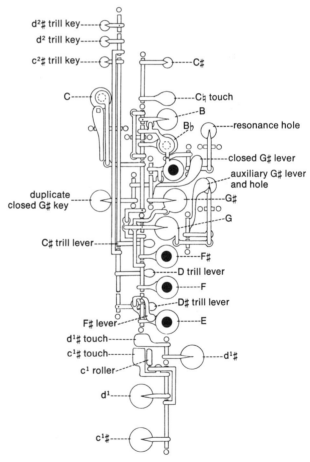

d²♯ trill key ----- C♯

d² trill key -----

c²♯ trill key ----- C♯

C ----- C♮ touch

----- B

B♭ ----- resonance hole

----- closed G♯ lever

----- auxiliary G♯ lever and hole

duplicate
closed G♯ key ----- G♯

----- G

C♯ trill lever -----

----- F♯

----- D trill lever

----- F

----- D♯ trill lever

F♯ lever ----- E

d¹♯ touch -----

c¹♯ touch ----- d¹♯

c¹ roller -----

d¹ -----

c¹♯ -----

[135

between the middle finger and the index and ring fingers of the left hand made these two alternations among the most difficult on the Boehm flute. Julliot's first remedy necessitated a supplementary lever for the right-hand middle finger. But then he found that, by linking the covers of the B♮, B♭, and near side duplicate G♯ holes to a right forefinger side lever, and the covers of the B and duplicate G♯ holes to the regular left-hand pinky G♯ lever, alternation between f^3 and a^3 could be obtained simply by trilling the G♯ lever with the pinky. Like the double F♯ lever, this arrangement was not compatible with the auxiliary G♯ lever mechanism.[9]

Julliot next attempted to improve the justice of the F♯ octaves; he considered F♯ to be one of the principal victims of Boehm's system of compromises. Ideally, f^3♯ should be vented only by the B hole, and not by the B♭ hole, also, as in Boehm's scheme. Thus, to ensure a reliable and correctly tuned f^3♯ in pianissimo passages, he installed a small F♯ lever for the right-hand ring finger that curved over the lowest trill lever, adjacent to the E key. The new key closed the B♭ hole along with the F♯ hole.[10]

However, the improvement of f^3♯ had a deleterious effect on f^2♯, and Julliot again adopted the expedient of a duplicate tone hole, installing an open "resonance hole" (Figs. 104 and 105), on the far side of the flute, which was closed by action of the left-hand ring finger on the G key. The new hole also improved f^3 and b^3, which had lost some of their sonority in the previous configuration.[11]

Julliot also sought to improve the C/C♯ trill; because the left forefinger helps to support the flute, an extended trill using that finger could be awkward, though not impossible. So Julliot added a new C♯ trill key, between the D♮ trill key and the C♮ thumb hole on the near side of the flute. It was controlled by a new lever for the right forefinger, placed between the F and F♯ holes, parallel to the usual two trill levers. Moreover, when used in combination with one or both of the other two trill keys, the new lever simplified or improved most of the third octave trills: g^3/a^3, for instance, in conjunction with the middle trill key, and $a^3♭/b^3♭$ by trilling all three together.[12] The 1901 patent went a step further, describing yet another supplementary trill key, placed adjacent to the middle trill lever. Designed primarily for the g^3/a^3 trill, it combined the action of the upper and middle trill levers, controlling both the C♯ and D trill keys.

Perhaps the most unusual aspect of Julliot's "system" was a long tenon for the body/footjoint connection. This construction allowed him to remount the d^1♯ hole closer to the embouchure, in its acoustically correct position, by lengthening the tenon and equipping it with an overlapping hole. In addition to remedying the flat tendency of d^1♯, the new construction permitted the joints to be fastened together more firmly.[13]

Julliot also devised several other mechanisms for the footjoint keys. The 1901 patent, for example, described a link between the c^1♯ lever, operated by the right pinky, and the cover of the E hole. This connection created a c^1♯/d^1♯ trill by playing c^1♯ and lifting the right ring finger to obtain d^1♯. In a slightly different vein, Julliot's catalog offered three types of connections between the footjoint and a supplementary left-hand pinky lever. If attached to the B key, the lever facilitated movement between B and C. If attached to the C key, it permitted passage from c^1 to e^1 without an intermediate d^1. Finally, if the lever were attached to the D♯ key, c^1♯/d^1♯ was considerably simplified. Of course, none of the latter three arrangements was compatible with the F♯ or G♯ pinky keys of the "Borne-Julliot System" flute; they were merely optional accessories for regular Boehm system instruments.

Julliot fully recognized that all of his devices could not be incorporated on one instrument, a fact acknowledged even in the first French patent. Consequently, his catalogs offered ten different models, with various combinations of supplementary apparatus. The ultimate instrument, however, in Julliot's estimation, was Model 10 (Figs. 104 and 105), which incorporated the long foot tenon, split E, C♯ trill, supplementary F♯ key, and left-hand double G♯.

Another early twentieth century modification of the Boehm system was developed by T. Van Everen of New York City (Figs. 106 and 107). His instrument featured an apparently experimental

Fig. 106. VAN EVEREN FLUTE.
Anonymous, United States, modified by T. Van Everen,
New York, early twentieth century.
Grenadilla, with German silver keys.
Modified Boehm system. Open G♯,
open D♯ foot key. (DCM 1213)

Fig. 107. VAN EVEREN FLUTE.
(Diagram by Jerry L. Voorhees from DCM 1213)

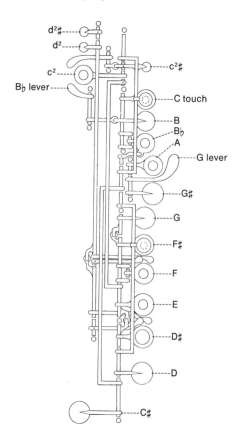

arrangement of finger touches, clutches, and adjusting screws. Its open G♯ was not unusual, but the open D♯ foot key necessitated a total redesign of the foot keys. Evidently the flute was never manufactured; the specimen in the Miller collection was the inventor's working prototype.*

A more fully developed instrument of the same era was the McAvoy flute (Figs. 108 and 109), the work of John William McAvoy of Bangor, North Wales. Miller categorized this instrument as a modified Boehm system. Acoustically, the appellation is correct, but the convoluted McAvoy mechanism is a far cry from the simplicity advocated by Boehm. In fact, Miller, the archespouser of Boehm's dogma of simplicity, dismissed the McAvoy key system as "very awkward and bungling, . . . with many complications, and heavy."[14] In short, whether one describes the McAvoy flute as a modified Boehm system depends on one's definition of the word "system."

In any case, some discussion of the McAvoy mechanism is warranted because of the musical significance of the inventor's intentions; namely, to provide simple chromatic fingering (an idea reminiscent of Siccama, Giorgi, Burghley, et al.) and a means of playing the same music in different keys without "material" change in the fingering. The instrument was therefore somewhat paradoxical, for it attempted to render an allegedly complicated fingering system simpler by making the mechanism more complicated.

In McAvoy's scheme, the holes are numbered from 1 to 16 beginning at the lower end of the flute. The sixteen open-standing "pad levers" or keys, which control the holes, were numbered

*The manner in which Miller acquired the Van Everen flute provides an interesting illustration of the unpredictability of collecting. Miller obtained the instrument from Arthur Gemeinhardt, who wrote, "I have . . . taken the liberty of sending to you a wooden flute (a freak) which an unemployed musician left with me with instructions to get anything I can for it. In other words if you wish to retain this . . . flute send on any thing you wish as I explained to the musician that it is practically worthless." Miller was of a different opinion, and eagerly seized the opportunity to broaden his collection. Gemeinhardt, obviously amused, promised to "be on the lookout for you from now on regarding freaks or experiments."

according to their corresponding holes and were arranged in the following configuration:

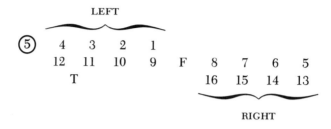

Lengthwise, the keys were grouped into four "manuals" of four keys each: 4-3-2-1, 12-11-10-9, 8-7-6-5, and 16-15-14-13. Keys 12 through 9 and 8 through 5 covered their holes directly; keys 16 through 13 and 4 through 1 were actually only finger touches, linked to their corresponding holes by axles. Crosswise, the keys were grouped in eight pairs; the keys of each pair were sufficiently close to permit one finger to control them simultaneously. Since none of the sixteen keys was connected in any way with any other, each could be worked independently.

Because the keys outnumbered fingers, McAvoy supplied two multiple closing levers: F (i^2 in the patent diagram, Fig. 109), operated by the right forefinger, simultaneously closed holes 9, 10, 11, and 12 when the left hand was needed for keys 4, 3, 2, and 1. Multiple closing lever T (i^1 in the patent diagram), controlled by the left-hand thumb, closed 13, 14, 15, and 16 together when the hands were needed for keys 12 through 1.

The fingering of the McAvoy flute is best illustrated by the following chromatic sequence: D was produced with all fingers off. Successively depressing keys 16 through 13 with the fingers of the right hand produced D♭ through B♭. Substituting T for 16 through 13 and successively pressing 12 through 9 with the left hand produced A through G♭. Replacing those four keys with F, still keeping down T, and successively depressing 8 through 5, gave F through D. Finally, retaining pressure on T, F, and 8 through 5 and successively adding 4 through 1 on the left hand gave D♭ through B♭.

McAvoy also suggested the possibility of "double fingering,"

Fig. 108. McAVOY FLUTE.
Rudall, Carte & Co., London (No. 6983), ca. 1926.
Ebonite with silver fittings. B foot. Open G♯. (DCM 1089)

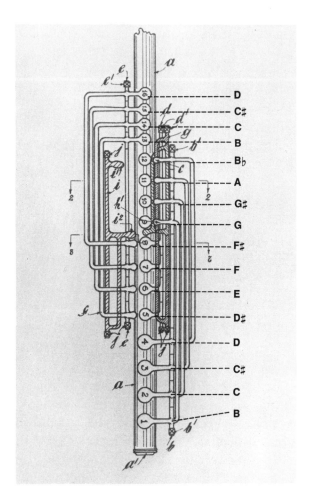

Fig. 109. McAVOY FLUTE.
U.S. Patent No. 1,643,463 (1927).
The tone holes are arranged in a straight line for clarity.
Vent and duplicate holes are not shown because their
control is unrelated to this mechanism. Pad levers *1–4*
are pivoted on axle *b* carried in bearings *b'*, coupled to
extensions *c*. Pad levers *5–12* are pivoted on axle *d*,
carried in bearings *d'*. Pad levers *13–16* are pivoted on
axle *e*, carried in bearings *e'* coupled to auxiliary
levers or extensions *f*. There are 3 bar levers
(*g, h, i*) and 2 multiple closing levers (*i'* for the
left thumb and *i²* for the right forefinger).

simultaneously depressing both keys of a crosswise pair—4 and 12, for instance—with one finger, a technique he considered useful in rapid passages. Moreover, this technique required that both hands be on the instrument only for the lowest four notes; for the remainder, one would suffice. What McAvoy was really doing, of course, was to sanction a mild form of digital cheating in a system whose complications were bound to be a deterrent to the prospective player. By avoiding hand shifts, fingering was greatly simplified. And because there would always be three open holes below the speaking hole, McAvoy claimed that the effect of double fingering on tone quality would be minimal.

Finally, to accomplish McAvoy's second goal, that of simple transposition, the flute was equipped with one additional key, marked ⑤ in the key scheme. It was to be used with key 13 when the hands were moved up one semitone to convert the concert (C) flute to a military (D♭) flute while retaining the same fingering.

THE MURRAY FLUTE

The only large-scale modification of the Boehm system executed in the second half of the twentieth century was begun in 1948 by Alexander Murray, then solo flutist of England's Royal Air Force Band, and initially developed in conjunction with flutemaker Albert K. Cooper and mathematician/flutist Elmer Cole. Having studied Boehm's treatise, Murray decided that the original open G♯ was more rational than the now-usual closed type. He listed four reasons: (1) the duplicate G♯ hole would be unnecessary; (2) the spring of an open key is lighter than for a closed key; (3) e^3 is improved when correctly vented with only the A hole; and (4) there is one finger and one key pad on G. Accordingly, Murray had his Haynes flute altered to open G♯.

Next, Murray became dissatisfied with the asymmetrical use of the little fingers and the necessity of depressing the right-hand little finger most of the time, so he experimented with an open D♯ key. He rotated the footjoint until the D♯ hole was within reach of the little finger, then unhooked the spring and held it open with a rubber band. This arrangement proved unstable, however, so he inserted a wedge of cork on the body above the right-hand thumb. Concluding that the open D♯ was indeed superior to the closed form, in 1959 he had Albert Cooper construct a more permanent open D♯ footjoint for his Hammig flute, placing the C♯, D, and D♯ holes in line from an axle on the near side of the flute (Fig. 110). The D♯ key was automatically closed by both of the other keys. The problem remained of how to trill c^1/d^1 or c^1♯/d^1, since d^1♯ sounded when the little finger was removed from either the c^1 or c^1♯ key. So Murray built a crescent-shaped key from the D♯ key around the front of the third finger key so that that finger could then close both keys. Later, Murray replaced this device with two parallel rollers so that the ring finger could move easily from D to D♯.[15]

Fig. 110. MURRAY'S OPEN D♯ MECHANISM, first version, on Hammig flute rebuilt by Albert K. Cooper (1959). (Diagram by Philip Bate)

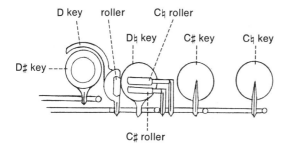

Now that the little finger was freed from venting E, F, and F♯, since the open-standing D♯ key served that purpose, Murray installed a new F♯ lever for the little finger, built on the same principle as the Carte, Brossa, Rockstro, and Julliot F♯ keys. By fingering F♯ with the lever, rather than with the cover of the E hole, all holes from E down remained open, thus ensuring better venting. Extending this concept, Murray split the left-hand A key so that the B♭ hole remained open when the A hole was closed. He then connected the A key to the F♯ lever, thereby ensuring correct venting for $f^3\sharp$. This "split F" or "split A" arrangement gave a good E/F$\sharp$ trill with no fingering change for F$\sharp$.[16]

Murray's third concern was the compromise C$\sharp$ hole of the Boehm flute, which made $c^2\sharp$ too high in relation to its neighbors. On the Boehm flute, because the C$\sharp$ hole must simultaneously serve as a tone hole for C$\sharp$ in the second, third, and fourth octaves and as the vent hole for d^2, d^3, d^4, $g^3\sharp$, a^3, and b^3, compromise was inevitable. Murray contrived a mechanism to divide these functions between an enlarged C$\sharp$ tone hole (now regular size) on top of the flute and a small D vent on the near side. It was necessary to reverse the thumb keys from the Briccialdi form to the original Boehm configuration, with the B lever above the B$\flat$ lever. Initially, the thumb keys were touches only, with both holes on the top of the flute. Finally, in order to avoid depressing the right-hand little finger for b^3, Murray linked the lower trill key to the D key, so that the D$\sharp$ hole was automatically closed when B was fingered normally.[17]

In 1960, Murray had Albert Cooper build a prototype flute embodying all of the changes that had been made on his rebuilt Hammig. The primary difference between the two instruments was the prototype's deviation from the Boehm *Schema*, using instead a scale perhaps best described as "Cooper experimental." Ultimately, the Cooper scale was adopted by several prominent flute manufacturers, most notably Powell. A few features of the prototype's mechanism, however, do deserve brief mention: Murray added a third thumb key, placed just below the B$\flat$ touch, which closed the C$\natural$ hole without closing C$\sharp$ to produce $g^3\sharp$. The finger plates were rectangular, to facilitate digital motion between keys, and the footjoint was extended to B$\natural$.

Around 1961–62, Cooper constructed the Murray "Mark I" flute (Fig. 111), which was written up in the journal of the Japanese Flute Club. Although the rectangular touches were retained on the right hand, the thumb keys were changed to a circular shape and the third thumb key was deleted. More importantly, those two keys now covered their tone holes directly (on the near side of the instrument), which made the Boehm configuration not just desirable, but absolutely necessary. Thus, when A was

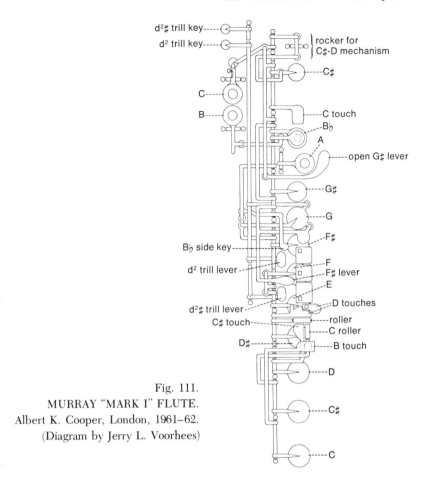

Fig. 111.
MURRAY "MARK I" FLUTE.
Albert K. Cooper, London, 1961–62.
(Diagram by Jerry L. Voorhees)

fingered, the left-hand middle finger key was linked with the Bb key (B hole) on the near (thumb) side. A Rockstro-like F♯ key was added for the right-hand ring finger, between the right-hand second and third finger touches, and the "split F" was also connected to a right-hand forefinger lever. The tone holes were uniformly large, on Rockstro's pattern. Similarly, the embouchure was constructed with an area measuring as close as possible to that of the tone holes. This latter decision was the result of Murray's hearing Severino Gazzelloni play a flute with an unusually large embouchure.

A 1964 Murray flute, Cooper No. 129 (Fig. 112), saw the Bb

hole returned to the top of the flute; the C hole remained under the upper thumb key on the near side. The "split A" key was of circular shape. The footjoint underwent major modification: two rollers were superimposed on the D♯ key, the D on top and D♯ below. A large rectangular D plate to the right of the D♯ key provided the most direct fingering for D. Thus D could be fingered with the third finger pressing both the D♯ and D rollers, thereby leaving the little finger free, or with the third finger pressing only the D♯ roller and the little finger on the D plate. The latter fingering was preferable for alternations between D and D♯ because the alternation could be made by raising the pinky rather than by sliding the ring finger. There were also two

Fig. 112. MURRAY FLUTE.
Albert K. Cooper, London (No. 129), 196
Cooper added a large D trill hole on the
top of the flute in 1974. (Photo of
full flute by Leslie Timmons; photo of
thumb keys courtesy of Alex Murray, fro
Michigan State University Photographic
Laboratory Information Services)

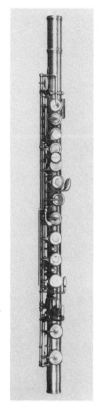

Fig. 113. MURRAY FLUTE.
Albert K. Cooper, London (No. 131), 1965.
(Photos courtesy of Alice Avouris)

rollers over the D key, C on top and C♯ below. To the right of the two rollers was a flat plate for C, intended for ordinary use; the C roller was to be used primarily for transition from C to C♯.

Cooper flute No. 131* (Fig. 113) built in 1965, reverted to the thumb key pattern of Murray's first modification (on the rebuilt Hammig of 1959). Although the two thumb keys were circular, they were again merely touches, B above B♭, controlling top-side keys. Murray reasoned that key leverage would be simpler in this configuration since directly controlled holes would require pillars, thereby fixing the key position, and he wanted more design flexibility on the near side of the flute. At the foot, the D♯ roller was removed from the D♯ key, and an additional roller to operate the optional B foot was added above the preexistent C♮ roller.

*The photograph of this instrument in Philip Bate's *Galpin Society Journal* article (1973) mistakenly labeled it Cooper No. 160.

Fig. 114. MURRAY FLUTE—
ARMSTRONG PROTOTYPE I.
W. T. Armstrong Co., Elkhart, Indiana
(built by Jack Moore), June 1971.
This instrument was donated by Armstrong
to the Dayton C. Miller Collection in 1977.

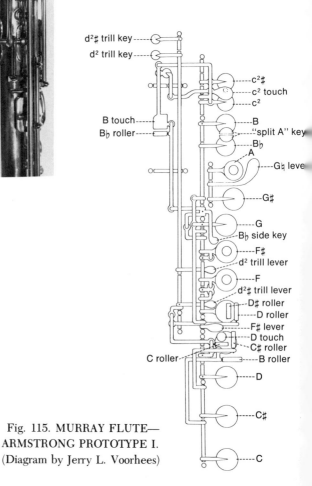

Fig. 115. MURRAY FLUTE—
ARMSTRONG PROTOTYPE I.
(Diagram by Jerry L. Voorhees)

Fig. 116. MURRAY FLUTE—ARMSTRONG PROTOTYPE II.
W. T. Armstrong Co., Elkhart, Indiana, 1972.
(Photos courtesy of W. T. Armstrong Co.)

In 1967, while teaching at Michigan State University, Murray arranged to have a prototype built by W. T. Armstrong Company of Elkhart, Indiana. This contact was the beginning of a fruitful collaboration with Jack Moore, then foreman of Armstrong's top-of-the-line Heritage division, who completed the first prototype* (Figs. 114 and 115) in June 1971. On this instrument, the shape of the thumb keys changed yet again; the shanks were lengthened, the actual touches reduced in area, and the B♭ touch made as a roller. At the foot, the D♯ roller was reinstated atop the D♯ key. A circular D touch was added atop the D key, and the positions of the C♮ and B rollers were altered so that both stood vertically on the lower side of the D key, a considerable improvement over the awkward B/C slide of Cooper No. 131.[18]

On the second Armstrong prototype† (Fig. 116), the shape of the B and B♭ thumb keys became trapezoidal and rectangular, respectively, but mechanically their functions remained the same. The split A plates together formed an oval rather than a circle. Because the foot extended only to C, the vertical disposition of the C roller was unnecessary and the form of Cooper No. 131 was readopted for the C♮ and C♯ rollers.

*The first Armstrong prototype was pictured in Murray's 1972 article in the *American Musical Instrument Society Newsletter* and in Walfrid Kujala's 1972 *Instrumentalist* article.
†The second Armstrong prototype was pictured in Kujala's 1973 *Music Journal* article and on the jacket of the Murray flute recording (Pandora 102).

Fig. 117.
MURRAY FLUTE
PRODUCTION MODEL.
W. T. Armstrong Co.,
Elkhart, Indiana (No. 8), 1972.
This instrument was donated
by Armstrong to the
Dayton C. Miller Collection
in 1977.

Later in 1972, Armstrong produced fifty production model Murray flutes (Figs. 117 and 118) and six Murray piccolos. Mechanically, they were almost identical to the second prototype except that the D♯ roller was eliminated. As a matter of elegance, not function, the thumb keys and D plate were modified in shape and the split A once again made circular. These "school model" flutes were made in two pieces, thereby avoiding the somewhat delicate mechanical connection between the body and footjoint of Armstrong Prototype I.

A slightly later version of the Murray flute is represented by Armstrong Heritage flute No. H-3002 (Fig. 119), built in 1973. A

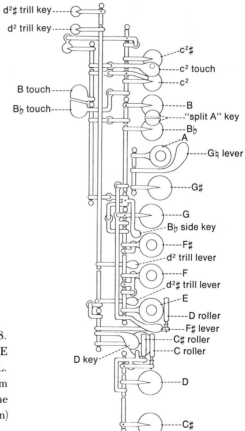

Fig. 118.
MURRAY FLUTE
PRODUCTION MODEL.
Diagram by Jerry L. Voorhees from
Armstrong-Murray No. 23, in the
collection of James M. Swain)

Fig. 119. MURRAY FLUTE.
W. T. Armstrong Co., Elkhart, Indiana
(Heritage No. H-3002), 1973.
(Photos by Leslie Timmons)

large D trill key was added on the top of the flute, as there was no room for it beside the D vent on the near side. At the foot, the D♯ roller reappeared once again. Atop the D key (D♯ hole), the three rollers for C♯, C, and B were placed in a parallel horizontal series, more or less like Cooper No. 131, except that the C♮ roller was considerably longer than the other two, thereby facilitating the progression C-D-E♭. This flute had a B foot, with the first gizmo key on a Murray flute, but the B key was detachable to allow the player to weigh the relative advantages of the two lengths for any given piece of music. Its current owner finds that, in general, the flute speaks better with the C foot; she uses the B foot only when that note is actually written in the music.

In 1974 Alex Murray took with him to the Pittsburgh convention of the National Flute Association a new, white gold flute (Fig. 120) identical to H-3002 except for the deletion of the gizmo (because the foot extended only to C) and the D♯ roller. The A key for the left-hand ring finger came equipped with a ring atop the hole cover; pressing the hole cover alone closed only that key; pressing the ring also closed the B♭ key. On the right hand, just below the B♭/C side key for the index finger was a parallel lever for the same finger for the C♯/D or G/A trill.

Nineteen seventy-six was a busy year for the Murray flute, or more accurately, flutes. Some time before the National Flute Association's convention in Atlanta in August, Tex Richardson of the Chicago Conservatory faculty had written Murray with regard to the possibilities of applying his concepts to the French model (open-holed) flute. Up to this point, the Murray flute had been made only on the plateau model because the split A pulled the left-hand middle finger too far to the left to enable it to cover a

Fig. 120. MURRAY FLUTE.
W. T. Armstrong Co., Elkhart, Indiana, 1974.
(Photo by Laura Santi)

perforated A key. A perforated plate had likewise been impractical for the right-hand third finger because of the double key arrangement. In any case, Murray sketched a possible solution and
Richardson brought an adapted flute to Atlanta, where avant-
garde specialist Robert Dick, author of *The Other Flute*, examined it. Dick had previously been critical of the Murray flute precisely because of the limitations of its closed holes.

The open hole version of the Murray flute was later modified
to become the "Multiple Option" or "M.O." model (Fig. 121), on
which all keys opened independently. A parallel bar in the thumb
key mechanism was eliminated (parallel to the trill key axle),
which gave it a simpler appearance. Originally, the instrument
had three trill keys, a large D and D♯ and small E, but the last
key was subsequently removed. Another mechanism, tried but
abandoned in favor of a simpler mechanism, was consciously modeled after the double-sprung Dorus G♯ key. This expedient, applied to the B♭ lever and F♯ key, involved a rocking motion of the
hands so that the hand slid backward toward the near side of the
flute to touch the lower portion of the Doruslike wishbone key.
Finally, the left-hand forefinger touch was made as an open ring,
which made it very light—merely a gimmick, the inventor ac-
knowledges, of no mechanical significance. The final M.O. model,
to be built in 1978, will reinstate the E trill desired by Robert
Dick for multiphonic use.

The Murray concept has also been applied to the F flute, and
No. 2 (Fig. 122), built for Murray's young daughter, was completed in December 1976. It was a hybrid instrument, with body
by Albert Cooper and keywork by Jack Moore. This flute had no
C♯ mechanism, only a single vent for C♯, because of the space limitations on the smaller flute. The left hand closely resembled
Boehm's design; like Cooper No. 129, the upper (B) thumb key
covered the C hole directly, while the lower thumb key, for B♭,
closed the B♮ hole on top. The axle construction, however, dif-
fered from Boehm's. Also because of space restrictions, the D
vent was placed on top of the tube. On the foot, the C♯ key
reverted from roller form above the D♯ hole to a crescentic touch
curving around the D♯ key, much in the shape of the D key on

Fig. 121. PROTOTYPE FOR
MULTIPLE OPTION MURRAY FLUTE.
Jack Moore, Elkhart, Indiana, December 1976.
(Photos courtesy of Alex Murray)

Fig. 122. MURRAY FLUTE IN F, No. 2.
Albert K. Cooper, London (body) and
Jack Moore, Elkhart, Indiana
(keywork), December 1976.
(Photos courtesy of Alex Murray)

Murray's 1959 model. The other keys also underwent minor changes in shape.

At about the same time—December 1976—Jack Moore produced the prototype for Murray's current (1977) flute (Fig. 123). The F flute had proved to be such a successful design that Murray had reconsidered the treatment of the C mechanism, and therefore, on this new flute, he moved the D vent to the top of the instrument. Unlike the F flute, however, it had open holes. The thumb key shape was altered once more and a large C♯ trill key was added between the C♮ hole and the D hole on the near side of the flute.

The latest model to date is Murray's own instrument, Jack Moore No. 33 (Fig. 124). (Moore had left Armstrong to establish his own shop.) Interestingly, Murray, who considers the closed holes acoustically superior, now prefers the open holes for the flexibility they allow, though he is not actively involved in the performance of avant-garde music. On this flute, the split F was initially controlled by the right-hand middle finger, but this connection was removed and the F♯ played with the A key. The foot rollers are of variable size, with B the largest, C♯ the smallest. The gizmo is unnecessary because the B roller can be reached without depressing either the C or the C♯ key. Though the B roller will, of course, also close the D key, the tone will not be affected because of the two intervening open holes.

Late in 1977, Murray made plans for still another modification, the addition of a ring key atop the B♭ thumb key. He considers the C hole to be the most useful hole on the instrument for venting purposes, and therefore envisions using the ring as an octave key for notes from b to f¹. Leaking the b with the ring, for instance, will produce b¹. In this sense, the ring would act as a subtle form of the octave key. Murray plans to add the new ring to his current instrument, Jack Moore's No. 33, and to the latest version of the Multiple Option flute, which, incidentally, will have a footjoint to low A.

The important question now is the Murray flute's chances of achieving acceptance. The early Armstrong prototypes received strong support in the United States from Walfrid Kujala, picco-

Fig. 123. MURRAY FLUTE.
Jack Moore, Elkhart, Indiana, December 1976.
Jack Moore modified this Armstrong flute as
a prototype for his No. 33 (Fig. 124).
(Photos courtesy of Alex Murray)

Fig. 124. MURRAY FLUTE.
Jack Moore, Elkhart, Indiana
(No. 33), May 1977.
(Photos courtesy of Alex Murray)

loist of the Chicago Symphony, and were played in England not only by Murray, who has used it in numerous London Symphony recordings and in a 1973 solo recording, but also by Christopher Taylor, former first flutist of the Royal Philharmonic, and Robin Chapman, piccoloist of the London Philharmonic. Kujala considered the primary advantages to be the flexibility of the right hand effected by the F♯ lever and the improvement of c¹♯ and d¹♯, which cannot be trilled with the regular Boehm key configuration. Philip Bate predicted in 1969 that the Murray flute "may possibly become the final Boehm flute;"[19] closer examination four years later led him to state that ". . . although the Murray flute may seem complicated it is in fact both logical and mechanically sound," and that furthermore, he expected to see it in the catalogs of leading manufacturers before long.[20]

Yet the Murray flute has also had many critics. Robert J. Baasch, for instance, considers the instrument to be another in the long series of "improvements" which deal with isolated mechanical aspects while losing sight of the basic principles of Boehm's work. Baasch attributes the Boehm flute's permanence to the inventor's willingness to accept compromise for the sake of simplicity. More specifically, Baasch made the following criticisms of the Murray flute: (1) the right-hand little finger must operate five keys; (2) the revised mechanism adds additional weight to the instrument; (3) the thumb key reversal is not necessary, and the delicacy resulting from the absence of a key under the thumb levers (the key is on the top of the flute) may be a source of trouble; and (4) the support or crutch for the left-hand forefinger is ungraceful.[21] Kujala replied that the second prototype, with a C foot, required only two positions for the little finger, that the weight was only two ounces more than that of a comparable Boehm flute, and that even this extra weight could be reduced by a new lighter key design. Furthermore, he stated, the first finger support is optional; in fact, Murray no longer uses it.[22]

Kujala did make the interesting observation, however, that the "corrected" C♯ may not be totally advantageous; the thin, veiled quality of the Boehm C♯ may well have influenced Debussy to select it for the beginning of *Afternoon of a Faun*. A concern for advanced technique is voiced by Thomas Howell, who, while admitting that the Murray flute solves the problems of e^3, $f^3\sharp$, and $g^3\sharp$ inherent in the Boehm flute, complains that the plateau keys severely limit the Murray flute's capacity to execute special techniques such as harmonics, whistle tones, and the like.[23]

From a pragmatic point of view, perhaps the most important opinions to consider are those of the manufacturers. It is revealing that Armstrong has made no more Murray flutes since the completion of the original group, evidently having concluded that commercial manufacture of the instrument was not feasible. One prominent flutemaker states that the Murray flute is almost impossible to build, terming it "a theoretical masterpiece and a practical monstrosity." A colleague considers the instrument "a dead issue." "You need a repairman sitting beside you," he says. It is logical that, without the confidence of flutemakers, no flute can succeed.

Today, Murray flutes are made solely as special orders by Jack Moore, obviously on a very small scale. The current distribution of Murray flutes is rather limited; most of those in use today are owned by Murray's students or by students of his students. Perhaps an omen of the fate of the Murray flute is the presence of several of the school models in formal instrument collections, where they are already relegated to the status of historical phenomena rather than working instruments.

This situation should not be surprising, though, because from a historical perspective, the Murray flute is a recapitulation of a century of mechanical development. Some of Murray's borrowings from his inventive predecessors were deliberate and acknowledged: the split A, based on Julliot's split E; the adaptation of Dorus's double-spring principle; and the return to Boehm's early thumb key configuration, for example. Other features, however, are better categorized not as borrowings, but as unconscious repetitions: the F♯ key, akin to those of Carte, Brossa, Rockstro, and Julliot; the open D♯ of Gordon and Van Everen; the C thumb ring similar in function to Boehm's *Schleifklappe*; and the rollers reminiscent of the German reform flute.

The Murray flute repeats history, too, in its evolution from simplicity (conversion of the Boehm flute to open G♯ and D♯) to complication (major redesign of the footjoint and thumb mechanisms) and a partial return to simplicity. Experience indicates that the last phase has been a healthy one. Moreover, in its latest incarnation the Murray flute has attracted interest in avant-garde circles, the performance specialty that is likely to have the greatest need for mechanical innovation. Thus it is conceivable that the Murray flute has not yet come into its prime, and that it will do so in the future as a specialized tool for the avant-garde repertoire. The inventor's continuing willingness to experiment, solicit criticism, and revise his designs makes this possibility all the more likely.

AUXILIARY MECHANICAL DEVICES

Not all twentieth century modifications of the Boehm system have been sufficiently large in scale to qualify as "named systems." But in a sense, these individual devices are even more symptomatic of the redirection of mechanical invention from major redesign toward rectification of relatively minor digital inconveniences, particularly trill fingerings.

Typical of the trend toward supplementary keys are three French patents dating from the first quarter of the twentieth century. The first, issued to J. Thibouville-Lamy & Cie. in 1902, covered three trill keys (Fig. 125). The first was a key for the left-hand pinky that closed the low C key, thereby facilitating the c¹/c¹♯ trill. Will the C♯ key closed by the right-hand pinky in the normal manner, the trill could be executed by the left-hand pinky. The second new key facilitated the B/C trill, which was likely to be uneven when fingered by the left-hand thumb. Often known as the side key, it was operated by the right-hand forefinger and controlled the C hole under the left-hand thumb. The third new trill key was placed adjacent to the side key, between the G and F♯ holes, and was also operated by the right-hand forefinger. It was linked with the cover of the B hole; when the left thumb was on the B key, pressing it gave a simple B♭/B trill.

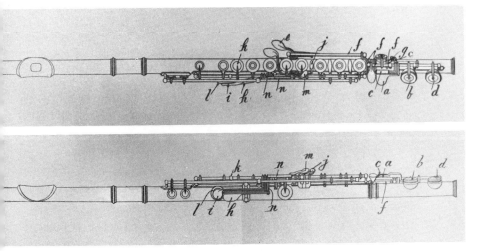

Fig. 125. THIBOUVILLE-LAMY PATENT. French Patent No. 326,145 (1902). Supplementary key (*e*) for left pinky closes low C key (*a*). Side key (*m*) controls C thumb key (*l*). New trill key (*j*) closes B hole (*k*).

In 1909, Mme. Cornélie Villedieu Laubé patented a mechanism to improve existing trills and add new trills to the Boehm flute (Fig. 126). She added a supplementary C# hole between the small C/D trill key (the lower trill key) and the left-hand thumb. This extra, large hole was controlled by a "side" lever for the right

Fig. 126. LAUBÉ PATENT. French Patent No. 409,922 (1909). Supplementary C# hole (*a*) controlled by side lever (*d*). Trill lever (*f*) closes C/D trill key (*b*); trill lever (*g*) closes C#/D# trill key (*h*).

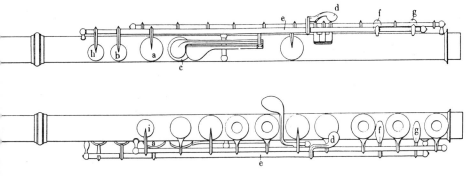

index finger. It improved five preexistent but difficult trills: $b^1/c^2\sharp$ and $b^2/c^3\sharp$ (or their enharmonic equivalents, $c^2\flat/d^2\flat$ and $c^3\flat/d^3\flat$); $b^1\sharp/c^2\sharp$ and $b^2\sharp/c^3\sharp$ (equal to $c^2/d^2\flat$ and $c^3/d^3\flat$); $f^3\sharp/g^3\sharp$ ($g^3\flat/a^3\flat$); and $g^3/a^3\flat$. The new key also gave a new trill, g^3/a^3, when operated in conjunction with the upper (C/D) trill lever.

In 1913, Louis-Fernand Vigué patented several mechanical features (Fig. 127), all with the aim of remedying specific fingering difficulties of the Boehm flute, particularly for first and third octave trills. The most unusual portion of the design was the reversal of the right-hand little finger touches for the $c^1\sharp$ and d^1 holes (c^1 and $c^1\sharp$ keys), thereby facilitating the c^1/d^1 trill. The addition of a second lever for the left-hand pinky, to control the $c^1\sharp$ key, created the $c^1/d^1\flat$ and $c^1\sharp/d^1\sharp$ trills, which are nearly impossible on the regular Boehm system.

Fig. 127. VIGUÉ PATENT. French Patent No. 459,169 (1913).
The footjoint touches are reversed: 1 controls the C key (A); 2 controls the C♯ key (B). Supplementary lever 6 controls the C♯ key (B). The B hole (L) is controlled by the E key (E) and the F key (F). The D key (D) controls the A hole (J). The G♯ lever (7) controls the linked covers of the G and A holes (G and I). A new touch (II) controls the cover of the C hole (M). A new lever (9) is linked to trill keys O and P; trill lever 4 closes trill key P, and trill lever 5 closes trill key O.

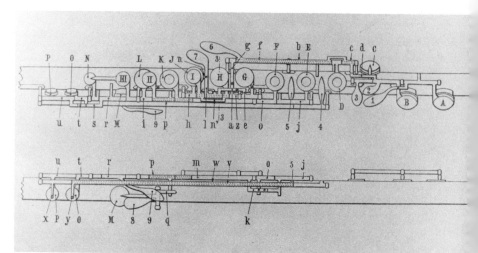

The cover of the B hole was controlled by the E key (right-hand second finger) as well as by the F key (right-hand index finger) in order to eliminate the double thumb key for B♭. The D key, operated by the right-hand ring finger, controlled the A hole; the G♯ lever for the left pinky controlled the covers of the G and A holes; and the G and A hole covers were linked together. This arrangement provided a new fingering for high D—closing all holes down to D♯, inclusive, except for F♯ and G—which permitted an easy d^3/e^3 trill with the left-hand middle finger. The mechanism also eliminated the necessity for the duplicate G♯ hole because the G♯ hole would always be open when the A hole was open.

The fourth feature of the Vigué patent was a new touch for the left-hand middle finger, placed atop the cover of the B hole. It controlled the cover of the C hole on the near side of the flute in order to make the left thumb dispensable for the a^3/b^3 and a^3/b^3♭ trills. The left thumb was given a new lever, placed to the right of the B key, which controlled the small D and D♯ trill keys simultaneously, thereby duplicating the joint action of the two right-hand trill levers. This apparatus, in conjunction with the G♯ lever and regular trill levers, facilitated six third octave trills: g^3/a^3, g^3♯$/a^3$, g^3♯$/a^3$♯, a^3/b^3♭, a^3/b^3, and a^3♯$/b^3$.

Another new contrivance was the Gage Articulated B-F♯ Device (Figs. 128 and 129), patented by Charles B. Gage in 1926 and manufactured by the Gage-Anderson Company of Wilkes-Barre, Pennsylvania. Its purpose was to eliminate the difficulty of sliding the left-hand thumb between the Briccialdi B♭ lever and the B♮ lever. Despite a more-than-usually lengthy and obscure patent description, the device was rather simple, consisting merely of a thin rod, and, in the first version, adjusting screws and a spring, all inconspicuously attached below the main bearing shafts of the flute. The device prevented the B♭ thumb lever from closing the B♭ hole on the top of the flute. Instead, the B♭ hole could be closed either by the G key or by the E key. Thus B♮ in the first and second octaves was produced by depressing the B thumb lever and either the third finger of the left hand or the second finger of the right hand.

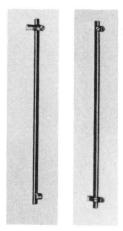

Fig. 128.
GAGE ARTICULATED B-F♯ DEVICE
from Gage-Anderson Co. brochure.
The device was invisible from the top,
inconspicuous from the side.
The adjusting screws were eliminated
from later models.

Gage acknowledged that the difficulty of sliding the thumb was not insurmountable even with the regular Boehm mechanism, since B♭ could be fingered with the B♮ thumb lever and the right index finger, and the B♭/B trill could be easily produced by trilling the right forefinger. As Gage admitted in his brochure, this was the usual B♭ fingering of most French players. But Gage also claimed that his invention automatically cleared f³♯ and b³ and produced an excellent third octave harmonic F♯ by overblowing B♮, fingered with the second finger of the right hand.[24]

Perhaps the ultimate embodiment of the availability of supplementary mechanical devices in the early part of this century is the 1931 catalog of Leipzig manufacturer Otto Mönnig (Fig. 130).

Fig. 129. GAGE ARTICULATED B–F♯ DEVICE. U.S. Patent No. 1,586,794 (1926).
To avoid withdrawing thumb from the touch (34) of the B thumb key (31),
yet permit unseating of the cover of the B hole (21), lever 42 is activated
by the cover of the E hole (14) through shaft 52. Lever 42 is offset as at 44,
with a slot (45) in which lever 32 lies. End 44 engages the free end 47
of spring 46. End 49 of spring 46 retains thumb key 31 in its normal position.

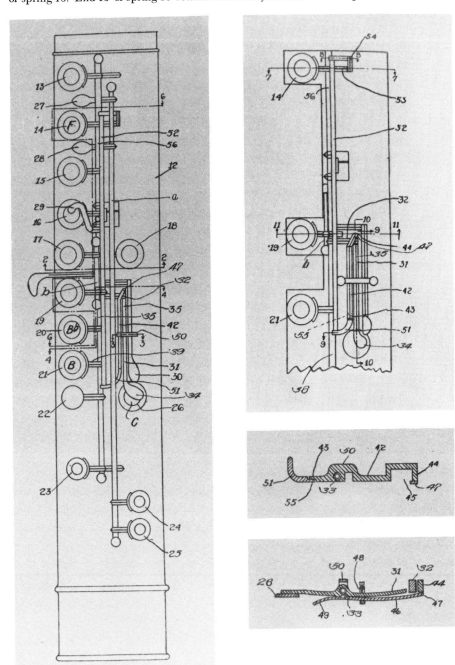

Fig. 130. MECHANICAL OPTIONS from catalog of Otto Mönnig, Leipzig, 1931.

Otto Mönnig, Leipzig S 3   Hardenberg-Straße 20 a

44 Jahre Spezialist im Bau v. Flöten u. Piccolos, System Böhm.   „Orthoton"-Holzblasinstrume

Beschreibung der Neuerungen für die Böhmflöten Nrn. 101–

Bestellnummern 1000 bis 1021 zur Katalogausgabe 1931

Meine Erfindungen sind durch viele Gebrauchsmuster gesetzlich geschützt.

Abb. Nr. 1000, betr. Best.-Nrn. 1000, 1002, 1004, 1008

Trillergriffe für b-h oder h-c, g²-a² und h¹⁽²⁾ - cis²⁽³⁾.

Diese 3 Trillergriffe werden bei Flöten mit geschlossener Gisklappe wie auch bei offener Gisklappe angebracht. Die Abbildung zeigt ausserdem noch die verbesserte enge Grifflage für die linke Hand.

Abb. Nr. 1001, betr. Best. Nrn. 1001,

Trillergriffe für b-h, h-c zugleich sowie g² - gis² - a² für offene Gisk

Nr. 1 dient zur Ausführung des h-c-Trillers für den b-h Triller. Werden beide Gr gleich gedrückt, so entsteht der b-c Nr. 3 Trillergriff für g gis-a.

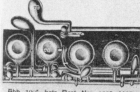

Abb. 1005, betr. Best. Nrn. 1005, 1007.

E-Mechanik,

in allgemeiner Ausführung, für das c^3, wodurch dasselbe reinstimmend und in allen Bindungen sicher gespielt werden kann. Der Gisklappendeckel 2 wird durch den Verbindungshebel 1 geschlossen. Nr. 3 zeigt einen Seitenhebel für den kleinen Finger der linken Hand zur Betätigung einzelner Fussklappen.

Abb. und Best. Nr. 1006.

E-Mechanik. Diese seitlich angebrachte Ausführt net sich für solche Instrumente, an denen die E-M *nachträglich* gewünscht wird.

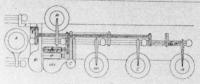

Abb. und Best.-Nr. 1007

Seitenhebel für den kleinen Finger der linken Hand.

(Nur für Flöten mit geschlossener Gisklappe!)

a) zum Öffnen der es-Klappe, für Triller cis-dis.
b) zum Schließen der cis-Klappe, für Triller cis-dis
c) zum Schließen der h-Klappe.
d) zum Schließen der h-Klappe und cis-Klappe, für Triller cis-dis und h-cis.
e) zum Öffnen der cis-Klappe und zum Schließen der h-Klappe.

Erläuterungen zur Ausführung e): in der gezeichneten Lage betätigt der Seitenhebel 1 die Verbindung 3 zur es-Klappe und öffnet diese, wodurch der cis-dis-Triller ausgeführt werden kann. Wird das Fussstück rechts nach aussen gedreht, sodass der schraffierte Hebel 2 auf Hebel 1 zu liegen kommt, so kann die h-Klappe geschlossen werden. Diese Verbindung ergibt die Triller h-c u. h-cis.

Abb. Nr. 1000, betr. Best. Nr. 1008.

Verbesserte enge Grifflage für die linke Hand.

Durch die Zusammenlegung der Griffteller der linken Hand bisherige Spannung beseitigt und die Fingerstellung eine r geworden. Die linke Hand, die ja den schwierigen Teil der Zu bewältigen hat, kann nicht mehr so ermüden. Die Beweg der Finger wird durch die Entspannung eine freiere. Ganz ders gilt dies für Spieler mit kurzen Fingern.

Abb. und Best. Nr. 1009

Rollengriffe für die es- und cis-Klappe.

Abb. und Best. Nr. 10

Stütze f. den rechten Da

Durch diese bekommt die eine ruhigere Lage und die der rechten Hand gewinnen die mehr gebogene Haltu Fertigkeit.

Bei Böhmflöten ist bisher das E¹ nicht befriedigend in der Ansprache gewesen. Eine diesbezügliche Erinnerung des Herrn Kammervirtuos Adolf Buchholz ist von mir übernommen und in der Konstruktion des Klappen-Mechanismus praktisch übertragen worden. Durch diese Neuerung ist die Ansprache so leicht geworden, dass man Stellen wie im Anfang der Mignon

Abb. und Best. Nr. 1021

Pedal-Mechanik für das hohe e²

Ouverture mit absoluter Reinheit bis zu einem ausklingen lassen kann. Erzielt wird dieser dadurch, dass zwischen d- und dis-Trillerloch Schallochklappe liegt, welche mit einem Pedal-Hebe sehen ist. Wenn die e-Daumenklappe geschlossen die d-Trillerklappe gedrückt wird, öffnet sich Letzterer gleichzeitig die erwähnte Schallochklappe

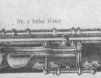

Nr. 1 linke Hand

Nr. 2 rechte Hand

Abb. und Best. Nr. 1012

Klappen-Mechanik, die das erschwerte Hinüber-
beim Tonwechsel vom fis² u. b²-ces² ausschaltet

Notenbeisp. IV

...schliessen des Daumen-B-Hebels 1 ist bekanntlich die H-Klappe
...sen. Um sie beim Liegenlassen des Daumens wieder zu öffnen,
...ieser ein Hebel 3 angebracht (s. Abb. Nr. 2), welcher mit dem
...r der rechten Hand nach rückwärts niedergedrückt wird.
...em leichten Druck öffnet sich die H-Klappe wieder. Diese
... ist in der Konstruktion ganz einfach und beim Spielen in
...eise hinderlich.

Abb. und Best. Nr. 1014

h¹⁽²⁾ - cis²⁽³⁾ - Triller.

Notenbeispiel I

H-Cis u.
H-Gis

Abb. und Best. Nr. 1015

h¹⁽²⁾-cis²⁽³⁾- Triller in Verbindung mit b¹-c²-Triller

Notenbeispiel I

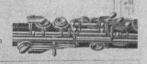

Abb. und Best. Nr. 1016

Trillerhebel für

g² - a², g² - gis², a² - h²

Notenbeispiel I

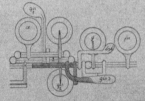

Abb. und Best. Nr. 1017

Trillerhebel für g²- gis²
verbesserter
Konstruktion

Abb. und Best. Nr. 1018

...ebel für cis¹-dis¹ an Flöten mit offener Gisklappe.

Die Bedienung des cis¹-dis¹-Trillers erfolgt mit dem 4. Finger der rechten Hand, ebenso das c¹-es¹-
Tremolo. Der Spieler stelle sich vor, dass aus dem Griff des tiefen d¹ durch Vorschieben des 4.
Fingers rechts der Ton cis und mittelst der es-Klappe der cis¹-dis¹ (des¹-es¹) Triller erreicht
wird. Durch weiteres Vorschieben des 4. Fingers rechts wird die c-Klappe geschlossen und kann
das c¹-es¹-Tremolo leicht gespielt werden, z. B.

Abb. und Best. Nr. 1019

cis¹-dis¹-Triller und c¹-es¹-Tre-
molo-Mechanik

v. R. Röhler, Freiburg (Brg)

*Alte, sonst in dieser Lage nicht ausführbaren Stellen
sind mittelst des cis¹-dis¹-Triller und c¹-es¹-Tremolo-
Mechanik spielbar.*

Abb. und Best. Nr. 1020

mechanik für einen reinen hohen g³-a³-Triller

Notenbeispiel III

Gleichzeitig für die Triller h²-cis³, h²-c³, gis³-a³. Diese
...ik kann nicht in Verbindung mit allen andern Verbesserungen
...acht werden.

Abb. und Best. Nr. 1021

Wechsel-Gis-Mechanik für die Alt-Flöte

Mittelst dieser Mechanik kann das Instrument wahlweise mit offener
oder geschlossener Gisklappe gespielt werden. Gleichzeitig wird der
B-Daumenhebel so angebracht, daß derselbe rechts oder links vom
Daumen C betätigt werden kann.

...nbeispiele

...u den

...uerungen

I   II   III   IV

laut Abbildungen
Nr. 1011, 1013
bis 1016, 1019.

This is an especially interesting document in that it reflects the juxtaposition of the German tradition of auxiliary mechanism, which was manifested primarily in the old system reform flute, and the comparatively streamlined Boehm system. The multiplicity of options is almost staggering, and the number is increased more than it might be today by the necessity of providing auxiliaries for both open and closed G♯ instruments.

In addition to an extensive assortment of "side" and trill keys for the right index finger, Mönnig offered two "E mechanisms" (split E and split G), a support for the right thumb, and a vent key for b^3 that was automatically opened when the C thumb key was closed and the D trill lever depressed. A lever for the left-hand little finger could be used to control any of several foot keys on a closed G♯ flute: to open the E♭ key, for the c^1♯/d^1♯ trill; to close the C♯ key, for the same trill; to close the B and C♯ keys, for the c^1♯/d^1♯ and b/c^1♯ trills; to close the B key; and simultaneously to open the E♭ key and close the B key. In addition, the E♭ and C♯ touches could be fitted with rollers, and two more rollers could be installed above the D key to facilitate the c^1/e^1♭ trill.

CONTEMPORARY MECHANICAL OPTIONS

Clearly, twentieth century inventors and manufacturers have not been idle with regard to mechanism. But the abolition of choice with regard to fingering system, culminating in the universality of the Boehm system, was followed, not illogically, by a decrease in the availability of multiple options with regard to details within the Boehm system. Largely, of course, this development resulted from the advent of mass production, but it is also evident in the catalogs of the leading makers of handmade flutes, Haynes and Powell. Those mechanical alternatives that do survive fall into three categories: additional keys, arrangement of the keys on the flute tube, and type of keys.

The first category perhaps most graphically demonstrates the movement toward simplicity. For, as the Boehm system approaches its sesquicentennial, it is instructive to note how few of the many supplementary mechanisms offered only forty years ago are still "live options."

Perhaps the most common additional key is the B♭ side key for the right-hand forefinger, which duplicates the action of the Briccialdi B♭ lever. In addition to the objective stated in the Thibouville-Lamy patent of providing an alternative B♭/B trill, this key also facilitates passages with sequences of G, A♯, B, A♯ because the side key, unlike either the F key or the B♭ thumb key, can be held down while fingering G, thus ensuring a clean transition from G to A♯. The side key may also be used for A♯ in G♯/A♯ trills.

In place of the B♭ side key, the player may order a B/C trill key for the right-hand forefinger. It, too, was covered by the Thibouville-Lamy patent. This key replaces the thumb trill for b ^{1}/c^2, b ^{2}/c^3, and f^3♯/g^3. A rather unusual fingering made possible by the B/C trill key is an alternative B♭/C trill in the first two octaves, whereby the right forefinger shakes the trill key and the second finger moves over one key to depress the F key.

The C♯ trill key, from the Laubé patent of 1909, may be added to either the B♭ side key or the B/C trill key, and is also placed within reach of the right index finger.

Of Djalma Julliot's many inventions, only the split E is regularly available from the leading manufacturers. Until about 1970 Powell also offered the split G; as of 1977, Haynes still did. With the split E, the G hole is closed automatically by the E key; with split G, the manual version, the G key may also be depressed independently of the G♯ key, but it must be operated directly by the little finger of the left hand. The 1977 catalog of W. T. Armstrong's Heritage Division includes a compromise between split E and split G, described as a "G key lever for first finger, right hand, plateau model only."

On standard footjoints, only the C♮ and B keys have roller touches, but most manufacturers offer a roller on the right side of the D♯ touch, as well. And Haynes still offers a left-hand pinky lever for low B.

The major choice regarding the footjoint, however, concerns its length. The "standard" Boehm foot extends to c^1, but a very common extension takes it to b by adding an extra key and touch. An obvious reason for such an extension is the existence of compositions which score the low B, a few examples being Kuhlau's Duet, Op. 39, Bartók's *Concerto for Orchestra*, Bloch's *Schelomo*, several Mahler symphonies, Prokofiev's *Classical Symphony*, and Respighi's *Pines of Rome*. Considerable objection has been raised, however, to the low B. Anthony Baines, for instance, rejects the compositional justification, noting that "In England, should these notes be indispensable to the music they are discreetly slipped in on bassoon or clarinet."[25] Others, such as Jean-Pierre Rampal, charge that the B foot upsets the balance of the flute and makes the low register and notes above c^3 more difficult to produce.

Nevertheless, the B foot is the preference of the majority of professional players and an increasing number of students in the United States. A major influence in its adoption was William Kincaid, who valued it not for the extra note, but for the added resistance and resonance which the increased length of the tube provides. The result is a fuller, darker sound.

Because the response of c^4 may suffer with the B foot, the high C facilitator or "gizmo" key is often applied (Fig. 131). The gizmo has the same effect as depressing only the B roller; it closes the B key independently, thereby cutting off the low C harmonic. The idea for the key was conceived in the late 1930s by Georges Barrère and conveyed by Arthur Lora to Verne Q. Powell, who designed it and implemented it on his own flutes. The gizmo was not patented and is therefore available from almost all

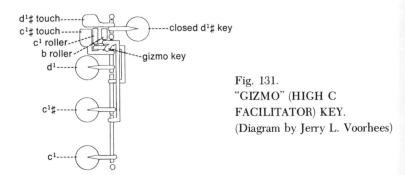

Fig. 131.
"GIZMO" (HIGH C
FACILITATOR) KEY.
(Diagram by Jerry L. Voorhees)

manufacturers. It is so much in demand, yet so simple to manufacture, that in 1976 Powell began offering the device at no additional charge.

Occasionally, the range of the flute has been taken down even farther than b. Dayton C. Miller's gold flute, which he built in 1905, has a footjoint to b♭ (Figs. 92 and 93, page 113), the same is true of Robert Cantrick's 1970 Powell, which was built to facilitate certain avant-garde techniques. In 1963, the K. G. Gemeinhardt Company introduced a b♭ footjoint, available on special order, with the avowed purpose of mellowing the tone of the low register. The B♭ key was operated by a lever for the left-hand little finger. The lower range may also be expanded by the addition of extension "sleeves." In emergency situations where a low note is required for a particular performance, a temporary sleeve is often fashioned of oaktag or other sturdy paper. Georges Barrère had two sterling silver extension sleeves made for him by Haynes; each extended the range by a semitone, thus allowing him to obtain low B♭ and A with his regular B foot.* The upper sleeve was cylindrical, the lower, bell-shaped.

The second category of keywork options involves the arrangement of the keys on the tube. For most of this century, Haynes offered its customers a choice of three thumb key arrangements (Fig. 132). Style A had the B♭ lever above the B♮ lever (Briccialdi's design, and the current preference); style B had the levers reversed, with a closed B♮ key; and style C also had the levers reversed, but with an open B♮ key, a la Boehm. Today, however, the only major alignment option concerns the placement of the A and G♯ holes, which are closed together to produce G♮. On keyless flutes, the holes were in a straight line; Boehm, however, offset the G keys to accommodate the third finger of the left hand. When Godfroy perforated the keys, he reverted to the straight line G; thus there has developed a tradition of offset keys on plateau models and straight or "in line" keys on the French. Today,

---

*These extensions are now in the possession of Arthur Lora. Lawrence Taylor mistakenly reported in his "Flute Facts" column of *The Instrumentalist* 3 (November–December 1948): 46, that Lora's extension sleeves took the flute to low G.

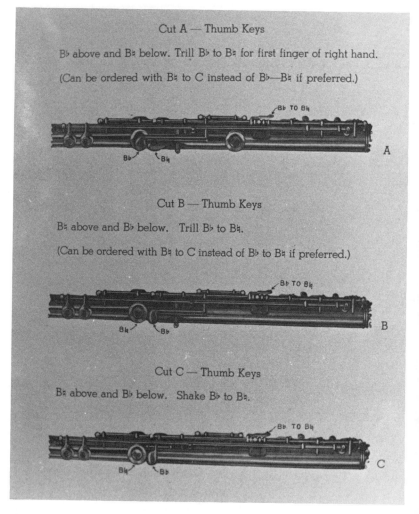

Fig. 132. THUMB OPTIONS from 1940 catalog of Wm. S. Haynes Co.

both Haynes and Powell confine their production almost exclusively to straight G keys, which are preferred by some players for the faster left-hand trills they permit. Yet both manufacturers agree that the offset configuration is mechanically better because it prevents the rods from binding.

The third category of mechanical options involves the type of

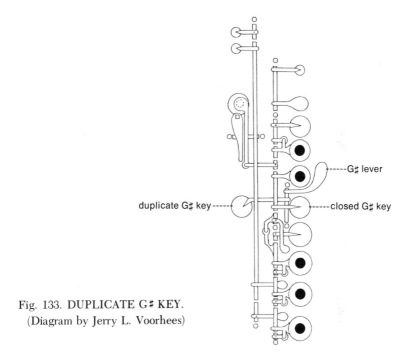

duplicate G♯ key------

-----G♯ lever

------closed G♯ key

Fig. 133. DUPLICATE G♯ KEY.
(Diagram by Jerry L. Voorhees)

key desired. For the G♯ key, this means a choice between a closed and an open key. Boehm's original design called for the open type; he claimed that it was acoustically superior, more logical in fingering, and produced a clearer e^3. Players accustomed to the closed G♯ of the old system demanded a return to that variety, but the Dorus key of the nineteenth century has been replaced by a first order lever with a duplicate G♯ hole on the near side of the flute for venting (Fig. 133). By 1920, William S. Haynes estimated, ninety-five percent of all players used the closed G♯, one reason being the simpler fingering in the third register. Today, the tradition of open G♯ is carried on in the Soviet Union, Israel, and Australia; the few Americans who still use it, such as Clem Barone of the Detroit Symphony, do so because of early training, primarily in Europe.

Today, the most important choice that a flutist must make is between the plateau or American (closed hole) and French (open hole) models. In 1930, the Haynes catalog stated that

> There is still a difference of opinion among the best authorities regarding the relative merits of the French Model (open hole flute) or the covered key instrument. The first chairmen of our leading Symphonies are about equally divided on the subject. . . . A few years ago it was a rare thing to see a French model flute in the United States. At the present time, the demand for them is increasing so rapidly they bid fair to outnumber the covered hole flutes.

The most common objection to the French model is the initial discomfort of accustoming one's fingers to covering the holes properly. Dayton Miller, however, marshaled science to the cause: "I think that the perforated key is the one acoustical crime that has been perpetrated against the Boehm flute," the primary disadvantage being the "non-uniform scale." In a diplomatically unmailed first draft of a letter to William S. Haynes, Miller wrote:

> It is notorious the country over that the performers with the perforated holes [sic!] are not as good as regards perfect intonation as the others. Specifically I think that Arthur Brooke, Jay Plowe and Harry Baxter play in better tune than Barrère, Laurent or Kincaid, and I believe that the perforated holes have something to do with this. Personally I think Barrère is the greatest living artist on the flute, but this is not due to the perforated keys, but because he is Barrère.

Despite Miller's objections, however, the French model is now played by the majority of professional flutists and by many avocational musicians and students as well. In 1958, Emil Eck gave the professional figure as eighty percent.[26] Closed hole flutes are used mostly by students and by "doublers" who find the American model more comfortable when switching between the flute and reed instruments.

Historically, many reasons have been given for adoption of the French model. The Haynes catalog claims "greater clarity and brilliance of tone" due to the greater venting afforded by the perforations. For students, especially, the French model assures proper finger positions, which in turn facilitate digital technique. To the advanced flutist, the greatest advantage of the open holes is the possibility of modifying tone color or intonation by "shading"—that is, partially or totally uncovering the perforation while pressing the rim of the key. Increasingly important in the latter part of the twentieth century is the use of extended "shading" for alternate fingerings that provide timbral variety; almost all of the altered fingerings listed by James J. Pellerite in his *Modern Guide to Fingerings for the Flute* (1972) require the French model, and it is essential for producing many of the multiphonics, quarter tones, and other special effects of avant-garde music.*

The tonal concerns of proponents of the French model are of great significance in that they are characteristic of the shift of attention from matters of digital technique to the interrelated factors of intonation and timbre. Only in the twentieth century, with the decline of the "fireworks" style, could a writer dare to suggest that "The tone is the soul of the flute."[27] As a result of this attitude, promoted especially by the French school, manufacturers have concentrated their efforts on such aspects of flute construction as tone hole dimensions, to regulate pitch; the bore, embouchure, and stopper of the headjoint, to produce a given tone quality; and most importantly, the materials of construction needed to project that quality.

PITCH

One of the less notable legacies of the nineteenth century was uncertainty, indeed confusion, over pitch standards. Dr. D. J. Blaikley's "Essay on Musical Pitch," appended to the *Catalogue* of the Royal Military Exhibition of 1890, includes a comparative table of contemporary musical pitch which records a range for a^1 from 457.9 to 435.0 vibrations per second. As in Quantz's time, even "official" standards were highly variable. Old Philharmonic Pitch, the standard of Victorian England, was $a^1 = 452$. This was followed, in England, by New Philharmonic Pitch of $a^1 = 439$, which

---

*Not long ago, however, James MacGillivray shortsightedly wrote that "[T]he perforated fingerplates . . . do not provide additional fingerings. . . ." ("The Woodwind," in *Musical Instruments Through the Ages*, ed. Anthony Baines [London: Faber and Faber, 1961], p. 238.)

prevailed until 1939. The contemporaneous standard of Europe, known as Continental or French Pitch, was a ^{1} = 435.

American flutemaking in the early twentieth century proceeded primarily on the French pattern with respect to both construction and tuning. By 1923, however, the catalog of the Wm. S. Haynes Company stated, "In our opinion, the A-435 pitch is too low, inasmuch as instruments of that pitch . . . have a much less brilliant and pleasing tone than those tuned to A-440." The following year, William S. Haynes told Dayton Miller that "all our flutes are A-440. We have no call for A-435." He hypothesized that the rise in pitch "may be a case of 'follow the leader.' We are absolutely certain that if George[s] Barrère used A-452 that all his pupils would follow suit whether they required an instrument of that pitch or not. The same is true of Laurent's followers. Personally, we wish very much that the pitch could be standardized." This desire was fulfilled in 1939 when the International Standard Pitch of A-440 was adopted at a London conference. Today, Haynes and Powell build their flutes to A-440 unless otherwise requested. Powell advises that the instrument has a tuning tolerance of two vibrations per second; that is, an A-440 flute can be played with "negligible distortion" at pitch levels ranging from A-338 to A-442. Powell offers models with A-440, A-442, or A-444 scale, but recommends the last only for those areas of Europe with a minimum standard of A-443. (Much of Europe tunes to A-444 or higher.)

An interesting attempt to adapt to unstable pitch levels was made by Nicholas Alberti in 1914. He devised a flute with a revolving inner tube (Figs. 134 and 135) whereby the instrument could, in effect, transpose itself from a C to a D♭ instrument or take any pitch between the two. Without his invention, musicians were often obliged to carry multiple instruments or even to transpose because pitch varied by as much as a semitone. The Alberti flute was constructed of two telescoping silver tubes, the inner one of which was provided with either round holes or helical slots. The outer tube contained the full Boehm mechanism; the only variation was in the shape of the key cups, which were more elongated than on the standard model. There were two guiding slots, one

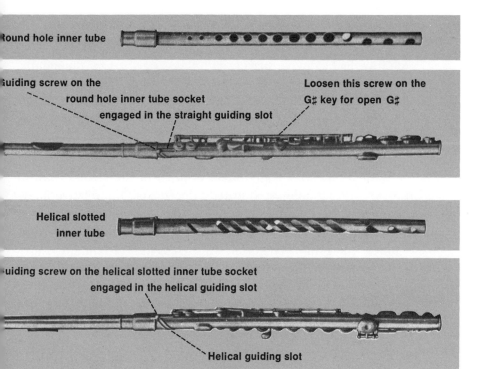

Round hole inner tube

Guiding screw on the round hole inner tube socket engaged in the straight guiding slot

Loosen this screw on the G♯ key for open G♯

Helical slotted inner tube

Guiding screw on the helical slotted inner tube socket engaged in the helical guiding slot

Helical guiding slot

Fig. 134. ALBERTI FLUTES
from *N. Alberti's Any Pitch and Transposing C and D-flat Flute.*
Both flutes are shown in position for low pitch (C). To convert the round hole
inner tube model to D♭, the guiding screw is shifted to the upper position.
The guiding screw must be set in either extremity of the straight guiding slot, not
in any intermediate position. To convert the helical tube model to D♭, the outer tube
is simultaneously pushed and turned to the right in the direction of the guiding slot.
The pitch will be higher in proportion to the distance the outer tube is moved up.

Fig. 135. ALBERTI PATENT. U.S. Patent No. 1,103,462 (1914).
Sleeve D moves longitudinally on tube B. Guide-pin d on sleeve D projects
into guide-slot b in tube B. Tube D is provided with oblong openings (d^2) covered
by valves (V); tube B is provided with helical slots (b^2).
Guide-slot b causes rotation of sleeve D so that it follows spiral slots b^2.

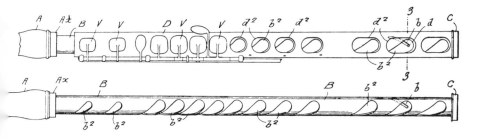

straight and the other helical, at the top of the outer tube. The inside tube had a double socket, with the upper part for the mouthpiece and the lower part, with a guiding screw engaged in the guiding slot of the outer tube, covering the extremity of the outer tube.[28] Another screw allowed the flute to be played with either open or closed G♯. The instrument won the gold medal at the San Francisco Exposition of 1915.

With the relative stabilization of pitch in the second third of this century, attention has turned to perfecting the relative internal pitch of the flute. Despite its enormous superiority to the ordinary German flute, the Boehm flute still contained certain inequities as a result of compromises such as the C♯ vent key. Early in this century, makers such as Julliot attempted to remedy the compromises by mechanical means. But the dominant trend has been toward acoustical, rather than mechanical, modification of acoustical problems. The first step in this direction was the reintroduction of graduated holes, which Boehm had abandoned after six years as being too difficult to manufacture. Haynes saw them as a great advantage, "as they bring the low tones out strongly and clearly and with great resonance." He also noted their role in improving the intonation and reponse of the third register, particularly above a^3.

Nevertheless, certain small pitch discrepancies have persisted. Roger Stevens summarizes such expected deviations as follows:[29]

GENERAL		PROBABLE	
b, c^1, c^1♯	low	f^1	low
c^2♯	high	f^2	low
d^3	low	e^3♭	high
b^3♭	low	f^3♯	low
c^4	high	g^3♯	high
		b^3	high

Various attempts have been made to adjust tone hole size and position to compensate for internal deviations. The most recent of these is the Cooper Scale, designed in 1973 by Albert Cooper, and now used, under a royalty agreement, by Powell Flutes.* The traditional scale, Cooper found, had a "wide octave"; that is, c^1 was flat and c^2 sharp in relation to a^1, with varying degrees of error in the remainder of the octave. The reason, he surmised, was that the scales used in flutemaking were based on pitches below A-440 and had not been sufficiently modified for modern pitch. Further defects that he noticed included an increasingly sharp third register and the tendency of G♯, c^2, and d^2 to be "out of character" with adjacent notes.

Cooper began his remeasurement by establishing accurate locations for the c^1 tone hole on the footjoint and for the thumb c^2 hole in relation to a^1, the result being a shorter octave length than in the traditional flute scale. However, with equal-sized holes, the third octave was still poor (since the venting required by harmonics differs from that for fundamentals), so he altered the size and location of holes accordingly. Advantages claimed by Powell are good intonation, smooth transition between registers, and the qualitative improvement of certain traditionally weak notes. A notable feature of the Cooper Scale is its consideration of the differences between plateau and French models due to the venting characteristics of open keys; thus, in fact, two different scales are employed.

THE HEADJOINT

A crucial determinant of the proportions of the flute is the position of the headjoint stopper in relation to the embouchure. John Coltman explains the importance of this factor as follows:

> The cork provides a small cavity above the mouth hole, which functions to maintain a reasonably constant acoustic end correction over the range of the instrument. Adjustment of the size of this cavity has most effect in the third register of the flute. Shortening the cork-to-embouchure distance produces a rising characteristic in the third oc-

*Lewis J. Deveau, general manager of the Wm. S. Haynes Company, claims that the Cooper Scale is "almost identical" to the Haynes closed hole scale, yet he also terms the Cooper Scale "a fad."

tave, the notes becoming successively sharper as the scale is ascended; withdrawing the cork has the opposite effect.[30]

In the early part of the century, the cap was often removed for cleaning; particularly with wood instruments, thorough swabbing is essential to remove all traces of moisture. The procedure was potentially perilous, however, for the plug had to be repositioned properly. In 1906, E. H. Wurlitzer devised a simple solution, counterboring or enlarging the end of the tube so as to form a shoulder (Fig. 136). The shoulder then acted as a stop for the removable plug, ensuring its proper replacement.

On modern flutes, the cork is not adjusted by the player for each performance; fine tuning of that sort is accomplished solely by moving the tuning slide between the headjoint and the body. Players are advised, however, to check the embouchure-cork distance periodically by means of the calibration provided on the instrument's cleaning rod.

Fig. 136. WURLITZER PATENT. U.S. Patent No. 859,714 (1907). Above the blow hole (5) of the headjoint (4), central passage 6 is counterbored at 7 to form a shoulder (8), which acts as a positioning stop for removable plug (9), which closes the end of the passage. Plug 9 has an extending stem (10), which carries at its end a head or button (11) that closes the end of the enlarged portion of the passage (7). The side walls of the flute (12) are made thinner at the end of the flute by enlarging the bore of the central passage at 7.

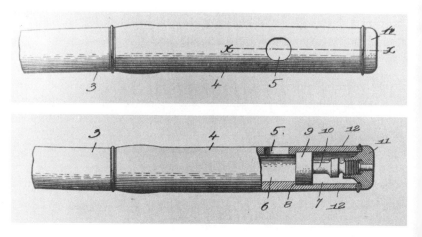

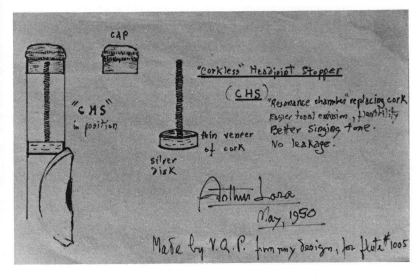

Fig. 137. "CORKLESS" HEADJOINT STOPPER.
Design by Arthur Lora, May 1950.

More recent concerns have centered on the cork stopper it-self. In 1950, for instance, Arthur Lora designed a "corkless head-joint stopper" (Fig. 137) that was executed by Verne Q. Powell for his flute No. 1005. With this arrangement, the cork was re-duced to a thin veneer covering the upper portion of a silver disc. Thus the space between the bottom of the stopper and the crown of the flute, previously occupied by a large cork, became a "reso-nance chamber." By this expedient, the inventor not only avoided the air leakage which might result from a shrunken cork, but also achieved "easier tonal emission, flexibility, and a better singing tone." The "corkless headjoint stopper" was never patented, nor did it ever see extensive commercial production.

Similar reservations about the acoustical efficacy of cork led to the invention of the "O" Ring (Fig. 138). Originally used by Ru-dall, Carte & Co. in the early part of the twentieth century, it was later altered by English headjoint maker Leslie Eggs to suit the modern silver flutes. The design was subsequently imported to the United States by James J. Pellerite, now professor of music at Indiana University. It is marketed as a separate flute accessory by Pellerite's company, Zalo Publications and Services. The device is made of neoprene, a synthetic rubber, which, though more expensive than cork, does not require replacement and makes a tighter seal. Bickford Brannen, formerly a partner in Powell Flutes, considers that, from the manufacturing standpoint, it is easier to make than a cork stopper. Pellerite's company promotes several advantages to the player: tonal improvement throughout the range of the flute, easier articulation and legato production, and an added vibrating quality in most headjoints.

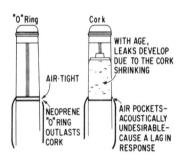

Fig. 138. "O" RING.
Zalo Publications & Services flyer, ca. 1975.

Moving down the headjoint, the next structural component is the embouchure, which is of great importance in that it is the first step in directing the airstream into the tube. On early wood flutes, the hole was oval shaped, and this design was continued for some early metal flutes. More recently, however, embouchures have been shaped as rounded rectangles. For student flutes, a compromise configuration has been adopted because, while the oval makes the upper register more responsive, the rounded rectangle assists the lower register. A similar problem is evident in determining the size of the hole; a large hole, though it makes the lower octave easier to produce, makes the upper register more difficult to control. A small hole, on the other hand, simplifies production of the middle and upper registers but considerably hinders the lower one, particularly for the beginner.

Still another factor in constructing the embouchure is the shape and dimension of the lip plate, which, of course, only became an issue with the introduction of the metal flute. At first, efforts were made to approximate the outer diameter of wooden flutes in order to ease the transition. Recently, the arc of the curvature has diminished. In general, there are three types of embouchure available: flat, concave, and winged or cusped (as on the German reform flute).

During 1958 and 1959, James Hopkinson, first flutist of the National Orchestra of New Zealand, conducted experiments with embouchures in order to compensate for the differences between individual players' lips. Following the precedent of Wilhelm Heckel, who had attempted to channel the air column through a bridge across the lip plate, Hopkinson had a thin silver plate, which tapered from $^1/_{16}$ to $^1/_{50}$ inch. A small platform or ledge with an indentation was built just below the hole and part of the plate. The structure was thus similar to a dental impression, in that it could be contoured to each player's mouth. It was designed to allow greater lip flexibility and to avert embouchure fatigue.[31]

Design of the headjoint itself has been the subject of much recent research, as it is the section of the flute where the tone originates. "[T]he flute body is mainly an acoustical resonator; it determines which of the frequencies generated at the embouchure section will be reinforced."[32] One important function of the headjoint is determining the tone color of a sound, or in acoustical terms, its harmonic content. Hermann Helmholtz attributed tone color solely to the presence and relative amplitudes of harmonic frequencies. In 1962, however, J. H. Craig and L. A. Jefress, writing in the *Journal of the Acoustical Society of America*, concluded that phase relationship is also influential in determining tone color. Boehm was aware that a taper in the headjoint bore was necessary for proper tuning and that, in general, the steeper the bore, the richer will be the generation of harmonics. Furthermore, the thicker the wall of the embouchure hole, the richer will be the harmonics of the lower register, within limits.

Raoul Fajardo, a professor of physics and electronics, has conducted research on wave form analysis in the flute and observed that "In a relatively simple sound, like that of the middle F of the flute, this shift in phase between the harmonics and the fundamental can make a noticeable contribution to tone color." Although he admitted that "The design characteristics that determine whether or not a flute head will produce phase shift in the harmonics is a question that remains unanswered," he has designed an experimental headjoint made of linen phenolic with ⅛-inch walls. Its bore changes smoothly from a circular cross section at the body joint to an ellipse at the cork. The resultant sonority is similar to that of the Baroque flute, with a quick response but weak dynamic range.[33]

MATERIALS

Undoubtedly the most controversial and most publicized aspect of modern flute construction is the choice of materials, a source of considerable acrimony between the musical and scientific communities. Viewing the situation with a humorous perspective, John Backus has written:

> For many years, there has been discussion and argument on the question of the influence of the wall material of a woodwind instrument on its tone quality. These arguments probably started in early Stone-Age musical circles with assertions that a flute made of a human thigh bone had a better tone than one fashioned from the rib of a sabre-tooth tiger.[34]

In his landmark article on the subject in a 1909 issue of *Science*, Dayton Miller recounted the change in attitude of the scientific community. Biot had suggested in 1817 that the variant production of harmonics by different substances determined timbre. Boehm, in 1871, wrote that "The greater or less hardness of the material has a very great effect upon the quality of tone." Yet Victor Mahillon countered with the statement three years later that "air is the only vibrating body in the flute," and that the tube therefore was only a container with no timbral influence. "This error," Mahillon continued, "is shared by nearly all artists who play wind instruments."[35]

Miller despaired, in 1909, that the question had still not been settled, and he therefore conducted his own experiments with zinc and wood organ pipes. As a result of the tubes being filled and surrounded with water and of being grasped, Miller concluded that ". . . the quality of a wind-instrument may be affected by the material of its body tube to the comparatively small extent claimed by the player." Moreover, he stated, because of its extreme thinness (between 0.2 and 0.3 millimeters), the flute was especially susceptible to this influence; "it is conceivable that the presence or absence of a ferrule or of some support for a key might cause the appearance or disappearance of a partial tone, or put a harmonic partial slightly out of tune."[36] In sum, Miller wrote:

> The traditional influences of the different metals on the flute are consistent with the experimental results obtained from the organ pipe. Brass and German silver are usually so hard, brittle and stiff as to have but little influence upon the air column, and the tone is said to be hard and trumpet-like. Silver is heavier and softer, and adds to the mellowness of the tone. The much greater softness and density of gold adds still more to the soft-massiveness of the wall, giving an approach to the organ pipe surrounded by water, and permitting a greater influence of the walls upon the tone, and increasing the richness of tone by augmenting the fullness of the partials, as was the case with the organ pipe. That the partials from the gold flute are actually fuller than from other, is proved by the photographic comparison of wave forms.[37]

Scientists were ultimately dissatisfied with Miller's findings, however, and in the last twenty years investigations have been resumed. John Backus, for instance, reporting in 1964, concluded as the result of his experiments that

> . . . although the walls of a woodwind instrument do vibrate when the instrument is sounded, these vibrations are insufficient to affect the steady-state tone quality either by radiating sound themselves or by altering the form of the internal air-column vibration. Therefore, it appears, that the material from which the instrument is made can be selected for other qualities such as dimensional stability, ease of fabrication, etc. and not because of any tone quality associated with the material.

> Some musicians claim to be able to tell the difference between a

wood and metal clarinet by the way it plays; this point is not within the scope of the above work.[38]

To evaluate this latter aspect, John Coltman set up still more experiments. Using three keyless flutes of silver, copper, and grenadilla wood, all fitted with Delrin plastic heads, he tested the differentiation of tone observed by listeners and players. His experiment was designed to take into account performers' subjective opinions regarding the responsiveness of the instrument, which he realized "brings into question the pertinence of laboratory measurement of steady tones." His conclusion, however, was that "No evidence has been found that experienced listeners or trained players can distinguish between flutes of like mouthpiece material whose only difference is the nature and thickness of the wall material of the body, even when the variation in the material and thickness are very marked." He conceded, however, on the basis of pitch deviations observed with the copper tube, that thermal mass, unlike tone quality or responsiveness, could be a legitimate reason for selecting one material over another.* [39]

Robert J. Baasch, in discussing the various precious metals used in flutemaking, delineated two physical qualities to be considered in making a choice. The first is density (mass divided by volume); Miller, among others, favored a denser material. A second factor is the resonant frequency, that is, the rate at which a vibrating body resonates, which is dependent on the ratio of the modulus of elasticity to the mass of the material; the higher the ratio, the higher the resonant frequency. Baasch writes: "Just which ratio should give the best tone is anybody's guess, although it does seem reasonable to want the flute to respond to the lower frequencies since that is where the musical sounds or frequencies are found—below 15,000 cycles per second." Thus, according to Baasch's figures for density, platinum is preferable; in terms of resonant frequency, gold ranks highest, platinum next, and silver third.[40]

---

*Coltman's experiments were severely criticized by Roger Mather in *Woodwind World* 11 (September 1972): 6–7, on the basis of the experimental flutes' dissimilarity to regular instruments. Moreover, Mather wrote, Coltman did not vary the material of the headjoint, which is the prime determinant of the tone.

As both Backus and Coltman perceived, however, flutists maintain strong, albeit nonscientific, opinions as to materials. Such views, not surprisingly, reflect closely the players' national affiliations; the British and Germans have retained wood well into this century. When silver flutes first appeared in his Bayreuth orchestra, Wagner is reported to have banished them, commenting, "Those are not flutes—they are cannons."[41] In England, the emphasis of orchestral playing on tonal blending makes wood appropriate, for the resultant sound is denser and reedier than that of metal. Americans were surprised to find the flutists of the Royal Philharmonic Orchestra playing wooden instruments during their 1950 United States tour. The French, in contrast, have used silver ever since its adoption by Dorus in 1855.

In the United States, where musical traditions have been formed by immigrants from many areas, the history is much more complex. At the turn of the century, wood flutes were the norm, though Edward Martin Heindl had brought the first metal flute to the United States in 1864 and had used it in the Boston Symphony, which he joined at its founding in 1881. A. G. Badger of New York made the first American silver flute in 1874. Nevertheless, during Wilhelm Gericke's tenure as conductor of the Boston Symphony, he ordered the players to change back to wood flutes.*

The turning point for the United States came in 1905, when Georges Barrère arrived with his coin silver flute, characteristic of the French school. In 1912, William S. Haynes began experiments to determine the relative merits of wood and silver. He eventually ruled in favor of silver as being more durable and having greater carrying power and better tone quality. The 1915

*The dates of Gericke's wood flute mandate and the subsequent return to silver instruments are unclear. Gericke conducted the Boston Symphony from 1884 to 1889 and 1898 to 1906, so it seems unlikely that he would have waited until 1905 to order wooden flutes, as the Haynes 1925 catalog states (p. 41). The same catalog reports that the wooden instruments were used only for the 1905–6 season. Paul Giroux wrote in his 1952 thesis on the history of the flute in the United States (p. 90) that, according to William Kincaid, the symphony used all metal flutes "as early as 1911," but the validity of this statement is also questionable since Giroux was apparently unaware of the Gericke situation.

Haynes catalog carried the following statement: "All honest makers of wood flutes are obliged to admit that the bore of the instrument becomes changed through warping and shrinking. . . ." Furthermore, it read, "The tones of the silver instrument respond much more readily throughout the entire compass," but especially in the third octave. Other objections to wood were originally published in a Boston medical journal and reprinted by the C. G. Conn Company:

> Wood flutes are losing their popularity because of their susceptibility to injury. Unless the wood is well seasoned and kept carefully oiled, it is liable to check in sudden changes of temperature and ruin the instrument. The oil frequently ruins the pads and is also objectionable because of its rancid taste and smell. Another grave reason why wood should not be used for a flute is its liability to become a hot bed of disease.[42]

The most important factor in the adoption of the silver flute, however, was its tone quality; its brilliance became a necessity in the context of the modern symphony orchestra, and the French school preferred it for the delicate control of tone color which it afforded. This attitude was perhaps best summarized by William Kincaid: "In my opinion a wood instrument has a very steady sound although it seems inflexible and stolid. To me a fine metal instrument has a sound which floats and is pliant."[43]

In 1913, more wood than silver flutes were played in the United States. Though the Boston Symphony had changed back to metal by that time, the New York Philharmonic did not switch to silver until 1914. The transition is graphically reflected by the stationery of the Wm. S. Haynes Company. A letter written by Haynes to Dayton Miller on March 18, 1914, pictures a wood flute with silver mechanism on the letterhead; his next letter to Miller, of April 6, 1915, has an embossed silver flute at the top. Haynes ceased making wood flutes in 1917, and by 1935 the *Literary Digest* reported that only five of thirty thousand flutists in the United States used wooden instruments.[44]

Not to be overlooked in the twentieth century are the compromise models such as cocuswood flutes with gold-lined headjoints. The prime example of this genre is the Conn Wonder Metal Flute (Fig. 139), developed by Charles T. Howe of Waterford, Connecticut, around 1895. Originally designed with a metal body and ebonite headjoint, it was also manufactured by Conn entirely in ebonite but with a metal lining. The latter instrument, a 1904 advertisement explained, ". . . is designed especially to supply those who have acquired, inherited or wish to cultivate a prejudice against metal Flutes." Though Conn did not claim any tonal advantages for ebonite, it did promote the substance's visual appeal because of its contrast with the silver- or gold-plated keys. The Wonder Flute won the Grand Prize at the Louisiana Purchase Exhibition in St. Louis in 1904 and was used by many

Fig. 139. HOWE MODEL FLUTE.
C. G. Conn, Elkhart, Indiana (No. 288), 1896.
Boehm system, closed G♯.
Metal, silver-plated ("Conn Wonder Metal").
Key cups and rods gold-plated.
Ebonite head with inset silver lip plate,
tips gold-plated. Ebonite knob for
left-hand knuckle joint. (DCM 1353)

Fig. 140. BOEHM FLUTE.
Gebrüder Mönnig. Markneukirchen, 1937.
Plexiglass with chromium-plated fittings.
Plexiglass plug instead of usual
screw cork. The instrument provides an
interesting visual perspective on the
Boehm mechanism. (DCM 1354)

prominent virtuosi, including J. S. Cox, a soloist with Gilmore's and Sousa's bands.

Today, silver is the usual material for American flutes,* but the use of other substances has also been explored. James Wilkins II, a student of Boehm, claimed that flutes of phosphor bronze were closest to Boehm's ideals, and considered a body of phosphor bronze with a grenadilla headjoint to yield the best tonal results. And in the 1930s, German manufacturer Gebrüder Mönnig, of Markneukirchen, experimented with Plexiglass construction (Fig. 140).

*Powell uses sterling silver (925 parts silver to 75 parts copper). Haynes used sterling until 1949, when the company switched to coin silver (900 parts silver to 100 parts copper).

In 1903, Henri-Émile Ehrmann took out a French patent for aluminum flutes, which, he claimed, afforded not only great economy, but also succeeded in uniting the sonority of metal flutes with the lightness of wood flutes. In wooden instruments, he explained, the depth of the holes is injurious to the sound. By using aluminum, the internal edges of the holes are joined to the internal walls by a curvature in the metal; moreover, the thickness of the tube was equivalent to that of a wooden flute. Finally, Ehrmann claimed, aluminum permitted the construction of an embouchure integral with the headjoint.

In 1913, William S. Haynes also experimented with aluminum tubes, which he patented the following year. He claimed that "aluminum makes an ideal instrument as far as tone and ease of blowing are concerned," but admitted its impracticability due to the tendency of moisture in the tube to form "salts" which ate into the tube.[45]

Of the so-called precious metals, gold is the most common in flutemaking. Louis Lot built such an instrument, now played by Jean-Pierre Rampal, in 1869. Rudall, Rose & Carte also made gold flutes at that time, but Montague S. George, director of that company, reported that they were not particularly popular with professionals. Two gold flutes made in 1896 by the John C. Haynes Company of Boston enjoyed quite a favorable reception. One customer, Hugo Wittgenstein of the Metropolitan Opera Orchestra, made the revealing comment that "The tone comes as near like that of a wooden instrument as is possible." The other customer, Henry Jaeger, solo flutist of the U.S. Marine Band and several Washington, D.C. theaters, wrote that "It has all the excellent points to be desired on any flute. The tone is rich, brilliant and mellow, surpassing in this respect even the best wooden flutes."[46]

The Wm. S. Haynes Company made its first gold flute in 1914, but finding the 18-karat gold of that instrument to be too soft, the company subsequently used 14-karat gold. Haynes gold flutes have been played by Georges Laurent of the Boston Symphony, John Kibburz of the St. Louis Symphony, Georges Barrère, and Jean-Pierre Rampal. Their very desirable qualities are considered to be density, affording great resonance, "mellow and golden" tone, and visual appeal. In comparison to silver, Dayton Miller decided in 1909, "The gold flute is, beyond all doubt, distinctly superior; its tone may be described as full, rich, less shrill when sounded loudly, and more liquid. . . ."[47] Soloist Elaine Shaffer preferred a gold flute because "it can take more—a silver flute has a limit."[48] In recent years, Haynes has made about ten gold flutes per year. In its 1975 catalog, however, Powell Flutes advised customers that "Due to the enormous increases in the price of gold, we no longer consider it practical to make solid gold instruments. In recent years, we have made several flutes with 14K gold bodies and silver mechanism, and now recommend this as a viable alternative to the solid gold flute."

The other precious metal used in flutemaking is platinum, a tin-white, malleable metal with a density of 21.45. Because of its softness, it is often alloyed with iridium (density 22.0 grams per cubic centimeter). Platinum flutes are frequently fitted with silver keys because the heaviness of an all-platinum flute makes it difficult to hold. As a result of his 1909 experiments, Dayton Miller outlined the optimum requirements for a flute tube: "The walls must be thin, soft and flexible, and be made relatively massive by increasing the density of the material. A tube of pure platinum would best fulfill these conditions."[49] Rudall, Carte first applied the qualities of platinum to lining cocuswood headjoints; in 1933, the company made its first all-platinum flute for a wealthy amateur. It was tested by such musical luminaries as Robert Murchie, professor at the Royal College of Music, "who said it was the best instrument he had [ever] played on." Perhaps the best publicized platinum flute was made by the Wm. S. Haynes Company in 1935 for Georges Barrère, and was debuted in the Bach *Suite in B Minor* at a Chautauqua Symphony concert on July 28, 1935. Barrère subjected his platinum flute to electronic testing at the Bell Telephone Laboratories and found that, in the low register, the odd harmonics were richer, while in the middle register, odd and even harmonics were equally rich. Barrère's testimony to the virtues of his new instrument was published by Haynes in November 1935 in connection with a New York demonstration.

I find that the platinum flute has great brilliancy in the high register, beautiful mellowness in the medium range and rich fullness in the lower notes. These qualities are very natural in the instrument without any change in the flute tone. In each register there is a somewhat higher "speaking quality" which enables the player better to legato and obtain prompter response in long intervals.

Because the metal holds its temperature steadily, I can depend upon keeping the same warmth in the column of air, thus insuring a perfect, even pitch through the performance of long selections in any auditorium.

Perhaps the most important factor, however, is that both the quality and the volume of tone are better. Such a double advantage has been practically unavailable before, since improvement in volume has meant sacrifice of quality and vice versa.[50]

Donald Peck's experimentation with flute materials is indicative of the interest of many contemporary flutists in materials. Peck had played a platinum flute for ten years when Chicago's Orchestra Hall was remodeled. The change in acoustics led him to seek a tone that was less dark, with "more glamour." He began by using a palladium headjoint, later combining a platinum body, a platinum headjoint with gold chimney wall, and a silver footjoint.[51] Currently, Peck is playing an all-silver flute. Bickford Brannen, formerly of Powell Flutes, which made Peck's instruments, commented, "I couldn't tell the difference between Peck playing a gold, platinum, or silver flute, but he can." Thus ultimately, at the professional level it is the player, not the scientist, who must be the judge of materials.

MANUFACTURING TECHNIQUES

The primary motivation for experimentation with the materials of flute construction was a concern for tone quality and projection, but such investigation has also exerted an important, albeit indirect, influence on the development of new manufacturing techniques. This effect is epitomized by the patent issued to William S. Haynes in 1914 for aluminum tubes, which, in turn, necessitated the construction of tone holes integral with the tube.

The technique of drawing tone holes directly from the flute tube had first been executed in 1898 by George W. Haynes, the patentee's brother, on a silver instrument (Fig. 141). The impracticability of soldering aluminum now made the procedure a necessity rather than an option. Previously, flanges for the tone holes had been cut to the proper length and individually wired to the side of the tube. A hole was then cut through the tube and the inner edges refined. Such a technique had several inherent perils, however, for the flange could slip without the craftsman's knowledge, and, once attached, the naturally soft lead solder could be affected by acid from the player's saliva or manual perspiration, thereby causing leakage. The immediate advantage of integral tone holes, because of their simplicity, was to increase production. Additionally, Haynes claimed, because the tube and flanges were of substantially equal thickness, whereas soldered flanges were five times thicker than the body metal, the resultant tone quality would be improved. The procedure was later refined by rolling the tone hole edges to decrease wear on the pads.

Fig. 141. INTEGRAL (DRAWN) TONE HOLES.
Alto flute in F. George W. Haynes, Los Angeles, 1898.
Tube made of Mexican silver dollars. According to Haynes, this was the first flute with drawn tone holes. (DCM 118)

Haynes's landmark patent was especially significant because it foreshadowed the enormous amount of research by twentieth century manufacturers and players into the construction of tone holes and pads. Twenty years later, Haynes himself experimented with curved keys in order to eliminate the space that the conventional tone hole leaves in the socket. The new tone holes were drawn and rolled, as before, but the sockets, instead of being flat on top, were rolled so as to follow the curve of the bore. The key cups and pads were also curved. Haynes found, however, that curved keys were impractical not only from the manufacturing standpoint, due to the extra time needed to seat the pads, but also because greater finger pressure was necessary to ensure adequate hole coverage.

Since 1928, the vast majority of American flute patents— twelve in fifty years—have covered the mounting of keys and pads. Some of these patents, such as the one issued to Harry Dytch in 1930 for sponge rubber pads, are also concerned with the use of new, synthetic materials. But most importantly, all are symptomatic of the modern aim of efficiency of both manufacture and instrumental performance.

PUBLIC SCHOOL MUSIC

A key factor in twentieth century musical life has been the role of public music education. Before the turn of the century, public school music had been synonymous with vocal music, but in the first decade of the twentieth century, several high-school orchestras were organized, albeit with rather miscellaneous instrumentation. The first school bands were started just before World War I, partially as a result of increasing athletic interest. The band movement's growth was indicated in the following years by the founding of several major music camps and the organization of the first contest.

Along with football games, instrumental music carried over into higher education. In the last decade of the nineteenth century, several universities in the South and Midwest formed orchestras. The University of Kansas announced the first flute major in 1891; in 1909 the University of Indiana offered lessons in reed, wood, and string instruments and Notre Dame announced orchestral and band training. In England, the demand for inexpen-

Fig. 142. AMAN MODEL FLUTE. Frank Aman & Co., Chicago, 1917.
Boehm system, open G♯. Silver-plated brass tube. Conical bore. (DCM 76)

sive instruments for school use came somewhat later, with the
passage of the Education Act in 1945.

The resultant growth of the flutist population has also had a
great effect on instrument construction, giving rise to the "student flute," which can be produced with greater efficiency and at
less expense than professional grade handmade models.

One of the earliest examples of this genre was the flute manufactured by Frank Aman & Co. of Chicago around the time of the
First World War (Fig. 142). Aman was obviously a better businessman than linguist when he wrote,

> [W]e intent to introduce this Flute in particular to amateurs who as
> I am informed are not verry much in favor of paying the enormous
> price for Flutes of Reputation.
>
> I was induced by many Teachers of Chicago Schools of Music
> and private Tuitors to make up some Flute that would be within the
> reach of poor pupils. I decided to improve the conical bore Flute to
> a greater extent in the lower register, and intonation in general,
> keeping in view to simplify the mechanism as to reduce the cost of
> making, and at the same time preserve the technic of the Boehm
> fingering, to enable a student of flute to take up a higher grade in-
> strument without a handicap as to applied technic or change of
> finger position.

In 1928, Carl Fischer, Inc. of New York advertised as the
newest item in the company's flute line "Scholastic Boehm System Flutes." Made of nickel silver, these instruments were "the
ideal instrument[s] for School Bands and other organizations of
similar character." Similarly, a contemporary catalog of Sherman,
Clay & Co. listed "American Perfection" and "Boston Wonder"
flutes at a considerably lower price than the top-of-the-line Wm.
S. Haynes instruments. "The saving is on the finish," the catalog

explained; although nickel silver produced a more brilliant tone than did sterling, the former material was "especially fine for use in band, or for work that does not call for the last word in refinement of tone."

A mechanically simple form of the student flute was proposed by the W. T. Armstrong Company in 1947. This instrument maintained all the essential features of the Boehm flute, but eliminated the c¹ and c¹♯ keys, trill keys, right hand B♭ lever, and the movable headjoint cork. It had only two joints, and was calibrated to assist the player in lining up the flute.[52]

Another instrument designed specifically for school use is the DeFord Marching Flute, introduced by the E. L. DeFord Company in July 1972. It is provided with a second, curved headjoint, reminiscent of the patents of Pfaff (1857), Wünnenburg (1889), and Guenther (1891), so that the flute can be held vertically in front of the player. It embodies no acoustical change from the regular Boehm model; the only addition is a clarinet-type thumb rest. Its attributes include comfort during marching band use and simplicity for clarinet doublers.

The identical headjoint was patented in France in 1926 by Alcide Allirol, who noted the additional advantage, during marching use, of avoiding the cumbersome underarm lyre to hold the player's music; the clip-on lyre used on clarinets, trumpets, and the like could easily be applied to the altered vertical flute.

One feature unique to student flutes is the presence of adjusting screws on the mechanism, which are necessary because of the rough treatment student instruments often must endure. Anywhere from two to seven such screws may be provided. Another accommodation to hard wear is the H. & A. Selmer Company's use of patented "Adjusta-Pads." These pads are made of synthetic material in order to avoid swelling, compression, or drying; they are center-mounted on tiny swivels so that they will seat properly even when the mechanism is out of regulation.

The majority of student instruments have been made with covered or plateau keys because of the small size of young players' hands. Recently, however, educators have looked more favorably on the open holes as promoting proper finger position, and manufacturers such as Armstrong, DeFord, Gemeinhardt, and Selmer now offer both French and plateau models.

The most distinctive aspect of student flutes is their materials, which are chosen primarily for their durability and low cost. Most are plated tubes of yellow brass (70 percent copper, 30 percent zinc); some are nickel silver, also called German silver, a similar alloy which includes ten to twenty percent nickel. Plating is either of nickel or silver. Nickel, which is harder, shinier, and more durable, is more resistant to corrosion, but its slipperiness may make it difficult to handle. Silver plating, on the other hand, tends to impart a more mellow sound, though it can tarnish easily. In general, plated instruments have a brighter timbre than do all-silver ones since the number of overtones is greater, but the result may be an unpleasantly rough or shrill sound. Moreover, the tubing may be unusually heavy to avoid mechanical damage, thus resulting in a "stiff" sound. Finally, the plating may wear through within a few years of purchase. All of these factors make plated flutes impractical for professionals, but eminently desirable for young students who will own them for a relatively short time and may not give the flute optimum care.

MUSICAL IMPLICATIONS

The standardization of the flute mechanism during the twentieth century has had the immediate effect of improving the quality both of instruments and of performance. Because manufacturers have not spent their time designing new fingering systems and have concentrated instead on the perfection of the existing Boehm system, instruments have been made more efficient and reliable. In turn, performers have increasingly been relieved from mechanical concerns and have turned their attention to tonal aspects of performance.

Moreover, the Boehm flute has musically proven itself in the twentieth century. Its first task, of course, was to simplify the execution of preexistent music. With that goal accomplished, the Boehm flute provided the flexibility requisite for an expanded mechanical and timbral technique. The fingering facilities are obvious, and composers have responded with increasingly more difficult works. Expansion of range has allowed composers to effect greater registral contrasts, a trend begun in the late nineteenth century. Milhaud took the flute up to $g^{4}\sharp$ in his Second Symphony, while Bartók, Stravinsky, and many others scored low bs.

Another technical possibility provided by the Boehm flute is a multiplicity of alternate fingerings for certain difficult passages, particularly in the upper register. Though these are often labeled "fake fingerings," they are considered legitimate by most contemporary flutists, especially those of the Kincaid "school." Some alternate fingerings fall into the category of harmonic fingerings; the note an octave or a twelfth below is overblown, sometimes with half-holing for venting. Finally, the immediate response of Boehm flutes, particularly those of metal construction, facilitates both subtle and extreme gradations of dynamics and tone color. To this end, the harmonics which so greatly facilitate upper register fingerings have been given inherent compositional status. One of the earliest examples occurs in Ravel's *Daphnis et Chloé*, where the harmonics are notated, as is the custom, with small circles above the notes. Another notation, "flag.," for flageolet or whistle tone, is used by Stravinsky in his *Sacre du Printemps*.

One of the most interesting forms of timbral sophistication is the specification of articulation, of which the best known and most important new type is *Flatterzunge* or flutter-tonguing, a special tremolo executed by rolling or trilling the tongue. Although this procedure is also designated for other instruments, the absence of a reed makes it more practical on the flute than on any other instrument. The earliest examples are found in the works of Strauss and Mahler; other notable passages occur in Ravel's *La Valse* and Schoenberg's *Pierrot Lunaire*. Walter Piston, in his classic orchestration textbook, described the technique, when used in a rapid chromatic scale, as Ravel does, as having "a certain picturesque quality."[53]

Indeed, as Gardner Read pointed out in his *Thesaurus of Orchestral Devices*, the majority of coloristic techniques have been used in pieces of impressionistic or programmatic character.[54] Since Read wrote that in 1953, however, these devices have evolved from the role of highlighting orchestral texture to serving as self-sufficient elements of solo composition. This is especially evident in works for unaccompanied flute. Moreover, the flute has now exceeded the other wind instruments in quantity and quality of solo music as a result of its technical versatility and particularly its adaptability to the special requirements of the avant-garde.

In short, twentieth century manufacturers of the Boehm flute, by making the technical essentials of performance thoroughly reliable, have allowed flutists to turn their attention to more sophisticated aspects of tone production such as articulation, timbral subtleties, and improvisatory decisions. In turn, composers such as Hindemith, Debussy, and Ibert have clearly subordinated digital display to the exploitation of the flute's unique timbre. No longer dependent on transcriptions of the violin or vocal literature, the flute has come into its own in the twentieth century; its mechanical perfection has earned it its own repertoire.

Notes]

1. *The Flutist* 1 (1920): 42.

2. Horniman Museum, *Wind Instruments of European Art Music*, ed. E. A. K. Ridley (London: Inner London Education Authority, 1974), p. 33.

3. Carl Fischer, Inc., *Something About Flutes* (New York, [1928]), p. 8.

4. Liz Roman Gallese, "Music Makers: Serious Flute Players Insist Two Companies Are Most Noteworthy," *The Wall Street Journal*, February 1, 1977, pp. 1, 34.

5. F[rançois] Borne and Djalma Julliot, *Notice Concernant les Améliorations apportées à la Flûte de Théobald Boehm* (Pacy-sur-Eure: Imprimerie E. Grateau, 1903), p. 31.

6. Ibid., pp. 41, 47, 49, 52.

7. Ibid., p. 61.

8. Ibid., p. 67.

9. Ibid., p. 65.

10. Ibid., p. 66.

11. Ibid., p. 72.

12. Clement Masson, successeur de D. Julliot, *Manufacture de Flûtes Système Boehm à Perce Cylindrique en Metal* (Paris: post-1898), p. 29.

13. Borne and Julliot, pp. 63–64.

14. Dayton C. Miller, Accession List of Flutes in the Dayton C. Miller Collection, MS, IV, no. 1089.

15. Alexander Murray, "The Murray Flute," *American Musical Instrument Society Newsletter* 1, no. 3 (1972): 6.

16. Walfrid Kujala, "The Murray Flute," *The Instrumentalist* 27, no. 4 (1972): 27. Hereafter cited as Kujala, "Murray Flute."

17. Murray, pp. 6–7.

18. Kujala, "Murray Flute," pp. 28–29.

19. Philip Bate, *The Flute* (New York: W. W. Norton & Co., 1969), p. 151.

20. Philip Bate, "The Alex Murray Flute," *Galpin Society Journal* 26 (1973): 52–53.

21. Robert J. Baasch, "The Murray Flute An Improvement?" *Music Journal* 31, no. 4 (1973): 18–19, 22.

22. Walfrid Kujala, "The Murray Flurry," *Music Journal* 31, no. 7 (1973): 73–74.

23. Thomas Howell, *The Avant-Garde Flute: A Handbook for Composers and Flutists* (Berkeley: University of California Press, 1974), p. 4.

24. Gage-Anderson Co., *The Gage Articulated B-F Sharp Device* (Wilkes-Barre, Pa., n.d.), pp. 2–3.

25. Anthony Baines, *Woodwind Instruments and Their History* (New York: W. W. Norton & Co., 1962), p. 67.

26. Emil Eck, "The Open Hole Flute," *The Instrumentalist* 13, no. 4 (1958): 39.

27. Richard Cameron, "The Flute—Its Story and Practice," *Etude Music Magazine* 49 (October 1931): 708.

28. Nicholas Alberti, *N. Alberti's Any Pitch and Transposing C and D-flat Flute* (Chicago, n.d.), p. 6.

29. Roger S. Stevens, *Artistic Flute Technique and Study,* ed. Ruth N. Zwissler (Hollywood, Calif.: Highland Music Co., 1967), p. 26.

30. John W. Coltman, "The Intonation of Antique and Modern Flutes," Part I, *The Instrumentalist* 29, no. 5 (1974): 55.

31. J. M. Thomson, "A New Look for the Flute," *Canon* 12, no. 7 (1959): 265–66.

32. Raoul Fajardo, "Tone Properties of the Flute Head Joint," Part I, *The Instrumentalist* 27, no. 2 (1973): 49.

33. Ibid., Part II, *The Instrumentalist* 27, no. 3 (1973): 45–46, 49.

34. John Backus, "Effect of Wall Material on the Steady-State Tone Quality of Woodwind Instruments," *Journal of the Acoustical Society of America* 36 (1964): 1881.

35. Dayton C. Miller, "The Influence of the Material of Wind-Instruments

on the Tone Quality," *Science*, n.s. 29, no. 735 (1909): 164–67. Hereafter cited as Miller, "Influence."

36. Dayton C. Miller, *The Science of Musical Sounds* (New York: Macmillan Co., 1916), pp. 180–82.

37. Miller, "Influence," p. 170.

38. Backus, p. 1887.

39. John W. Coltman, "Effect of Material on Flute Tone Quality," *Journal of the Acoustical Society of America* 49 (1971): 520.

40. Robert J. Baasch, "The Precious Metal Flutes," *Woodwind World* 4, no. 2 (1961): 5–6.

41. H. W. Schwartz, *The Story of Musical Instruments* (Garden City, N.Y.: Doubleday, Doran & Co., 1938), p. 83.

42. C. G. Conn, *C. G. Conn's Flute and Piccolo Players' Handy Pocket Book of Reference* (Elkhart, Ind., ca. 1903), p. 3.

43. Paul Henry Giroux, "The History of the Flute and Its Music in the United States" (M.A. thesis, School of Music, University of Washington, 1952), p. 105.

44. "Flutes: From Reed to Platinum," *Literary Digest* 120, no. 22 (1935): 15.

45. Wm. S. Haynes Co., *Modern Flute Construction* (Boston, ca. 1915–16), p. 15.

46. John C. Haynes Co., *A Notable Achievement in Flute-Making at the "Bay State" Factory* (Boston, ca. 1897): pp. 9, 7.

47. Miller, "Influence," p. 170.

48. "14-Carat Flute," *Newsweek*, December 3, 1962, p. 64.

49. Miller, "Influence," p. 170.

50. *The Platinum Flute and Georges Barrère* (New York: [Wm. S. Haynes Co.], 1935), p. 3.

51. William Barry Furlong, *Season with Solti* (New York: Macmillan Co., 1974), p. 257.

52. "That New Flute," *The Instrumentalist* 2, no. 2 (1947): 2.

53. Walter Piston, *Orchestration* (New York: W. W. Norton & Co., 1955), p. 124.

54. Gardner Read, *Thesaurus of Orchestral Devices* (New York: Putnam Publishing Corp., 1953), p. ix.

CHAPTER V

The Avant-Garde Flute

The history of the woodwind instruments, E. A. K. Ridley has observed, divides itself rather neatly into alternating centuries of development and stability with regard to organological structure. In the seventeenth century, Ridley writes, instrument makers met the compositional demand for differentiation of instrumental timbre and expanded concepts of range and dynamics. During most of the eighteenth century, in contrast, the emphasis was on music rather than on construction. By the end of that century, the addition of chromatic keywork began to reflect the increasing demands being made on it by composers and consequently by performers. Nineteenth century makers responded with a multitude of new models, and as an economic necessity, devoted much of their time to public relations; the players, except for those who were themselves flutemakers, afforded the manufacturers little assistance. In the twentieth century, the trend has again been toward mechanical standardization; as in the eighteenth century, players have attempted to improve their skills using existing instruments.[1] The enthusiastic attitude of contemporary composers toward the flute is even more significant, however, for the revolution of rising technical expectations which characterizes the avant-garde repertoire is perhaps the ultimate testimony to the capabilities of the Boehm flute.

Prior to the twentieth century, the goal of both instrument makers and players was the attainment of timbral homogeneity; the aim was not to create new sounds for each instrument, but merely to satisfy existing musical requirements of pitch, dynamic differentiation, and the like. Such ideals sufficed when the criteria of musical composition were purity and "beauty" of sound, but this concept is no longer fully applicable in the twentieth century. The new compositional framework, an extension of Schoenberg's "melody of tone colors," makes three new demands on the flute: the production of monophonic sounds with varying timbres, the production of smaller intervals than those of the tempered chromatic scale, and the production of polyphony by a single instrument.[2]

There is some historical precedent, however, for many of these new techniques. "Special effects," such as finger vibration, harmonics, and the famous "glide," were a trademark of Charles Nicholson's performance in the early nineteenth century. Even multiphonics were reported well before the age of the avant-garde, albeit as a physical feat rather than as a musical technique. What is important, however, is not merely to recognize the prior existence of such skills and devices, but also to analyze their musical function in historical perspective. Vibrato is perhaps the prime example; developed by the French school of Taffanel et al. as a means of enhancing the flute tone, it has been described as "Superficial to the tone itself, the frosting on the cake [that] nevertheless adds a lyrical quality and an element of freedom to the flow of sound."[3] The use of vibrato as an auxiliary expressive resource, however, was only a beginning, for vibrato, like so many other coloring techniques, was to become an integral element not only of performance, but also of composition.

In the largest sense, then, tone color has evolved, in the last century and a half, from a subordinate component of the compositional process to an influence upon it. The progress of symphonic composers in this regard is reflected in a comprehensive manner by Gardner Read's *Thesaurus of Orchestral Devices*, in which the author writes, "Orchestrating is not just arranging music for the orchestra; it is composing for the instruments. It is thinking first and foremost in terms of instrumental color, balance, and sonority. . . ."[4]

The decline of timbral homogeneity implied by the blossoming of orchestration has been accompanied by a parallel deemphasis of regularity and continuity in other aspects of musical composition. From a rhythmic perspective, the regular, symmetrical meter system has lost its universality; proportional notation, with its irregular placement of accents, has become an option. Melodically, intervals have become larger, and like rhythms, unsequenced. Microtones and pitches below the "normal" range have been discovered and new means have been explored to reach them. Dynamics, similarly, tend to be characterized not by continuity of volume or a process of change, but by frequent and drastic contrasts that are emphasized by timbral effects including articulation. In short, all musical elements join to extend the range of available tone colors; melody, harmony, rhythm, and dynamics, rather than maintaining their traditionally equal or superior status in relation to tone color, have, in their individual ways, become subordinate to it.

This development has involved a total rethinking of the capabilities of the flute, a change in attitude that includes the recognition that traditional conceptions, while valid, are restricted. The new flute techniques that prove the shortsightedness of those conceptions (or misconceptions) may be organized into six large categories: (1) alteration of pitch and timbre by fingering, (2) alteration of pitch and timbre by embouchure and breath control, (3) percussive effects, (4) noise effects, (5) extension of the lower range, and (6) multiphonics.

ALTERATION OF PITCH AND TIMBRE BY FINGERING

Thomas Howell, in his treatise on the avant-garde flute, has divided this category into five subdivisions, which this chapter will follow: simple harmonics, complex reinforced harmonics, inflected pitches, weak tones, and strong fingerings.[5]

Harmonics have long been recognized as a crucial acoustical component of a musical instrument's tone. Bernard Hague, for instance, attributed the more brilliant and reedy tone of the Boehm flute, as compared to the simple system conical flute, to the richer concentration of harmonics in its sound. Anthony Baines echoes the point: "Tone-colour, or tone-quality, is almost entirely due to the proportionate strength and number of the component harmonics."[6] Teachers, similarly, have recognized that even in traditional fluteplaying, the performer has some control over the production of harmonics and can modify the tone accordingly. John Krell, for instance, reflecting the philosophy of William Kincaid, has written:

> However appropriate it may be, [the] fundamental is a pure tone; as such, it can be bland and colorless. . . . While the flute is relatively deficient in harmonics when compared to the clarinet or oboe, it is still quite possible, particularly in the lower two registers, to manipulate the lips, air pressure, and directions of air so as to add (or subtract) a considerable complex of overtones with their interacting resultant, summation, and difference tones.[7]

The composers of the avant-garde have extended this concept to include the conscious separation of the harmonics by the player so that the upper partials, rather than forming a component part of the fundamental tone, are heard as distinct tones whose quality makes them timbral alternatives to the regular fingering for their respective notes. Natural or simple harmonics are produced by overblowing the regular fingerings from b to d^2#. It will be noticed, however, that the octave harmonics for the pitches from e^1 to c^2#, though technically harmonics, do not behave as such in terms of pitch and intonation due to the construction of the bore; in other words, the octave harmonics of e^1 through c^2# are the regular fingerings for e^2 through c^3#. All other octave harmonics will sound slightly flat because only the lowest note of the instrument is perfectly vented; for all other notes, the partials are flattened in relation to the fundamental. Except for a^2 and f^2 (and f^2# on flutes with C footjoints), there are as many as five alternative timbres, all readily differentiable from the regular fingerings, which may be obtained through the use of natural harmonic fingerings. This diversity of timbre is possible because the variant fingerings of the fundamental affect the relative strengths of each of the harmonics or partials.

A frequent by-product of natural harmonic fingerings is residual tones, which consist of a noiselike fundamental with several weak upper partials. Robert Dick suggests that these residuals may be exploited as polyphonic effects. They are easily produced, can be played at any dynamic level, and blend well with whisper tones.[8]

Each level of harmonics has its own timbral characteristics. Octave harmonics generally have a "closed" timbre; that is, they have few additional overtones, and they speak rather slowly. Third partials, those harmonics a perfect twelfth above the fundamental, range from f^2♯ (or g^2 on flutes with C footjoints) to a^3. Above c^3♯, third partials become increasingly flat; g^3, for example, is almost fifty cents flat and cannot be raised by manipulation of the embouchure. Others of the twelfths are certainly usable, but appear breathy when the pitch is sufficiently adjusted. In all cases, the fundamental is heard with the twelfth.

For notes above the twelfth (the fourth and higher partials), the playing resistance of the flute is so great that simple harmonics above a^3 or b^3 are, in the estimation of Thomas Howell, "virtually impossible." The only exceptions are the high partials of b (or c^1 with a C foot), which may be executed without difficulty; in this case, b^3 or c^4♯ (or b^3♭ or c^4 with a C foot) may be obtained. Upper partials of fundamentals close to c^1 are fairly reliable in intonation, but, Howell notes, the intervals are related to the fundamental by just, rather than by tempered, intonation. Thus the fifth partial (seventeenth from the fundamental) and the seventh partial (twenty-first from the fundamental) will be flat in twelve-tone temperament, while the third and sixth partials (twelfth and nineteenth from the fundamental) will be slightly sharp. Finally, the upper partials of those fundamentals that use short tubing, the notes e^1 and above, are noticeably flat.

Complex harmonics are defined by Howell as fingerings that support a common harmonic of two or more fundamentals. For example, the third octave fingerings for d^3♯ through g^3♯ are normally played as fifteenths, or fourth partials, of the fundamentals d^1♯ to g^1♯. However, those fundamentals are vented by the same hole that vents the pitch a twelfth below the tone produced. Thus

f^3 is fingered as f^1, but the highest hole that vents b^1b (the twelfth below f^3) is also opened. For notes between $d^3\sharp$ and $g^3\sharp$, inclusive, complex harmonic fingerings yield accurate tempered pitches with normal tonal focus. For all other notes, however, they lend a very bright timbre lacking in normal depth and the pitch is often slightly sharp. This latter characteristic is exploited by using complex harmonics for passages that must be played softly and lightly without going flat.[9] In an interesting historical precedent, Charles Nicholson used sharp-tuned fingerings for a slow legato; these were notated in his scores by stars or crosses.

The third category of pitch and timbre alterations is that of inflected pitches, designed primarily, though not exclusively, for French model flutes. A very simple form of inflected pitch is the technique of key vibrato, another device used by Nicholson, which effects very slight changes in pitch by means of rapid alternations between standard and nonstandard fingerings, the latter including both natural and complex harmonics. Large pitch changes by means of key vibrato are better categorized as quarter-tone trills; still larger pitch differentials are standard trills and require no special explanation.[10] A related effect is that of "random" effects by rapid key movement; for instance, wiggling the first, second, and third fingers of the right hand will result in random alternations of G, F♯, F, E, and D♯ in the first octave. These pitches may in turn be overblown into their own harmonics for additional timbral variation.[11]

The most important form of inflected pitches is the quarter-tone scale, a topic which has perhaps evoked more argument with regard to its adaptability to the flute than any other. In the early part of this century, the very suggestion of quarter-tone production was regarded as nothing short of ridiculous; Haydn Matthews made the following assertion in a 1922 issue of *The Flutist:*

> I do not think you need ever worry about the quarter-tone scale becoming popular. The great majority of our public is so ignorant in matters musical that it is unable to say when one is playing in tune or out of tune, with our present tone system. How then could untrained ears note such fine shakes of pitch as fractions of quarter-tones?

The flute can never be made practical to quarter-tone use. I rarely say 'It can't be done,' but a quarter-tone flute seems an impossibility. Take all of the keys off the instrument and see if there is room for more holes. Use under side? How would you transmit power to the keys? Impossible.[12]

As Matthews suggested, the production of quarter tones by structural modification of the flute is not practical, but contemporary flutists have developed them by means of a methodical study, often computer-assisted, of all available fingering combinations. To the traditionally trained flutist, such fingerings are not easy; indeed, they may be rather a strain in extended passages.

In general, however, flutists and composers have succeeded in using the standard Boehm flute for such techniques. Bruno Bartolozzi provides a quarter-tone scale from d¹ to c³♯♯ that is complete except for f¹♯♯, g¹♯♯ , and a¹♯♯ , whose omission he attributes to the coupling of hole covers.* He suggests a need for structural modification of the instrument to produce those notes. All fingerings provided by Bartolozzi may, according to the author, be executed on a plateau model flute.[13] Howell, however, judges most of Bartolozzi's fingerings to be such poor approximations as to render them useless; it is not possible, says Howell, to obtain a full set of quarter tones with the plateau system. The French model provides many more fingerings that are also of better quality in terms of pitch, but the requisite finger sliding (a practice that Boehm sought to eliminate) renders execution both difficult and unsafe.[14] Moreover, Howell's own quarter-tone scale, which ranges from b to f⁴♯, omits the following eight quarter-tone pitches as unplayable on the flute: b♯, c¹♯, d¹♭, d¹♯, b¹♭, d²♯, e⁴♭, and f⁴♯.[15] Robert Dick, however, provides full quarter-tone scales from d¹ to e⁴ for both closed and open hole flutes. The only qualification he makes is that the first five tones (d¹♯, e¹d, e¹♯, f¹♯, and g¹♯) require the low B key to be closed; with a C foot, these tones will be sharp and must be lipped down.[16]

Microtones are often combined to form microtonal segments,

*The following notation is used for the quarter-tone scale: c† is the quarter tone between c and c♯. c♯♯ is the quarter tone between c♯ and d. d d and d♭ are equivalent to c♯♯ . See Appendix II for a complete listing of avant-garde notations.

which are short scalar passages produced by leaving one upper hole open and fingering downward chromatically as if playing a regular chromatic scale. The resultant intervals may be as small as a thirty-second tone. Dick provides two charts for microtonal segments, one for French model flutes, the other for all flutes. A full microtonal scale, composed of microtonal segments, is unevenly spaced due to the system of linked keys and hole covers that characterizes the Boehm flute. For example, the G key is linked to the duplicate G♯ hole cover and the F key closes both the F♯ hole and the G♮ hole cover; thus the G♯ hole cannot be closed without closing the A key, and the G key cannot remain open when the F♯ hole is closed. Such complications preclude a large number of microtonal fingerings. Because of such complications, Howell suggests that the Boehm flute, particularly the French model, is better adapted to 31-tone equal temperament than to quarter tones within 12-tone temperament.[17]

An extension of microtonal segments is the glissando, a technique which actually dates from the early nineteenth century, when the holes of the old flute were covered directly by the fingers. The "glide," as the technique was then called, was a portamento made by gradually sliding the fingers off the holes, thereby producing quarter tones and smaller intervals. It was used, according to Fitzgibbon, "to express great tenderness or pity, or anguish or despair." But Fitzgibbon reflected the rising critical standards of the late nineteenth and early twentieth centuries in deploring the use of the glide as a mere gimmick of the virtuosi: "It is now happily impossible," he wrote, "on modern flutes with solid metal 'touches.' "[18]

True glissandi on the Boehm flute are possible, for obvious reasons, only on the French model. They are accomplished by successively sliding the fingers off the holes of the open keys and then lifting the rims of the keys. Howell cites possible glissandi from d^1 to b^1b, using fundamentals; from d^2 to b^2b, using second partials; and from b^2b to f^3, using third partials. Above f^3, he says, short slides are possible but "tricky." Fingered glissandi are possible in both ascending and descending passages, but the latter are more difficult.[19]

A second form of glissando is achieved with the headjoint alone, holding it in the left hand and closing the end with the right hand. There are three ways of doing this: (1) placing the end of the headjoint between the thumb and forefinger of the right hand and covering the opening by adding the fingers one at a time; (2) placing the heel of the right hand on the rim of the open end and moving the right hand toward the embouchure; and (3) inserting a finger or cigarlike object such as a soft wood dowel into the end of the tube. Because it takes approximately five seconds to remove the headjoint from the body of the flute, Dick suggests that the performer use a separate headjoint for this technique.[20]

A fourth type of timbral alteration effected by fingering changes is that of "weak tones," also known as "hollow tones" or, colloquially, "funky fingerings." These nonstandard fingerings give a rather empty, nonresonant tone quality; their principal use is to effect a certain continuity of timbre when normal chromatic pitches are played contiguously with multiphonics or timbrally distorted monophonic pitches. Weak tones are available between d^1# and d^3, inclusive.[21]

The opposite timbral alteration is produced by "strong fingerings," of which Howell lists sixteen, designed for unusual projection. With these fingerings, the respective pitches can be played extremely loudly and are therefore especially useful for *sforzandi*. Most of these fingerings produce a flat pitch at normal volume but are in tune when blown forcefully.[22]

ALTERATION OF PITCH AND TIMBRE BY EMBOUCHURE AND BREATH CONTROL

Physiologically speaking, the fingers contribute at most half of the effort necessary for fluteplaying; the remainder is accomplished by the breathing mechanism (lungs and diaphragm) and the organs of the pharyngeal cavity (throat, lips, and tongue). In any case, the fingers perform only a secondary operation upon the airstream created and directed in these two other areas. Indeed, the throat, lips, tongue, and diaphragm are capable of quite sophisticated alteration of pitch and timbre with no assistance from the fingers, the principal variables being breath pressure, which affects the pitch, tonal focus or intensity, and dynamics; and lip position and aperture, which determine the direction of the airstream and consequently the timbre and dynamics of the tone. Effects produced by the breath and lips are supplemented by variation in the angle of the flute, which is determined by jaw and arm as well as lip movement.

The most important variant of pitch and timbre is vibrato, one of the most controversial aspects of traditional performance technique. Early Boehm flutes were played without vibrato; the technique was introduced as a tonal modifier by Taffanel in the late nineteenth century. In fact, Howell states, very few flutes made outside France before World War I are suitable for vibrato production due to minor discrepancies in tone hole size and placement and in the construction of the lip plate; such instruments, he says, are little better for vibrato production than are wood ones. Key vibrato had been known and practiced prior to the Boehm era, but this technique was not suitable on the Boehm flute for traditional music of the time because of the noise element produced by its mechanical interconnections.

In Howell's analysis, modern flute vibrato is an intensity rather than a pitch vibrato; pitch variations tend to remain within a tolerance of five cents and exist only as a by-product of intensity fluctuations. Vibrato serves to emphasize the "brightness" or "darkness" of tone obtained through manipulation of the embouchure. It is a highly variable—some would say erratic—device, very much dependent on the individual performer. It is a largely intuitive technique that can be given only the vague physiological description of regulation of the airstream by the combined action of throat, lips, and diaphragm. Accordingly, it is difficult for a composer to be specific in scoring the effect. Howell warns: "Optimal vibrato production is unique to the particular note, the dynamic, the tone blown, the instrument, and the player. Structural compositional interference with this fragile 'ecology' is asking for trouble, unless much careful study and experimentation is undertaken with the intended performer."

Some composers, however, have specified desired speeds or intensities of vibrato. Roger Reynolds, for instance, in his *Four Etudes* and *Mosaic*, specifies no vibrato (nv), normal vibrato (v), and stressed vibrato (sv). Harley Gaber, in *CHIMYAKU*, uses a sliding scale of 0 to 10. Originally, the numerals denoted the number of pulses per second; later, because of the unpredictability of the player's perception of vibrato in relation to its actual amplitude or frequency, the scale was applied as a relative measurement ranging from no vibrato to maximum intensity.[23] Sheridan Stokes and Richard Condon suggest four notation levels for vibrato: Very Fast (VF), Very Slow (VS), Very Wide (VW), and Very Narrow (VN).[24] Bartolozzi uses a similar scale, but the various degrees are represented graphically by means of straight or wavy lines.[25] Stokes and Condon also mention that forcible vibration of throat and lips produces a sort of growl in the tone, which they notate as *bz*.[26]

Lip oscillation is an extension of vibrato, but it pertains more to pitch than to timbre. It is executed by alternately tensing and relaxing the pressure of the lips or by varying the degree to which the lips cover the embouchure hole. Pitch fluctuations produced by lip oscillation may be as large as a semitone and may be precisely specified as to range.[27] Still another variant of vibrato is labeled by Bartolozzi as *smorzato;* this is a dynamic vibrato produced by movement of the jaw and is most effective in the upper and middle registers.[28]

Whistle or whisper tones, individual notes of the harmonic series of a fundamental, are very high, clear pitches produced by blowing extremely gently across the embouchure hole. Pioneered by William Kincaid as a warm-up exercise for embouchure control, they can be produced by every fingering but are difficult to sustain individually at low dynamic levels. The best whistle tones range from g^3 to b^3; c^4 and above are also good, with the range from a^2 to $f^3\sharp$ next in quality. Below a^2, Howell states, they are "sometimes possible but not worth the effort" because the sound is too weak. Partials of low fundamentals, particularly b, c^1, and $c^1\sharp$, are the easiest to produce. The acoustical reason is clear; the longer air columns of the lower fundamentals yield high partials more easily. Evaluations of the projection capability of whistle tones vary; Howell comments that "Tiny as this sound is, it will nonetheless . . . project through very large halls."[29] Stokes and Condon, in contrast, state that whistle tones are barely audible beyond twenty feet and therefore require electronic amplification; Dick also mentions their lack of projection.[30]

Another timbral element is articulation. Because of the absence of a reed or mouthpiece, flute tone production actually occurs outside the mouth, thereby imparting great oral flexibility to the flutist. In the low register, however, response or "speech" tends to be slow, so that all varieties of attack are less reliable there. In traditional music, the flutist has a choice of single, double, or triple tonguing, generally initiated by the consonants T, T-K, and T-K-T, respectively, or occasionally, in legato passages, by combinations of D and G. Recently, however, articulation has evolved from the exclusive province of the performer to a matter of collaboration between performer and composer. Almost any syllable may be used to articulate a tone; such syllables are generally indicated by the International Phonetic Alphabet, though even this system sometimes proves inadequate. Six of the most common consonants used, as listed by Howell, are: *t*, for normal middle and upper register attacks; *T*, a forceful version of *t*; *d*, actually a voiced *t* that is softer and suitable for low register and quasi-legato use; *h*, a breath attack that may be used easily up to a^3; *p*, for soft attacks on high notes only; and *k*, normally used in alternation with *t* or *d* in double and triple tonguing but also available alone as a less distinct version of *t*.

The most distinctive form of articulation is the *Flatterzunge* or flutter-tongue, which is analogous to the string tremolo. The resultant sound ranges from a slight pulsation similar to vibrato to a loud buzz. Two pronunciations are possible: the Spanish or dental "r," produced by rolling the tip of the tongue on the hard palate, works best with high air pressure in loud or high passages; the French "r" is made by vibration of the uvula against the back of

the tongue and is most effective with low air pressure in soft passages.[31] Flutter-tonguing can profitably be applied in combination
with almost any other avant-garde techniques, including whisper
tones and multiphonics. It is generally notated by means of
slashes through the note stem and *fl.* or *RR* above the notehead, but Dick suggests a more specific graphic notation to represent variations of speed and intensity.[32]

PERCUSSIVE EFFECTS

The increasing attention being paid by composers to woodwind
articulation for rhythmic emphasis is symptomatic of the escalating importance of percussion in twentieth century music. Curt
Sachs views this development as an extension of nineteenth century "thoroughrhythm" structure analogous to the seventeenth
century thoroughbass; the trend is most obvious, he observes, in
the glorification of rhythm in jazz and swing.[33] Interestingly, Robert Dick explains that one of the purposes of his book, *The Other
Flute,* is to enable the flute to participate in musical innovations
not only of the "classical" avant-garde, but also of jazz and rock.[34]

The most widely used percussive technique for the flute is the
key click or key slap. Its origin may be traced to a trick of the
trade that performers have long used to alleviate the slow speech
of the lower octave; by slapping down the keys at the same instant
as the tongue attack, they found that the air column was more
easily activated, thereby making the sound more audible.[35] The
key slap was introduced as a compositional element in 1936 by
Edgard Varèse in *Density 21.5.* It is usually notated by a plus sign
(+) over the notehead. The key slap can also be played alone,
that is, "without air," although, in reality, this procedure necessi-
tates a small amount of air to lend resonance. The primary sound,
however, must be the percussive click. John Heiss, writing in
Perspectives of New Music, suggests that the best method of producing airless key slaps is to finger the desired note and then to
raise and slap the G key. This technique is applicable, however,
only from low B up to G. To obtain pitches an octave below,

Heiss recommends covering the embouchure hole with the curve under the lower lip (between the mouth and chin) and using the same G-key slap. The resultant pitch in this case will sound approximately a major seventh (rather than the expected octave) below the fingered note. Key slaps on fingered pitches above G, which have sounding pitches of ab and above, may be produced by slapping the lowest available key with the right index finger.[36]

Several variations may be made on the key slap. Dick notes that timbral alteration may be obtained by mediating between an open and closed embouchure hole, for which he suggests a graphic U notation to represent the angle of the flute, and specification of the vowel shape that the mouth should assume.[37] Howell recommends closing the embouchure hole with the tongue to produce low register tones. To obtain a louder and more definite pitch, he suggests placing the mouth over the lip hole, blowing air into the flute, and suddenly ramming the tongue into the hole in order to block it completely. Such tongue stops may also be executed without key-slap accompaniment.[38]

A similar device is the tongue click, which may also be executed alone or with a key slap. With the embouchure hole open, it produces residual tones at the lowest two pitches yielded by each fingering. With the hole between the lips, strong resonances are produced approximately a major third to an octave below the fingered pitch; the interval cannot be predicted because of variations in mouth shape.[39] A final percussive technique is key rattling; the keys are not closed as in key vibrato, but are jiggled slightly to produce small metallic noises.

NOISE EFFECTS

Closely related to percussive effects are various types of noise, for which the flute is amazingly well suited. Howell cites two reasons for its "colored noise" capability: the option of an open or closed mouth hole or intermediate gradations, and the short air column and ready access to it from the embouchure.[40]

The first type of colored noise is that of unpitched air sounds, which may be produced either with the lips in the normal position, but with an unfocused airstream, or with the lip plate covered by the lips. In the latter case, blowing forcefully into the mouthpiece, as if to warm up the instrument, results in "breathy, semi-pitched resonances of the flute's tube" that may vary from "short, violent 'shrieks' . . . to very soft, sustained sonorities."[41] Volume, pitch, and timbre are determined by the angle of the embouchure hole, the vowel shape of the mouth, fingering, and breath pressure. Such sounds are frequently referred to as "jet whistles" after the composition of that title by Heitor Villa-Lobos, scored for flute and cello. Covered-embouchure tones may be further modified by inhaling, a procedure that is useful for extending tones of exhaled colored noise.

The second category of colored noise is comprised of those techniques that combine internal and external tone production. One such technique involves whistling through the teeth while producing a normal flute tone; the sound of the whistle is reinforced by the flute tube. More commonly, the player may be required to sing and play simultaneously. This technique was introduced by jazz flutist Herbie Mann and is quite common in jazz and popular music. It is extremely difficult to perform; Howell suggests a very moderate vocal range of c^1 to d^2, which can accommodate both female and male flutists, the latter in falsetto. Unison humming and playing result in good acoustical reinforcement; if the two pitches are slightly different, beats are produced.[42] Speech sounds may also be added to the tone both to articulate and to sustain it; for the latter purpose, this procedure is especially helpful in the lower register.

LOWER RANGE EXTENSION

Avant-garde flute technique not only modifies the instrument's timbre in its normal compass, it also extends the compass. Lower range extension has already been mentioned with respect to key slaps, but this is not its exclusive domain. With normal embouchure and fingering, the lowest tone of the instrument (b or c^1) may be lowered one octave by covering the open end of the tube with a cork or the side of the right knee. The lowest pitch may be lowered to a small degree by paper or metal extenders at the bottom of the foot, or, quite simply, by pulling the headjoint out about an inch and fingering the lowest note.

The most sophisticated means of extending the lower range involves a radical alteration of the embouchure; by pressing the lips into the mouth hole and buzzing them as if playing a trumpet, pitches well below the normal range will result. This technique is an integral compositional element of Patrick Purswell's *It Grew and Grew* and Robert Cantrick's *Three Mimes*. Cantrick describes the tone quality as resembling "a cross between a muted French horn and a clarinet."[43] Howell, however, maintains that the uncertainty of pitch placement that results from the lack of harmonic reinforcement creates a timbre that is "extremely vulgar, not at all unlike a Bronx cheer."[44]

The literature is divided as to the range of buzzing. William Brooks writes in the *Dictionary of Contemporary Music* that buzzing produces a pitch approximately a sixth below the fingered note.[45] Stokes and Condon state that buzzing extends the lower range to c, implying that, with a B footjoint, the interval between the fingered note and resultant buzz is a major seventh.[46] Howell, similarly, says that the interval varies between a major and minor seventh. For open fingerings such as c^2, the interval will be a major seventh; for closed fingerings such as c^1, it will be a minor seventh. For partially open fingerings such as g^1, the interval will be somewhere between the two.[47] Cantrick, however, claims a much larger range. He asserts that, even when using a C footjoint, there is a complete chromatic buzz range from AA to a^{3}b, the only exception being d♭, which can only be played with a B♭ footjoint. Cantrick's own flute, specially designed for such techniques, has a B♭ footjoint and platinum headjoint. Combined with the normal range, which Cantrick designates as c^1 to f^4, the total flute compass is therefore AA to f^4, almost six octaves. In the overlapping range from c^1 to a^{2}b, he notes, an additional timbre is thereby provided.[48] Further advantages of the buzz technique are its capability for an especially powerful fortissimo and its adaptability to jazz effects such as the scoop, smear, and lip glissando.

MULTIPHONICS

Perhaps the most astonishing aspect of avant-garde flute technique is the production of multiphonics. Yet multiple sonorities were known as long ago as the early nineteenth century. In Vienna in about 1810, virtuoso Georg Bayr (1773–1833) reportedly played double notes on the flute, and the effect was so extraordinary that a special commission was appointed to determine the validity of his performance. Rockstro wrote disdainfully that "It will hardly be necessary to inform the flute-playing reader that the effect which created so much surprise was simply the result of playing a moderately soft 'running' or *arpeggio* accompaniment between strong detached notes at some distance either above or below the accompaniment."[49] Rockstro may well have been correct—we will never know—but in 1882 a very reliable source, W. S. Broadwood, published the following account of the performance of a flutist named Koppitz:

> I was present at the Philharmonic rehearsal, and well remember the brilliant and rapid staccato articulation with which the special wonder was ushered in. Presently came a pause; then amid deep silence and breathless expectation, the player emitted three several [*sic*] simultaneous sounds . . . which were greeted by the orchestra and its conductor (Sterndale Bennett) with one vast, irrepressible shout of laughter. When this subsided, the Dutchman had fled.[50]

Similarly, various 1924 issues of *The Flutist* carried accounts of teachers who demonstrated multiphonics to their students, but the technique was considered a mere physical trick that had no musical value.

The contrast with twentieth century multiphonic composition is obvious. Contemporary composers have discovered that the flute is eminently suited to multiphonic production—indeed, better so than the reed instruments. This capability is attributable to its metal construction, which is not as susceptible as wood to changes of temperature and humidity; to the international uniformity of its fingering system;* and to the clear distinction between fundamental and resultant frequencies. As defined by Howell, "A multiphonic fingering is a fingering that generates a group of two or more pitches sounding simultaneously, together with the additive and differential frequencies they generate—some of which may be supported by the air column itself."[51] They are produced by fingerings that, in effect, provide two or more tube lengths for tone production. Consequently, many multiphonics are produced by opening one or both of the trill keys, whose holes are nearest the headjoint, while closing a succession of lower holes; thus the tone may be produced by a single tube length or by two or more tube lengths together. The provision of a third trill key, as on the Murray flute designed for Robert Dick, further extends the possibilities of this technique.

"Double stops" are played by aiming the airstream "between" the two specified tones, a procedure that, like vibrato, is largely intuitive. Triple and quadruple stops are played with a "spread" tone created by a wide lip aperture; by this expedient the airstream may simultaneously be directed both high and low.[52] As a result, many multiphonic sounds are "relatively soft, not sharply focused, and, of necessity, short."[53] Multiphonics are of two basic types: those with fundamental and harmonics of equal volume and those with partials of distinctive timbre and volume.

Because of their large number (Howell lists 1826) and their infrequency in the hitherto standard literature, multiphonics require individual notation for each occurrence. In its simplest form, this notation may be merely the provision of a conventional fingering diagram in the margin of the score. The fingering chart given by Robert Dick, however, is much more detailed, for in addition to providing a representational fingering diagram, he gives information on ease of response, starting time, stability, dynamic range, timbre, modulation, residual tone, and class. While his

---

*Even so, Samuel Baron, an experienced performer of the avant-garde repertoire, complains of a "frustrating" lack of uniformity in the way different instruments, and also players, produce multiphonics.

charts are designed primarily for the composer, the additional information is also helpful to the inexperienced player.

Lawrence Singer has recently suggested a new form of multiphonic notation designed to consider multiphonic textures from a "coloristic and numerical point of view." He divides multiphonics into three categories, those with dominating high, medium, and low intensities. They are notated by a

> . . . rectangle with pre-designed color columns of various shades of red and blue indicating light and dark tones respectively. The parts of the color columns not used could be penciled out. The relative scale of intensity for the tones composing the multiphonic would appear longitudinally outside the rectangle but adjacent to the nearest color column. Beginning with number one on the bottom, the intensity range would continue to number six for a top or more if needed. The actual tones of the woodwind multiphonic would appear on a pre-designed pentagram near or within the rectangle.[54]

The usual fingering diagram is placed below the rectangle. From a printing perspective, the use of color seems impractical owing to its cost, but it is conceivable that a slightly simplified version of Singer's system could be devised using cross-hatching, the procedure used by *Woodwind World* for the publication of Singer's article. (See Appendix II, page 239.)

IMPLICATIONS

To date, the majority of avant-garde flute techniques have been used in solo composition. This state of affairs is logical; just as a conscientious ensemble player learns his part alone before rehearsing with the group, so composers often master their craft in a solo medium before applying new skills to ensemble composition. It is possible, therefore, that the coming years will see an entirely new role for the woodwinds in the orchestral texture. Historically, they began by doubling the string parts, and later were assigned the task of sustaining the harmony behind the string melody. With the discovery of registral capabilities beginning in the late eighteenth century, the woodwinds outgrew their supporting role and became dominant elements of modern orchestration. The greatest possibility for the future lies in the woodwinds', and particularly the flute's, newly recognized capacities both of timbre and of multiphonic production, which, Bartolozzi suggests, may well begin a new phase of orchestral history.

In large part, the responsibility for such a development lies with performers, for, as Howell notes, many of the new techniques are "unpredictable except by experience."[55] The example of cooperation between composers and flutists has already been set admirably by such performers as Severino Gazzelloni, and the work of flutist-composers John Heiss and Harvey Sollberger perhaps signals the necessity of a reunification of labor, at least temporarily. But even after completion of the initial composition process, when a performer's advice is essential, the player is often required to share in the process of composition through various sorts of improvisation or decision. The performer has become more than just an interpreter; he is also a cocreator with the composer.

The immediate problem of the avant-garde is to familiarize the general flutist population with the new techniques. The pioneering publications in this field, those of Heiss and Bartolozzi, were necessarily directed more to the musicological community than to performers. In the early 1970s, however, the first steps toward a widening of the "audience" were provided by the publication both of Stokes and Condon's manual of new sounds, designed, apparently, for quite a young audience, and of the second edition of James J. Pellerite's fingering guide, with its revised sections on alternate fingerings, quarter tones, multiphonics, and other special sonorities. The status of avant-garde techniques was definitely established in 1974 and 1975 with the publication of Howell's and Dick's handbooks and Aurèle Nicolet's compilation of the first étude book for the study of such techniques. Instructional literature of this sort, along with a large collection of avant-garde flute music, is now housed in the University of Arizona Music Library under the auspices of the National Flute Association.*

*The catalog of this collection, as of 1973, was published in Philip J. Swanson, "Avant-Garde Flute Music: A Partial Bibliography," Woodwind World, 11 (December 1972): 19–20, 22, and 11 (June 1973): 6.

Thus, from the point of view of literature, the avant-garde flute seems to have been well launched. But a large remaining hurdle is the elimination of misconceptions regarding potential effects of new techniques on the traditional embouchure. Even Howell, for instance, warns that buzzing may cause irritation or swelling of the lips and that saliva may interfere with the mechanism;[56] less informed individuals are likely to be even more conservative. Yet techniques such as whistle tones and difference tone production were initiated by perhaps the most influential flute teacher ever, William Kincaid. This history is reflected in the hopes of Robert Dick for the avant-garde literature: ". . . many flutists may find working with the new sonorities and techniques beneficial to their traditional playing, especially in the area of tone development. Quite simply, practice of the new sonorities serves to develop both the strength and suppleness of the embouchure."[57]

Another important factor in determining the future of avant-garde technique is critical musical evaluation. At the present time, not surprisingly, opinion is divided, but once again there is abundant historical precedent. Fitzgibbon wrote of the new genre of flute music of the early twentieth century:

> As for the eccentric, unmelodious, indefinite productions of those Bolshevists of music—the continental ultra-modernists—they appear to me to be quite meaningless and often absolutely painful; making me feel as if I (or my accompanist) was not playing the right note or keeping time. They endeavor to make up for the lack of ideas and inspiration by disregarding all the accepted rules, and trying novel experiments. . . . The greatest composers never found it necessary to attract attention by such usages.[58]

Yet Louis Fleury wrote of the same literature: "It is true that more difficult music is now being written, but this is because a more perfect instrument allows greater latitude, and not because everything is sacrificed to virtuosity."[59] From the perspective of fifty additional years, Fleury's evaluation has proven its validity; Fitzgibbon's has not.

With respect to the avant-garde, however, no decision has yet been reached. There has been considerable criticism of the Fitzgibbon variety; Paul Giroux wrote in 1952 that recent American composers "are still quite unable to resist the 'fatal facility' of the flute, and have exploited that facility in the production of angular and bizarre melodic skips to the apparent detriment of musical purpose."[60] Lyle Merriman made a similar observation in 1963: "With all of these 'exotic' effects at their command, many flutists and flutist-composers have shown a disturbing tendency to ignore the necessity of moderation, by using these devices at every opportunity."[61] Such charges have provoked spirited defenses by such innovators as Robert Cantrick, who wrote, "Buzzing the flute is a technique, not a 'gimmick,' and lends itself to a flute-like approach. In the hands of an imaginative performer, buzzing can yield genuinely musical results. It is not a mere trick."[62]

Thus we return to the necessity of full and progressive involvement of the performer in the compositional process, which must include not only a willingness to experiment, but also the exercise of critical faculties with veto power. Otherwise, given the increasingly high levels of technical ability of contemporary flutists that have been made possible by the perfection of the Boehm flute, we may see a repetition of the unfortunate musical situation of the nineteenth century, when virtuosity superseded, rather than enhanced, musical standards.

And finally, how will the avant-garde movement affect the development of the flute? Will the sine curve of musical and organological development suggested by Ridley take another turn, with manufacturers again experimenting with mechanism to suit the new literature? Some small steps, such as Robert Cantrick's use of the Bb footjoint, have been made in this direction, but Alex Murray's collaboration with Robert Dick on the Multiple Option Murray flute is the only such large-scale project to date. Will manufacturers attempt to remedy Howell's and Baron's objections to the instrument's unpredictability in multiphonic production? Will they work on developing a quarter-tone or all-glissandi flute? Will they strive for louder and clearer key percussion by means of harder pads or larger keys? But these intriguing possibilities raise still other questions: If key percussion is made more obvious, how will this alteration affect the performance of traditional literature, particularly in the recording studio? Will the performer be obliged to use two separate instruments or interchangeable accessories?

Unfortunately, these questions may have to be answered not by musicians, or even manufacturers, but by economists. In the uncertain inflationary economy of the late 1970s, it is reasonable to assume that experimentation will not be the long suit of any major manufacturers simply because it is too expensive. In the future, therefore, any such mechanical investigation is likely to come either from flutists with a mechanical bent or from the relatively few remaining independent flute craftsmen who are financially able to devote the time to such a project. Perhaps the economic strictures will foster a new brand of Yankee ingenuity. The maternal propensities of necessity are well known, and the next twenty-five years may once again affirm the accuracy of the proverb.

Notes]

1. Horniman Museum, *Wind Instruments of European Art Music*, ed. E. A. K. Ridley (London: Inner London Education Authority, 1974), p. 30.

2. Bruno Bartolozzi, *New Sounds for Woodwind*, trans. and ed. Reginald Smith Brindle (New York: Oxford University Press, 1967), pp. 3, 5.

3. John Krell, *Kincaidiana: A Flute Player's Notebook* (Culver City, Calif.: Trio Associates, 1973), p. 14.

4. Gardner Read, *Thesaurus of Orchestral Devices* (New York: Putnam Publishing Corp., 1953), p. ix.

5. Thomas Howell, *The Avant-Garde Flute: A Handbook for Composers and Flutists* (Berkeley: University of California Press, 1974), p. 14.

6. Anthony Baines, *Woodwind Instruments and Their History* (New York: W. W. Norton & Co., 1962), pp. 33–34.

7. Krell, p. 8.

8. Robert Dick, *The Other Flute: A Performance Manual of Contemporary Techniques* (New York: Oxford University Press, 1975), p. 12.

9. Howell, pp. 14–16.

10. Sheridan W. Stokes and Richard Condon, *Special Effects for Flute* (Culver City, Calif.: Trio Associates, 1970), p. 2.

11. Howell, p. 34.

12. "Questions and Answers," *The Flutist* 3 (1922): 646.

13. Bartolozzi, p. 28.

14. Howell, p. 18.

15. Ibid., pp. 50–51.

16. Dick, pp. 52–57.

17. Howell, pp. 18–19.

18. H. Macaulay Fitzgibbon, *The Story of the Flute*, 2nd ed., rev. (London: William Reeves Bookseller; New York: Charles Scribner's Sons, 1928), p. 98.

19. Howell, p. 33.

20. Dick, p. 79.

21. Howell, p. 19; Stokes and Condon, p. 7.

22. Howell, p. 20.

23. Ibid., pp. 10–11.

24. Stokes and Condon, p. 18.

25. Bartolozzi, p. 25.

26. Stokes and Condon, p. 18.

27. Bartolozzi, pp. 25–26.

28. Ibid., p. 22.

29. Howell, pp. 26–27.

30. Stokes and Condon, p. 17; Dick, p. 132.

31. Howell, pp. 24–26.

32. Dick, p. 128.

33. Curt Sachs, *The History of Musical Instruments* (New York: W. W. Norton & Co., 1940), pp. 445–46.

34. Dick, p. v.

35. Howell, p. 21.

36. John Heiss, "The Flute: New Sounds," *Perspectives of New Music* 10 (1972): 153–55.

37. Dick, p. 131.

38. Howell, p. 22.

39. Dick, p. 131.

40. Howell, p. 27.

41. Dick, p. 133.

42. Howell, p. 30.

43. Robert B. Cantrick, "Buzzing the Flute," *The Instrumentalist* 27, no. 9 (1963): 53.

44. Howell, p. 29.

45. William Brooks, "Instrumental and Vocal Resources," *Dictionary of Contemporary Music*, ed. John Vinton (New York: E. P. Dutton & Co., 1974), p. 346.

46. Stokes and Condon, p. 19.

47. Howell, p. 29.

48. Cantrick, pp. 53–54.

49. Richard Shepard Rockstro, *A Treatise on the Construction the History and the Practice of the Flute*, 2nd ed., rev. (1928; reprint ed., London: Musica Rara, 1967), pp. 570–71.

50. W. S. Broadwood, Preface to Theobald Boehm, *An Essay on the Construction of Flutes* (London: Rudall, Carte & Co., 1882), p. ix.

51. Howell, pp. 62–63.

52. John C. Heiss, "For the Flute: A List of Double-Stops, Triple-Stops, Quadruple Stops, and Shakes," *Perspectives of New Music* 5 (1966): 139.

53. John C. Heiss, "Some Multiple-Sonorities for Flute, Oboe, Clarinet, and Bassoon," *Perspectives of New Music* 7 (1968): 136.

54. Lawrence Singer, "Woodwind Development: A Monophonic and Multiphonic Point of View," *Woodwind World, Brass & Percussion* 14, no. 3 (1975): 15.

55. Howell, p. 16.

56. Ibid., p. 19.

57. Dick, p. v.

58. Fitzgibbon, p. h.

59. Louis Fleury, "The Flute and British Composers," Part II, *Chesterian*, n.s. no. 4 (January 1920), 116.

60. Paul Henry Giroux, "The History of the Flute and Its Music in the United States" (M.A. thesis, School of Music, University of Washington, 1952), p. 123.

61. Lyle Clinton Merriman, "Solos for Unaccompanied Woodwind Instruments: A Checklist of Published Works and Study of Representative Examples" (Ph.D. diss., State University of Iowa, 1963; Ann Arbor, Mich.: University Microfilms, 1964), p. 124.

62. Cantrick, p. 53.

Flute Systems Used by Leading Players

This bar graph illustrates the fingering systems used by leading European and American players between 1770 and 1930. Because the diversity of mechanisms is most evident in the nineteenth century, the graph is centered on that period, but a 30-year span on either side is included in order to demonstrate the rise and fall of the competitive spirit in flute design. Data is based on biographical notes in numerous histories of the flute and on iconographic evidence.

The following symbols are used:

(Birth date
| Change of systems—date definitely established
- - -→ Change of systems—exact date unknown
⌐ Death date*
⊃ Death occurred after 1930

*The date of Camus's death has not been firmly established. Rockstro reported that he retired in 1849 and was never heard from again.

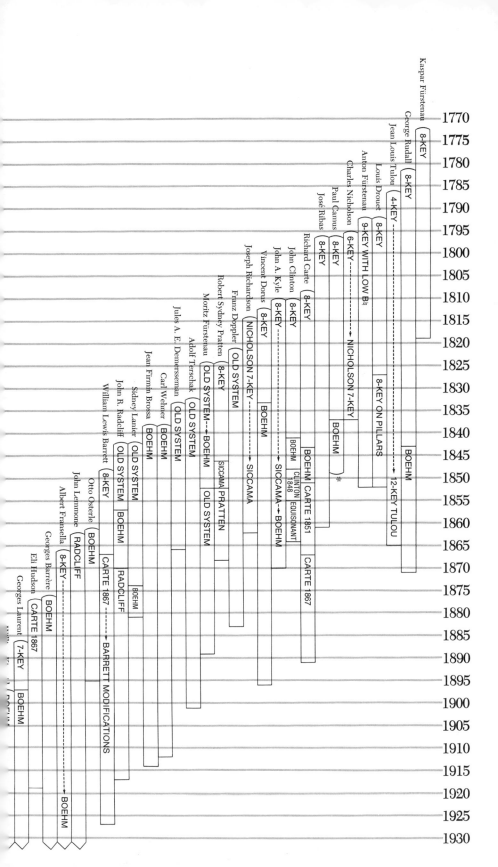

Avant-Garde Notation

The following list of avant-garde flute notation is compiled from many individual compositions and from the following sources: Complete citations are found in the Bibliography.

Bruno Bartolozzi, *New Sounds for Woodwind* (1967)
David Cope, *New Music Notation* (1976)
Robert Dick, *The Other Flute* (1975)
John C. Heiss, "The Flute: New Sounds," *Perspectives of New Music* (1972)
———. "For the Flute: A List of Double-Stops, Triple-Stops, Quadruple-Stops, and Shakes," *Perspectives of New Music* (1966)
———. "Some Multiple-Sonorities for Flute, Oboe, Clarinet, and Bassoon," *Perspectives of New Music* (1968)
Thomas Howell, *The Avant-Garde Flute* (1974)
Aurèle Nicolet, ed., *Pro Musica Nova* (1974)
James J. Pellerite, *A Modern Guide to Fingerings for the Flute*, 2nd ed. (1972)
Gardner Read, *Music Notation*, 2nd ed. (1969)
Howard Risatti, *New Music Vocabulary* (1975)
Lawrence Singer, "Woodwind Development: A Monophonic and Multiphonic Point of View," *Woodwind World, Brass & Percussion* (1975)
Harvey Sollberger, "The New Flute," *Selmer Bandwagon* (1975)
Sheridan W. Stokes and Richard Condon, *Special Effects for Flute* (1970)

Because of the continuing evolution of the avant-garde literature, this list is necessarily incomplete. Indeed, its purpose is not to be encyclopedic, but rather to demonstrate the scope of the subject and the contradictions in contemporary notational usage and to suggest the necessity for standardization of avant-garde notation.

Proportional rhythm:

As rapidly as possible   🎵

Accelerando

Ritardando

Harmonic or flageolet tone   ♩   OR   ♩ ---- pitch desired / ---- fingering

Harmonics with different timbres
(same pitch, different fingerings)   ♩   OR   ↑   OR   ↑   OR   ♦

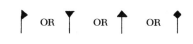

Harmonic/natural trill, same pitch   0+0+
tr ∿∿∿
♩

Key vibrato   **(KV)**   OR   **KV(↓)**   OR   **(↓)**

Quarter-tone trill   ¼T(↑)   OR   ¼T(↓)

Quarter tones:
¼ tone higher than base tone   OR   ⧣   OR   ♮↑
OR   ↑   OR   ↟

¾ tone higher than base tone   ♯   OR   ♯↑   OR   ⧣

¼ tone lower than base tone   ♭   OR   ♭   OR   ↋
OR   ♮   OR   ♭   OR   ♭
OR   ↓   OR |

¾ tone lower than base tone   ♭   OR   ↋   OR   ♭

Quarter tones—cents system (100 cents per semitone):

¼ tone higher   .5   ¾ tone higher   .75
than base tone   than base tone

¼ tone lower   ¾ tone lower
than base tone   than base tone
.5   .75

Pronounced pitch variation   ⅛↓, ½↓, ¼↓, etc.

Pitch variation:
    Slightly sharp ↑   Slightly flat   ↓

    Almost ¼ tone sharp ⬆   Almost ¼ tone flat   ⬇

    Microtonal pitch slightly lower than note to left
    and slightly higher than note to right

Glissando:

    Smooth

    Slightly broken

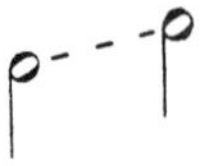

Portamento

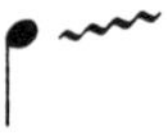

     OR 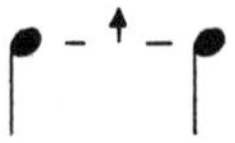   OR

Bending—up, then down

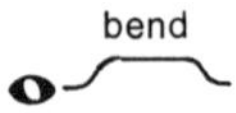

Bending—rolling flute inward
    and lipping downward

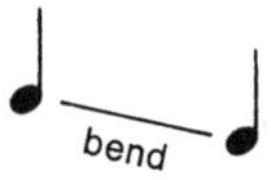

Lower pitch by inward rotation of flute

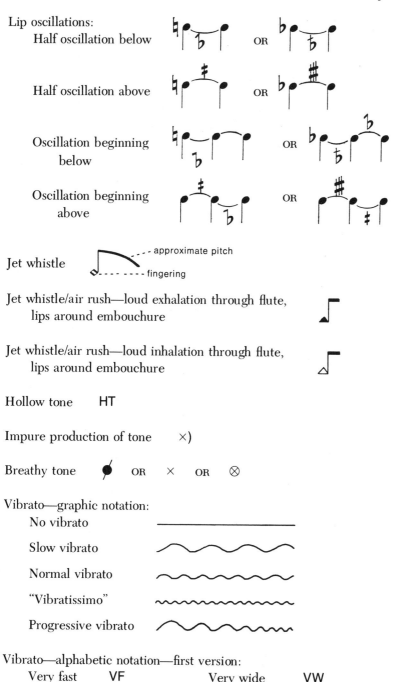

Lip oscillations:
　Half oscillation below　　　　　　　OR

　Half oscillation above　　　　　　　OR

　　Oscillation beginning　　　　　　　OR
　　　　below

　　Oscillation beginning　　　　　　　OR
　　　　above

Jet whistle　　　　　　　- - - approximate pitch
　　　　　　　　　　- - - - - - - fingering

Jet whistle/air rush—loud exhalation through flute,
　lips around embouchure

Jet whistle/air rush—loud inhalation through flute,
　lips around embouchure

Hollow tone　　　HT

Impure production of tone　　×)

Breathy tone　　　　OR　×　OR　⊗

Vibrato—graphic notation:
　No vibrato

　Slow vibrato

　Normal vibrato

　"Vibratissimo"

　Progressive vibrato

Vibrato—alphabetic notation—first version:
　Very fast　　VF　　　　　Very wide　　VW
　Very slow　　VS　　　　　Very narrow　　VN

Vibrato—alphabetic notation—second version:
    Nonvibrato   n.v.
    Slow vibrato—slow speed, variable bandwidth   s.v.
    Ordinary vibrato   **vibr.**
    Fast vibrato—fast speed, narrow bandwidth   f.v.
    Molto vibrato—fast speed, wide bandwidth   m.v.

Vibrato—alphabetic notation—third version:
    Nonvibrato   *nv*
    Normal vibrato   *v*
    Stressed vibrato   *sv*

Vibrato—numerical notation (sliding scale)   ∅ OR 1∅

Quarter-tone vibrato

Throat vibration/buzz   **bz**

Whistle/whisper tone   **(WT)** OR W.T. OR W.T.

Flutter-tongue

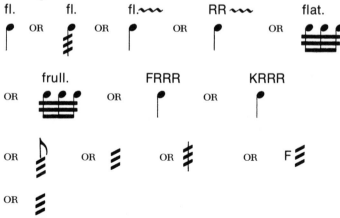

Flutter-tongue intensity

Flutter-tongue without producing definite pitch

Flutter-tongue without sound

Flutter-tongue on consonant "r"

Flutter-tongue with lips covering embouchure

Key slap, pitch sounding

OR   OR

Key slap alone (without air)

OR   OR

OR   K   OR   OR   OR

Rattle keys

Rattle keys without blowing

Tongue click   K

Tongue click into embouchure hole   (K)

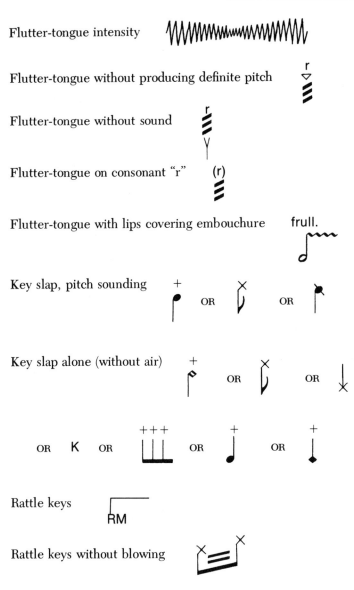

Slap or tongued pizzicato   **pizz.**   OR   **+**   OR   **slp.**

OR   **ϕ**

Simultaneous tongue click and key slap   **K+**

Tongue-blocked key slap   OR

Simultaneous tongue click into   **(K+)**
     embouchure and key slap

Tongue stop   **(T)**

Tongue ram

Simultaneous playing and singing

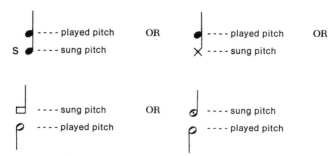

S ---- played pitch   OR   ---- played pitch   OR
   ---- sung pitch   ---- sung pitch

---- sung pitch   OR   ---- sung pitch
---- played pitch   ---- played pitch

Simultaneous playing and humming

---- hummed pitch
---- played pitch

Trumpet attack   T

Enclosing embouchure with mouth,
    blow without producing tone

Enclosing embouchure with mouth,
    blow producing a tone

Increase air pressure to produce
    glissando into highest tessitura

Attack as above, striking tongue on
    middle of blow hole

Normal attack, but playing tonelessly

Normal attack, very little tone but
    much sucking of tone

Blow without tone   OR   OR   OR   +

Subtones   ST

Exhaling   ↓   OR   S

Inhaling   ↑   OR   ꙅ

Soft or throat attack   —

Soft or windy attack   wh

Attack in back of throat   ⋎

Sharp attack, with exaggerated "T"   ∧

Attack with "th" sound as in "the"   th

Tongue without pitch

Breath attack, then tongued "ht"
    with lips enclosing embouchure   HT

Accents:

Blowing	bl	Harmonic	
Breath	br	Key	+
Flutter	fl	Singing	sing

Lip pressure:

Relaxed	○	Increased	● OR +
Slightly relaxed	☉	Slightly increased	
Very relaxed	▭	Much increased	▬

Air pressure:

Normal air pressure	N.Pr.
Much air pressure	M.Pr.
Little air pressure	P.Pr.
Augment air pressure	A.Pr.
Diminish air pressure	D.Pr.

Angle of flute:

Normal playing angle   U

Slightly turned out

Slightly turned in

Turned out as far as possible
    without pitch breaking   ⊏

Turned in as far as possible
    without pitch breaking   ⊐

Lip aperture—first version:

Wide	⬭	Small	○
Moderate	⬯	Very small	●

Lip aperture—second version:

Large   ○

Very wide, completely relaxed   ▭

Moderately reduced   ◑

Small   ●

Very small   ▬

Multiphonic notation of Lawrence Singer

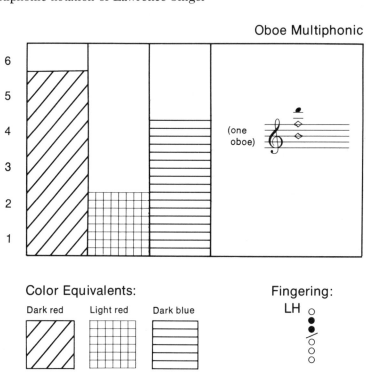

Note: Singer's article does not give any examples for flute, but the notation is identical in format.

Bibliography

BOOKS AND PAMPHLETS

Agricola, Martin. *Musica instrumentalis deudsch.* Wittemberg: Georgen Rhaw, 1542.

Ayars, Christine Merrick. *Contributions to the Art of Music in America by the Music Industries of Boston, 1640 to 1936.* New York: H. W. Wilson Co., 1937.

Badger, A. G. *An Illustrated History of the Flute.* New York: A. G. Badger, 1853.

Baines, Anthony. *Victoria and Albert Museum: Catalogue of Musical Instruments.* London: Her Majesty's Stationery Office, 1968.

———. *Woodwind Instruments and Their History.* New York: W. W. Norton & Co., 1962.

Bartolozzi, Bruno. *New Sounds for Woodwind.* Translated and edited by Reginald Smith Brindle. New York: Oxford University Press, 1967.

Barzun, Jacques. *Berlioz and the Romantic Century.* 3rd ed. 2 vols. New York: Columbia University Press, 1969.

Bate, Philip. *The Flute.* New York: W. W. Norton & Co., 1969.

The Bate Collection of Historical Wind Instruments. Oxford: Faculty of Music, University of Oxford, 1976.

Bayr, Georg. *Practische Flöten-Schule.* Vienna: Tranquillo Mollo, 1823.

Becker, Heinz. *History of Instrumentation.* Translated by Robert Kolben. Anthology of Music, edited by K. G. Fellerer, vol. 24. Cologne: Arno Volk Verlag, 1964.

Boehm, Theobald. *An Essay on the Construction of Flutes.* Edited by W. S. Broadwood. London: Rudall, Carte & Co., 1882.

———. *The Flute and Flute-Playing.* Translated and revised by Dayton C. Miller. 2nd ed., rev. 1922. Reprint. New York: Dover Publications, 1964.

Borne, F[rançois], and Julliot, Djalma. *Notice Concernant les Améliorations Apportées à la Flûte de Théobald Boehm.* Pacy-sur-Eure: Imprimerie E. Grateau, 1903.

Brooks, William. "Instrumental and Vocal Resources." In *Dictionary of Contemporary Music,* edited by John Vinton, pp. 339–49. New York: E. P. Dutton & Co., 1974.

Carse, Adam. *The History of Orchestration.* New York: E. P. Dutton & Co., 1925.

———. *Musical Wind Instruments.* 1939. Reprint. New York: Da Capo Press, 1965.

Carte, Richard. *A Complete Course of Instructions for the Boehm Flute.* London: Rudall, Carte & Co., 1845.

———. *Sketch of the Successive Improvements Made in The Flute.* 3rd ed. London: Rudall, Rose, Carte & Co. and Keith and Prowse, 1855.

Clinton, John. *A Code of Instructions for the Fingering of the Equisonant Flute.* London: Clinton & Co., ca. 1860.

———. *A Theoretical & Practical Essay, on the Boehm Flute.* 2nd ed. London: R. Cocks & Co., ca. 1843–46.

———. *A Treatise upon the Mechanism and General Principles of the Flute.* London: H. Potter, [1852].

Coche, Victor. *Examen Critique de la Flûte Ordinaire comparée à la Flûte de Boehm.* Paris: The Author, 1838.

———. *Examen Critique de la Flûte Ordinaire comparée à la Flûte de Boehm.* Translated by Edith E. Miller. Cleveland: TS, n.d.

Cope, David. *New Music Notation.* Dubuque, Iowa: Kendall/Hunt Publishing Co., 1976.

Day, C. R., comp. *A Descriptive Catalogue of the Musical Instruments Recently Exhibited at the Royal Military Exhibition, London.* London: Eyre & Spottiswoode, 1891.

De Lorenzo, Leonardo. *My Complete Story of the Flute.* New York: Citadel Press, 1951.

Dick, Robert. *The Other Flute: A Performance Manual of Contemporary Techniques.* New York: Oxford University Press, 1975.

Diderot, Denis, and d'Alembert, Jean. *Encyclopédie. Supplément: Suite du Receuil des Planches.* Paris: Panckoucke: Stoupe & Brunet, 1777.

Ehrlich, D. *The History of the Flute from Ancient Times to Boehm's Invention.* New York: D. Ehrlich, 1921.

Ferrari, Gustave. "(Claude) Paul Taffanel." In *Grove's Dictionary of Music and Musicians,* vol. viii, p. 289. New York: St. Martin's Press, 1954.

Fitzgibbon, H. Macaulay. *The Story of the Flute.* 2nd ed., rev. London: William Reeves Bookseller; New York: Charles Scribner's Sons, 1928.

Furlong, William Barry. *Season with Solti.* New York: Macmillan Co., 1974.

George[s] Barrère Flutist. New York: Henry Wolfson Musical Bureau, n.d.

"Georges Barrère." *International Cyclopedia of Music and Musicians.* 9th ed. Edited by Robert Sabin, p. 149. New York: Dodd, Mead, & Co., 1964.

Gilliam, Laura E., and Lichtenwanger, William. *The Dayton C. Miller Collection: A Checklist of the Instruments.* Washington, D.C.: Library of Congress, 1961.

The Giorgi Flute: Instructions how to play, and the Scale. London: Joseph Wallis & Son, n.d.

Girard, Adrien. *Histoire et Richesses de la Flûte.* Paris: Librarie Gründ, 1953.

Goldberg, Adolph. *Biographieen zur Porträts-Sammlung hervorragender Flöten-Virtuosen, Dilettanten und Komponisten.* Berlin: privately printed, 1906.

Harrison, Frank, and Rimmer, Joan. *European Musical Instruments*. New York: W. W. Norton & Co., 1964.

Hawkins, Sir John. *A General History of the Science and Practice of Music*. 2 vols. 1776. Reprint. London: J. Alfred Novello, 1853; reprint, New York: Dover Publications, 1963.

Horniman Museum. *Wind Instruments of European Art Music*. Edited by E. A. K. Ridley. London: Inner London Education Authority, 1974.

Hotteterre-le-Romain. *Principes de la Flûte Traversière, ou Flûte d'Allemagne*. Paris: Christophe Ballard, 1707.

Hotteterre le Romain, Jacques. *Principles of the Flute Recorder and Oboe*. Translated and edited by David Lasocki. New York: Praeger Publishers, 1968.

Howell, Thomas. *The Avant-Garde Flute: A Handbook for Composers and Flutists*. Berkeley: University of California Press, 1974.

Krell, John. *Kincaidiana: A Flute Player's Notebook*. Culver City, Calif.: Trio Associates, 1973.

Langwill, Lyndesay G. *An Index of Musical Wind-Instrument Makers*. 3rd ed. Edinburgh: Lyndesay Langwill, 1972.

Leonhard, Charles, and House, Robert W. *Foundations and Principles of Music Education*. 2nd ed. New York: McGraw-Hill, 1972.

McDiarmid, Ellis. *The Story of the Flute and How to Play It*. Elkhart, Ind.: H. & A. Selmer, Inc., 1929.

MacGillivray, James A. "The Woodwind." In *Musical Instruments Through the Ages*, edited by Anthony Baines, pp. 216–50. London: Faber and Faber, 1961.

Majer, Joseph F. B. C. *Neu-eröffneter Theoretisch und Prakticher Music-Saal*. Nürnberg: Berlegts Johann Jacob Cremer, 1741.

Mersenne, M[arin]. *Harmonicorum Libri XII*. Paris: G. Baudry, 1648.

Miller, Dayton C. *Anecdotal History of the Science of Sound*. New York: Macmillan Co., 1935.

———. *Catalogue of Books and Literary Material relating to the Flute and Other Musical Instruments*. Cleveland: privately printed, 1935.

———. *The Science of Musical Sounds*. New York: Macmillan Co., 1916.

The Murray Flute. Elkhart, Ind.: W. T. Armstrong Co., [1975].

Nicholson, Charles. *Nicholson's Complete Preceptor for the German Flute*. London: Preston, 1834.

———. *Preceptive Lessons for the Flute*. London: The Author and Clementi & Co., 1821.

———. *A School for the Flute*. London and New York: Wm. Hall & Sons, 1836.

Nicolet, Aurèle, ed. *Pro Musica Nova: Studies for Playing Avant-garde Music for Flute*. Cologne: Musikverlag Hans Gerig; New York: MCA Music, 1974.

Pellerite, James J. *A Modern Guide to Fingerings for the Flute*. 2nd ed., rev. and enl. Bloomington, Ind.: Zalo Publications, 1972.

Piston, Walter. *Orchestration*. New York: W. W. Norton & Co., 1955.

The Platinum Flute and Georges Barrère. New York: [Wm. S. Haynes Co.], 1935.

Praetorius, Michael. *Syntagmatis Musici Tomus Secundus De Organographia.* Wolffenbüttel: Elias Holwein, 1619.

————. *Theatrum Instrumentorum seu Sciagraphia.* Wolffenbüttel, 1620.

Pratten, R. Sidney. *A Complete Series of Scales and Exercises for R. S. Pratten's Perfected Flute.* London: Boosey & Sons, ca. 1855.

Prof. Giorgi's Patent Flute. London: Joseph Wallis & Son, n.d.

Putnik, Edwin. *The Art of Flute Playing.* Evanston, Ill.: Summy-Birchard Co., 1970.

Quantz, Johann Joachim. 1752. *On Playing the Flute.* Translated by Edward R. Reilly. London: Faber and Faber, 1966.

Radcliff, John. *School for the Flute, A Practical Instruction Book by Charles Nicholson, with the Original Appendix to his Preceptive Lessons, Altered and adapted with additions for the Modern Flute (Radcliff's Model).* London: Rudall, Carte & Co., 1873.

Read, Gardner. *Music Notation.* 2nd ed. Boston: Allyn and Bacon, 1969.

————. *Thesaurus of Orchestral Devices.* New York: Putnam Publishing Corp., 1953.

The Ridley Collection of Musical Wind Instruments in Luton Museum. Luton, England: Corp. of Luton Museum and Art Gallery, 1957.

Risatti, Howard. *New Music Vocabulary.* Urbana: University of Illinois Press, 1975.

Rockstro, Richard S[hepard]. *A Description of the "Rockstro-Model" Flute.* London: Keith, Prowse & Co. and Rudall, Carte & Co., 1884.

————. *A Treatise on the Construction the History and the Practice of the Flute.* 2nd ed., rev. 1928. Reprint. London: Musica Rara, 1967.

Sachs, Curt. *The History of Musical Instruments.* New York: W. W. Norton & Co., 1940.

Scale and Description of Boehm's Newly-Invented Patent Flute. London: Gerock and Wolf, ca. 1831–32.

Schwartz, H. W. *The Story of Musical Instruments.* Garden City, N.Y.: Doubleday, Doran & Co., 1938.

Schwedler, Maximilian. *Flöte und Flötenspiel.* Leipzig: J. J. Weber, 1910.

Sconzo, Fortunato. *Il Flauto e I Flautisti.* Milan: Ulrico Hoepli, 1930.

Skeffington, T. C. *"The Flute" in its Transition State.* London: William Walker & Co., 1862.

Stevens, Roger S. *Artistic Flute Technique and Study.* Edited by Ruth N. Zwissler. Hollywood, Calif.: Highland Music Co., 1967.

Stokes, Sheridan W., and Condon, Richard. *Special Effects for Flute.* Culver City, Calif.: Trio Associates, 1970.

Virdung, Sebastian. *Musica getutscht und auszgezogen.* 1511. Reprint. Berlin: Rob. Eitner, 1882.

Ward, Cornelius. *The Flute Explained.* London: The Author, 1844.

Welch, Christopher. *History of the Boehm Flute.* 3rd ed. London: Rudall, Carte & Co.; New York: G. Schirmer, 1896.

Wysham, Henry Clay. *The Evolution of the Boehm Flute.* New York: C. G. Conn, 1898.

Young, J. Harrington, ed. *Charles Nicholson's School for the Flute With Exer-*

cises and examples selected from his "Preceptive Lessons" with additional Scales for the Boehm, Carte & Boehm, and Radcliff Flutes. London: Howard & Co., n.d.

PERIODICALS

Baasch, Robert J. "The Flute: Yesterday and Today." *Woodwind Magazine* 7, no. 2 (1954): 4–5; no. 3 (1954): 6–7; no. 4 (1954): 6, 9, 10; no. 5 (1955): 6–7; no. 6 (1955): 6–7; no. 7 (1955): 6–7, 9–10.

————. "The Murray Flute An Improvement?" *Music Journal* 31, no. 4 (1973): 18–19, 22.

————. "The Precious Metal Flutes." *Woodwind World* 4, no. 2 (1961): 5–6.

Backus, John. "Effect of Wall Material on the Steady-State Tone Quality of Woodwind Instruments." *Journal of the Acoustical Society of America* 36 (1964): 1881–87.

Bate, Philip. "The Alex Murray Flute." *Galpin Society Journal* 26 (1973): 47–54.

Browne, James A. "The Fate of the Flute." *Monthly Musical Record* 40, no. 477 (1910): 198–99.

"Buzz Flute." *Musical America* 82, no. 10 (1962): 50.

Cameron, Richard. "The Flute—Its Story and Practice." *Etude Music Magazine* 49 (1931): 708, 741.

————. "Possibilities of the Woodwind Instruments." *Etude Music Magazine* 51 (1933): 813, 847, 862.

Cantrick, Robert B. "Buzzing the Flute." *The Instrumentalist* 27, no. 9 (1963), 53–54.

Coltman, John W. "Effect of Material on Flute Tone Quality." *Journal of the Acoustical Society of America* 49 (1971): 520–23.

————. "Effect of Material on Flute Tone Quality." *Woodwind World* 11, no. 2 (1972): 20, 26.

————. "The Intonation of Antique and Modern Flutes." *The Instrumentalist* 29, no. 5 (1974): 53–55; no. 6 (1975): 43–47; no. 7 (1975): 47–50, 52; no. 8 (1975): 77–80.

Eck, Emil. "The Open Hole Flute." *The Instrumentalist* 13, no. 4 (1958): 39.

Fajardo, Raoul. "Tone Properties of the Flute Head Joint." *The Instrumentalist* 27, no. 2 (1973): 46, 48–49; no. 3 (1973): 44–46, 48–49.

Fedderson, Jack. "Tradition and Music Instrument Technology." *The Instrumentalist* 16, no. 10 (1962): 35–36.

Fleury, Louis. "The Flute and British Composers." *Chesterian*, n.s. no. 3 (December 1919), 79–82; no. 4 (January 1920), 115–117.

————. "The Flute and Its Powers of Expression." Translated by A.H.F.S. *Music and Letters* 3 (October 1922): 383–93.

"Flutes: From Reed to Platinum." *Literary Digest* 120, no. 22 (1935): 15.

"14-Carat Flute." *Newsweek*, December 3, 1962, p. 64.

Gallese, Liz Roman. "Music Makers: Serious Flute Players Insist Two Companies Are Most Noteworthy." *The Wall Street Journal*, February 1, 1977, pp. 1, 34.

"Gemeinhardt Flute Low B♭." *Woodwind World* 5, no. 1 (1963): 11.

Giroux, Paul H. "The History of the Flute and Its Music in the United States." *Journal of Research in Music Education* 1 (Spring 1953): 68–73.

Harrop, Fred. "That Troublesome High E-Natural." *The Flutist* 9 (1928): 171.

Hegvik, Arthur. "An Interview with Jean-Pierre Rampal." *The Instrumentalist* 27, no. 4 (1972): 30–34.

Heiss, John [C.]. "The Flute: New Sounds." *Perspectives of New Music* 10 (1972): 153–58.

———. "For the Flute: A List of Double-Stops, Triple-Stops, Quadruple-Stops, and Shakes." *Perspectives of New Music* 5 (1966): 139–41.

———. "Some Multiple-Sonorities for Flute, Oboe, Clarinet, and Bassoon." *Perspectives of New Music* 7 (1968): 136–42.

Higbee, Dale. "Needed: A Gold Flute or a Gold Lip." *Woodwind World* 13, no. 3 (1974): 22.

Hullinger, William E. "Intonation, Harmonics, Etc." *The Flutist* 5 (1924): 105–7.

James, W. N. *Six Essays on Fingering the Flute. The Flutonicon* 13 (1846), supplements.

Kujala, Walfrid. "A Brief History of Flute Design." *The Instrumentalist* 27, no. 4 (1972): 24–25.

———. "The Murray Flurry." *Music Journal* 31, no. 7 (1973): 40–41, 72–75.

———. "The Murray Flute." *The Instrumentalist* 27, no. 4 (1972): 26–29.

Lesueur, Alexander. "To Be or Not to B." *The Instrumentalist* 25, no. 3 (1970): 43.

"Marching Flute Introduced at Texas Bandmaster Meet." *DeFord Digest* 1, no. 3 (1972): 1–2.

Mather, Roger. "The Flute Sound of Georges Laurent." *Woodwind World Brass & Percussion* 15 (March 1976): 12–14; 15 (May 1976): 30–31, 47.

———. "Flute Tube Material and Thickness." *Woodwind World* 13 (April 1974): 24–27; 13 (June 1974): 19–21, 27–28.

———. "The Influence of Tube Material and Thickness on Flute Tone Quality." *Woodwind World* 11, no. 4 (1972): 6–7.

Mignolet, J. "More About the Split-E Key." *The Flutist* 9 (1928): 232.

Miller, Dayton C. "Flutes of Glass." *The Flutist* 6 (1925): 151–55.

———. "The Influence of the Material of Wind-Instruments on the Tone Quality." *Science*, n.s. 29, no. 735 (1909): 161–71.

Moore, T. W. "Recent Developments in Flute Design." *Musical Opinion* 76 (1953): 599.

Murray, Alexander. "The Murray Flute." *American Musical Instrument Society Newsletter* 1, no. 3 (1972): 6–8.

"Musicians and Designers of Instruments Differ." *Science News Letter* 53 (1948): 361.

Pellerite, James. "The French-Model Flute: A Reappraisal for Music Educators." *The Instrumentalist* 18, no. 5 (1963): 62–64.

Phillips, Elsie A. "New Center for Flute Music." *Woodwind World* 13, no. 3 (1974): 17–18.

Poor, Mary Louise. "The Case for the Off-set G." *Woodwind World* 13, no. 4 (1974): 16, 24, 29.

———. "A Conversation With Severino Gazzelloni." *Woodwind World* 11, no. 5 (1972): 17–18.

"Questions and Answers." *The Flutist* 1 (1920): 117–19; 1 (1920): 140–44; 1 (1920): 164–68; 3 (1922): 645–46; 5 (1924): 21–22; 5 (1924): 45–46; 7 (1926): 81.

"Recently Patented Inventions." *Scientific American* 77 (1897): 395–96.

Redfield, John. "Some Woodwind Defects and Improvements." *Etude Music Magazine* 50 (1932): 704, 737, 756.

Sable [pseud.]. "The Flute and Its Vicissitudes." *The English Mechanic* 11 (1870).

Sachs, Curt. "Music and the Musical Inventor." *Musical America* 74, no. 4 (1954): 20–21, 146.

Sheppard, Leslie. "The Boehm Flute." *Music Teacher* 48, no. 2 (1969): 19, 40.

Singer, Lawrence. "Woodwind Development: A Monophonic and Multiphonic Point of View." *Woodwind World Brass & Percussion* 14, no. 3 (1975): 14–16.

Sollberger, Harvey. "The New Flute." *Selmer Bandwagon*, no. 76 (1975): 14–18; no. 77 (1975): 10–18.

Standish, H. "The Giorgi Flute." *Proceedings of the Musical Assn.* 24 (1898): 57–62.

Swanson, Philip J. "Avant-Garde Flute Music: A Partial Bibliography." *Woodwind World* 11 (December 1972): 19–20, 22; 11 (June 1973): 6–8.

Swift, Frederick Fay. "Early Efforts at Instrumental Music in American Schools and Colleges." *Woodwind World Brass & Percussion* 15, no. 1 (1976): 14–15, 50.

Taylor, Laurence. "The B-Natural Footjoint." *The Instrumentalist* 9, no. 7 (1955): 59–60; no. 8 (1955): 29.

———. "Curious Flutes." *The Instrumentalist* 10, no. 3 (1955): 34–35.

———. "Flute Facts." *The Instrumentalist* 3, no. 2 (1948): 46; 5, no. 5 (1951): 51.

———. "Flute Facts: Special Flute Keys." *The Instrumentalist* 12, no. 4 (1957): 43–45; 12, no. 5 (1958): 60–61.

Terry, Kenton. "William Kincaid." *Woodwind World Brass & Percussion* 16, no. 3 (1977): 20–21, 23, 34.

"That New Flute." *The Instrumentalist* 2, no. 2 (1947): 2.

Thomson, J. M. "A New Look for the Flute." *Canon* 12, no. 7 (1959): 265–66.

"The Thumb Crutch." *The Flutist* 1 (1920): 128–29.

Zlotnick, Henry. "Distortion and the Playing of Flute." *Woodwind Magazine* 3, no. 4 (1950): 4–5.

MANUSCRIPTS

Miller, Dayton C. Accession List of Flutes in the Dayton C. Miller Collection. 5 vols. MS. Dayton C. Miller Collection, Music Division, Library of Congress, Washington, D.C.

———. "The Evolution of the Wood-Wind Instruments." TS. Dayton C. Miller Collection, Music Division, Library of Congress, Washington, D.C.

————. "The Modern Flute: Its History and Construction." TS. Dayton C. Miller Collection, Music Division, Library of Congress, Washington, D.C.: 1906.

Powell, William, and Powell, Sidney. *The Flautist's Guide*. MS. Birmingham, England: 1906. Dayton C. Miller Collection, Music Division, Library of Congress, Washington, D.C.

THESES

Baasch, Robert J. "Modern Flutes and Their Predecessors." Ed.D. dissertation, Teacher's College, Columbia University, 1952.

Fossner, Alvin Koenig. "Significant Changes and Improvements in Certain Woodwind Instruments Since 1860." Ed.D. dissertation, Teacher's College, Columbia University, 1952.

Giroux, Paul Henry. "The History of the Flute and Its Music in the United States." M.A. thesis, School of Music, University of Washington, 1952.

Mellott, George K. "A Survey of Contemporary Flute Solo Literature with Analyses of Representative Compositions." Ph.D. dissertation, State University of Iowa, 1964. Ann Arbor, Mich.: University Microfilms, 1964.

Merriman, Lyle Clinton. "Solos for Unaccompanied Woodwind Instruments: A Checklist of Published Works and Study of Representative Examples." Ph.D. dissertation, State University of Iowa, 1963. Ann Arbor, Mich.: University Microfilms, 1964.

PATENT SPECIFICATIONS

FRANCE]

Allirol, Alcide. "Application d'un nouveau système cintré à la grande flûte ou à tout autre genre de flûte d'orchestre." No. 624,703 (November 16, 1926).

Buffet, Jeune [Louis Auguste]. "Flûte." No. 6339 (October 10, 1838).

Ehrmann, Henri-Emile. "Perfectionnements aux flûtes." No. 330,592 (March 25, 1903).

Julliot, Djalma. "Perfectionnements apportés à la flûte à clefs système Boehm." No. 245,108 (February 13, 1895).

————. "Perfectionnements apportés à la flûte à clefs système Boehm." No. 317,433 (December 31, 1901).

Laubé, Cornélie Villedieu. "Perfectionnements aux flûtes Boehm." No. 409,922 (March 1, 1909).

Laurent, Claude. "Flûte du Nouvelle Fabrication." No. 3847 (September 10, 1806).

————. "Perfectionnements apportés à la flûte allemand descendant jusqu'au sol d'en bas." No. 5643 (January 9, 1834).

Thibouville-Lamy, J. & Cie. "Perfectionnement apporté aux flûtes cylindriques système Boehm." No. 326,145 (November 6, 1902).

Vigué, Louis-Fernand. "Perfectionnements aux flûtes Boehm." No. 459,169 (June 12, 1913).

GREAT BRITAIN]

Carte, Richard. "Flutes, Clarionets, Hautboys, and Bassoons." No. 12,996 (1850).

———. "Flute." No. 3208 (1866).

Clinton, John. "Flutes." No. 12,378 (1848).

———. "Manufacture of Wind Musical Instruments." No. 3192 (1857).

———. "Flutes." No. 886 (1862).

Monzani, Tebaldo. "Flutes." No. 3074 (1807).

———. "Clarionets and Flutes." No. 3586 (1812).

Nolan, Frederick. "Flutes, Flageolets, &c." No. 3183 (1808).

Potter, Richard. "German flute, &c." No. 1499 (1785).

Potter, William Henry. "German Flutes, &c." No. 3136 (1808).

Rose, John Mitchell. "Flutes, Clarionets, &c." No. 11,853 (1847).

———, and Rudall, George. "Flutes." No. 6338 (1832).

Scott, Thomas. "German Flute, Clarionet, and Oboe." No. 3314 (1810).

Siccama, Abel. "Manufacture of Flutes &c." No. 10,553 (1845).

Steckel, Joseph Louis Réné. "Wind Musical Instruments." No. 2943 (1868).

Townley, Charles Gostling. "Key to Regulate the Tone of Flutes, &c." No. 3159 (1808).

———. "Flutes, Organ Pipes, &c." No. 3182 (1808).

Ward, Cornelius. "Flutes." No. 9229 (1842).

Wood, James. "German Flutes, Clarionets, and Bassoons." No. 3797 (1814).

UNITED STATES]

Alberti, Nicholas. "Wood Wind Instrument." No. 1,103,462 (July 14, 1914).

Berteling, Theodore. "Improvement in Flutes." No. 76,389 (April 7, 1868).

Conn, Charles G. "Wind-Instrument." No. 378,771 (February 28, 1888).

Dytch, Harry. "Musical wind instrument." No. 1,786,833 (December 30, 1930).

Fajardo, Raoul J. "Noncircular head joint for a concert flute and method of manufacture." No. 3,866,507 (February 18, 1975).

Gage, Charles B. "Flute." No. 1,586,794 (June 1, 1926).

Giorgi, Carlo T. "Flute." No. 594,735 (November 30, 1897).

Guenther, Karl Frederick W. "Flute." No. 444,830 (January 20, 1891).

Haynes, William S. "Musical Wind Instrument." No. 1,119,954 (December 8, 1914).

Julliot, Djalma. "Flute." No. 901,913 (October 20, 1908).

McAvoy, John William. "Wood-wind and like musical instruments." No. 1,643,463 (September 27, 1927).

Pfaff, J. "Flute." No. 17,054 (April 14, 1857).

Wurlitzer, Eduard H. "Flute." No. 859,714 (July 9, 1907).

TRADE CATALOGS

Nicholas Alberti. *N. Alberti's Any Pitch and Transposing C and D-flat Flute.* Chicago, n.d.

W. T. Armstrong Co. *Price List, Area 1.* Elkhart, Ind., May 1, 1974; January 1, 1977.

Boosey & Co. *Flutes and Piccolos*. London, ca. 1900.

C. G. Conn. *Flute and Piccolo Players' Handy Pocket Book of Reference*. Elkhart, Ind., ca. 1903.

E. L. DeFord, division of King Musical Instruments. *E. L. DeFord Flutes & Piccolos*. Elkhart, Ind., January 5, 1976.

Carl Fischer, Inc. *Something About Flutes*. New York, [1928].

Gage-Anderson Co. *The Gage Articulated B-F Sharp Device*. Wilkes-Barre, Pa., n.d.

Godfroy, ainé [Clair]. *Prix-Courant*. Paris, ca. 1878.

Hawkes & Son. *Price List of Flutes and Piccolos*. London, ca. 1905, 1926.

John C. Haynes Co. *A Notable Achievement in Flute-Making at the "Bay State" Factory*. Boston, ca. 1897.

Wm. S. Haynes Co. *Boehm Flutes and Piccolos of Improved Construction*. Boston, 1930, 1932.

———. *Boehm Flutes and Piccolos of Modern Construction*. Boston, 1923, 1925.

———. *Improved Boehm System Flutes and Piccolos*. Boston, 1940, 1945.

———. *Modern Flute Construction*. Boston, ca. 1915–16.

———. Untitled catalog. Boston, ca. 1975.

Wilhelm Heckel. *Preisliste über feine Instrumente*. Leipzig, Ausgabe 202, n.d.

Florent Hofinger. *Manufacture d'Instruments de Musique Brevetés*. Brussels, 1927.

Louis Lot. *Prix-Courant*. Paris, 1870, 1887, 1896, 1905, 1928.

Lyon & Healy. *Catalogue of Musical Merchandise*. Chicago, ca. 1898–99.

Clement Masson, successeur de D. Julliot. *Manufacture de Flûtes Système Boehm à Perce Cylindrique en Metal*. Paris, post-1898.

Moritz Max Mönnig. *Preisliste über Boehmflöten, Reformflöten und Flöten alten Systems*. Leipzig, [1930].

Otto Mönnig. *Orthoton*. Leipzig. 1931.

Verne Q. Powell Flutes. *Price List*. Arlington Heights, Mass., February 1, 1970; August 15, 1975; February 1, 1976.

———. Untitled brochure. Arlington Heights, Mass., 1975.

A. Rampone & B. Cazzani & Co. *Listino speciale per Flauti e Ottavini sistema Boehm e sistema Ziegler per Concertisti*. Milan: Maggio, 1921.

Rudall, Carte & Co. *List of Concert Flutes and Piccolos*. London, 1872, September 1895, April 1903, April 1904, June 1907, April 1911, January 1916, September 1922, October 1924, May 1926, October 1927, December 1928, October 1932, February 1934, October 1934, August 1936, August 1937.

Selmer Division of Magnavox Co. *Selmer Flutes and Piccolos*. Elkhart, Ind., 1975.

Sherman, Clay & Co. *Musical Instrument Catalog*. San Francisco, ca. 1928–29.

Index